Light

Light

Edited by Kerryn Greenberg

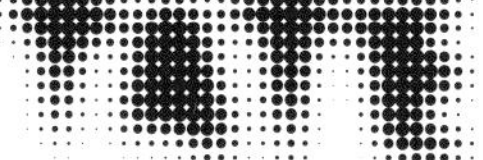

Published 2022 by order of the Tate Trustees
by Tate Publishing, a division of Tate Enterprises Ltd,
Millbank, London SW1P 4RG

A catalogue record for this book is available from the British Library

ISBN 978 1 84976 804 7

Distributed in the United States and Canada by Abrams, New York

Library of Congress Control Number applied for

Senior Editor: Emma Poulter
Production: Bill Jones
Picture Researcher: Roz Hill
Design: Lizzie Ballantyne
Cover typography: Johanne Lian Olsen
Colour reproduction by Evergreen Colour Management Ltd
Printed and bound in China by C&C Offset Printing Co., Ltd

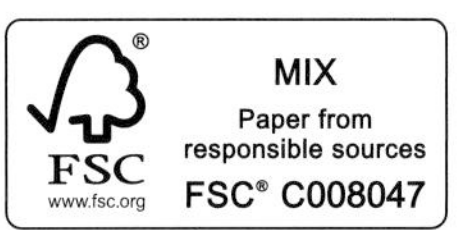

Cover: John Brett *The British Channel Seen from the Dorsetshire Cliffs* 1871 (detail). See p.79
p.2: György Kepes *Circles and Dots* c.1939–40 (detail). See p.137
pp.32–3: Joseph Mallord William Turner *Sun Setting over a Lake* c.1840 (detail). See p.75
pp.146–7: Yayoi Kusama *The Passing Winter* 2005 (detail of interior). See p.145

Measurements of artworks are given in centimetres, height before width

The Contributors

Kerryn Greenberg is an art historian and curator, and former Head of International Collection Exhibitions at Tate.

David Trigg is an independent writer, critic and art historian.

Matthew Watts is Curatorial Assistant at Tate.

The texts on pp.35–194 were authored by David Trigg and Matthew Watts, but draw on previously published catalogue texts. Many thanks to the following past and present colleagues in particular for their kind contributions: Ronald Alley, Lucy Askew, Simon Baker, Achim Borchardt-Hume, David Blayney Brown, Martin Butlin, Mary Chamot, Stuart Comer, Emma Dexter, Judy Egerton, Rachel Farquharson, Dennis Farr, Frances Fowle, Andrea Fredericksen, Matthew Gale, David Hodge, Cathy Johns, Evelyn Joll, Jo Kear, Emma Lewis, Anne Lyles, Elizabeth Manchester, Richard Martin, Shoair Mavlian, Kyla McDonald, Martin Myrone, Leslie Parris, Diane Perkins, Roy Perry, Sean Rainbird, Terry Riggs, Alice Sanger, Olga Smith, Rachel Taylor, Toby Treves and Beth Williamson.

Contents

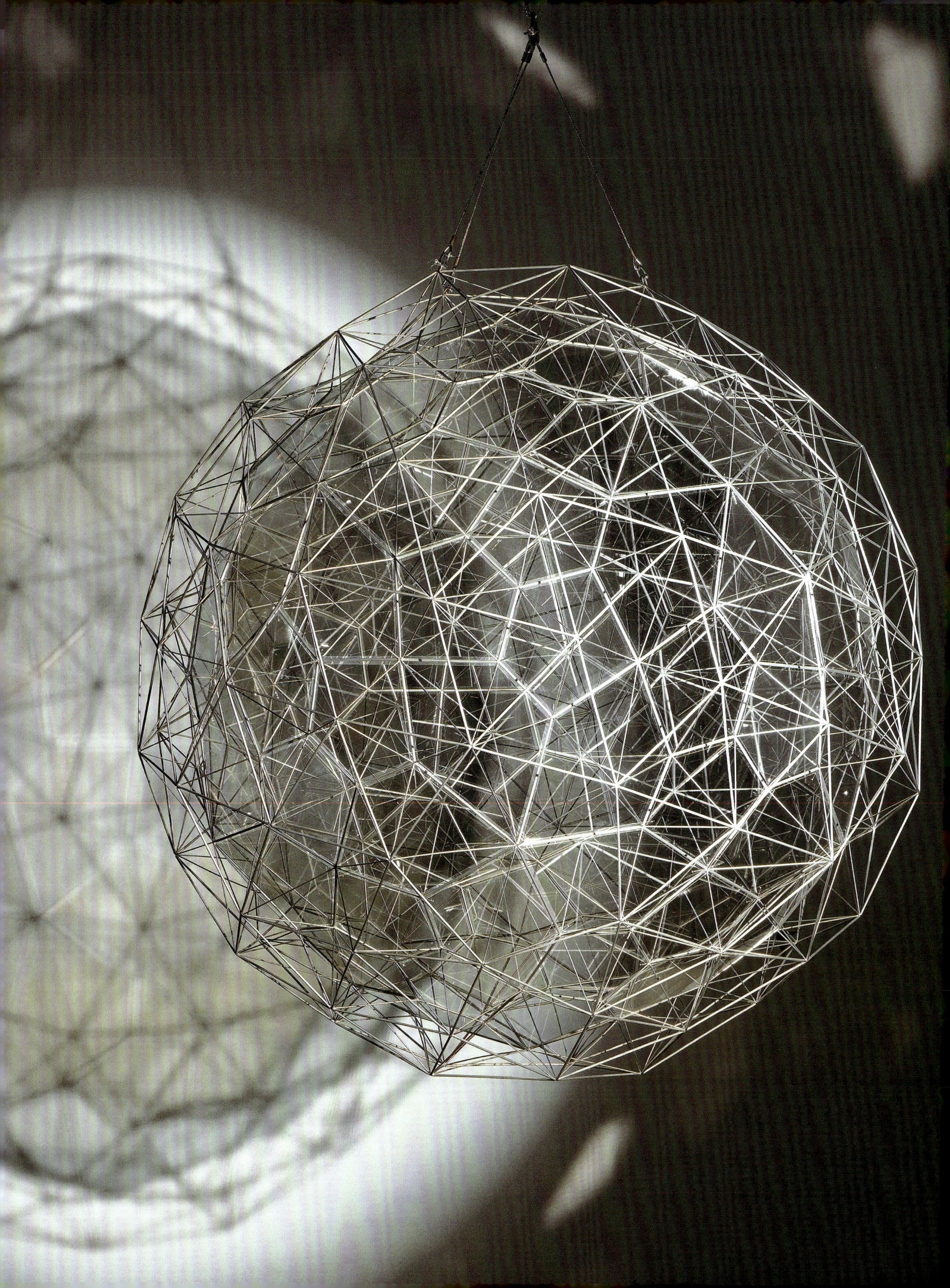

Olafur Eliasson *Stardust particle* 2014 (detail).
See p.191

The Colours of Light

Humankind has always observed the succession of day and night, the waxing and waning of the moon, and the changing seasons. Ancient civilisations studied the sun and other celestial bodies, built religious and funerary structures to align with their movements, and created myths to explain astronomical events. With time, philosophers around the world began to seek scientific explanations for natural phenomena and attempted to define the relationship between light and vision. Light has been a subject not only for scientists, but for philosophers, artists and poets too, who have all, in different ways, contributed to how we understand, capture and replicate its effects today.

In Europe in the seventeenth and early eighteenth centuries there was an explosion of scientific interest in light. For some – notably astronomers and microscopists – light served as a tool for observing and analysing nature, but for scientists like René Descartes (1596–1650), Christiaan Huygens (1629–95) and Isaac Newton (1642–1727), light was a subject worthy of study in its own right. Descartes thought everything physical in the universe was made of tiny 'corpuscles' of matter, a theory closely related to atomism. In his book *Le Monde* (*The World*) 1664, he began by distinguishing between the sensation of light (what we perceive) and the things that produce light (the stars, sun and fire), recognising light as a manageable material and attempting to define its properties.[1] At the time, the advancement of the natural sciences was regarded as the main exemplification of, and fuel for, intellectual progress, and Descartes's rationalist system of philosophy became a founding pillar of Enlightenment thought.

While Huygens and Newton both owed a great deal to Descartes, they disagreed fundamentally with each other about the nature of light. In 1690 Huygens published *Traité de la lumière* (*Treatise on Light*), in which he outlined his theory that light was a wave-like disturbance (centrifugal force).[2] In 1704, Newton argued in his book *Opticks* that light consisted of particles that moved in straight lines and bounced in predictable ways (the corpuscular theory of light).[3] By the early

Fig. 1 Olafur Eliasson *Your rainbow panorama* 2006–11
Rainbow coloured glass, diam. 150 m
ARoS Aarhus Kunstmuseum, Denmark

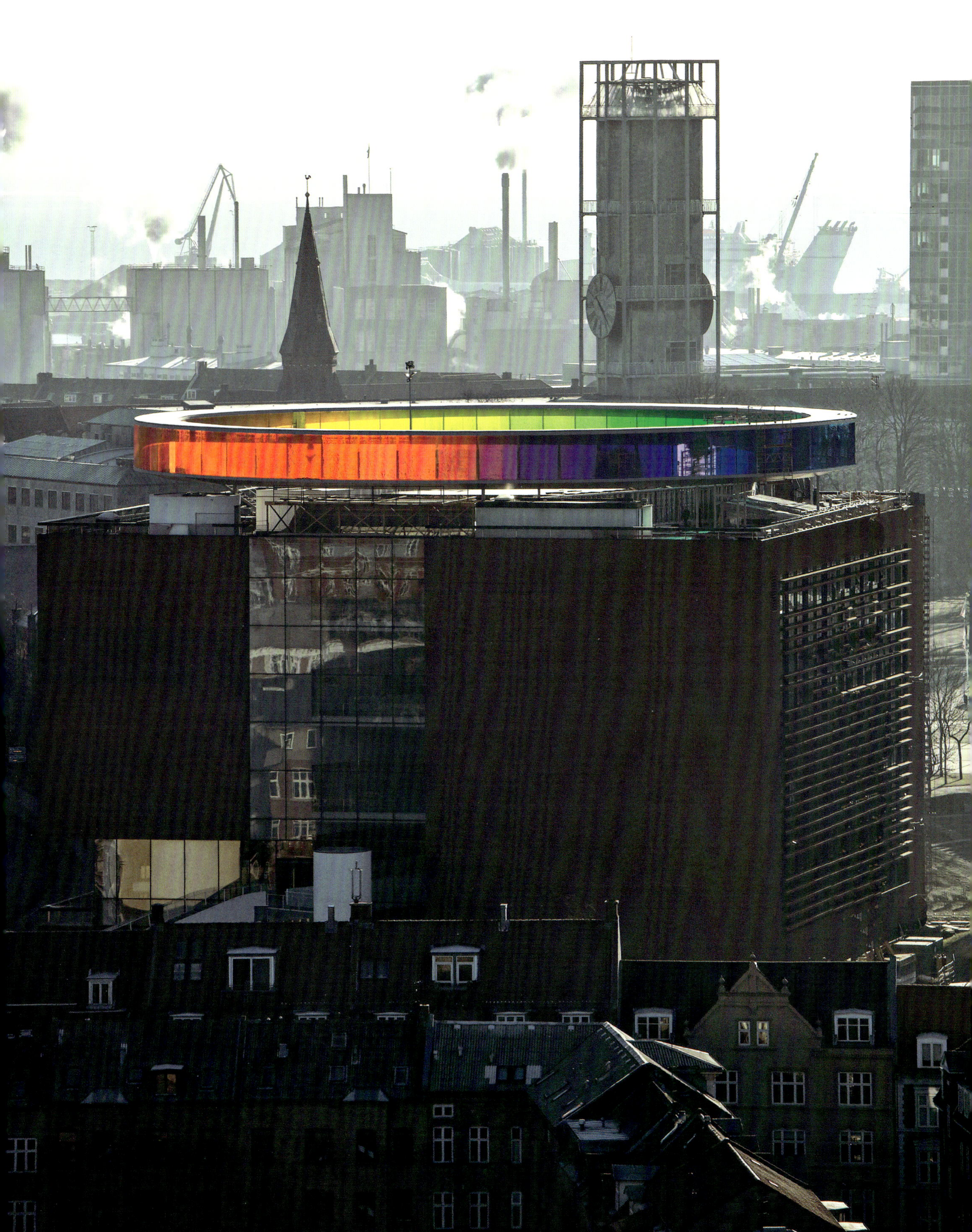

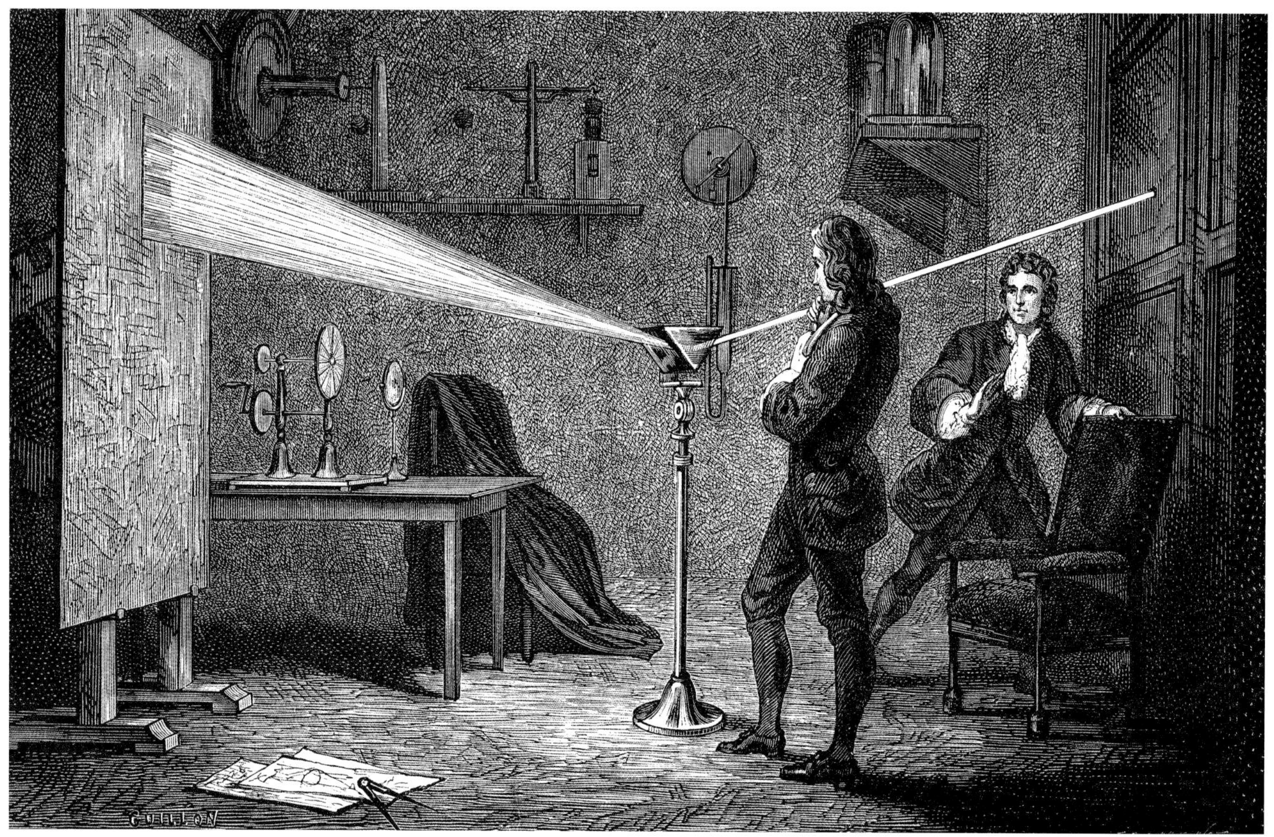

nineteenth century it was evident that both men were, at least in part, correct: Newton's early conception of the particle theory of light foregrounded modern understandings of the photon, but it could not explain refraction, diffraction and interference, which required knowledge of Huygens's wave theory of light.

Of Newton's many discoveries, the prism experiment became the most significant for artists. By shining a beam of sunlight through a prism, Newton was able to demonstrate how 'light refracts, with different coloured rays refracting at different angles, creating a spectrum'.[4] Newton identified the seven colours he observed: red, orange, yellow, green, blue, indigo and violet. Although it took decades for his ideas to be widely disseminated, his explanation of the spectrum eventually became the basis for every important colour theory until 1900.[5]

Despite Newton being one of the most influential scientists of all time, some artists were critical of his approach, which they felt was reductive. The English poet, painter and printmaker William Blake (1757–1827) portrayed Newton crouched naked on a rock absorbed

Fig. 2 Isaac Newton and the Prism Experiment
From Louis Figuier *Vies des Savants Illustres* 1868

Fig. 3 Goethe's symmetrical colour wheel with associated symbolic qualities, 1809

in a diagram, which he draws with a compass.[6] This implied that the scientist was so focused on following the rules of the compass that he was blind to everything else around him.

Blake was not the only person who believed Newton's error was trusting mathematics over the sensations of his eyes. The German writer and statesman Johann Wolfgang von Goethe (1749–1832) was also highly critical of Newton. In his book *Zur Farbenlehre* (*Theory of Colours*) 1810, Goethe combined the objective reason of the eighteenth-century Enlightenment with the subjective intuition of nineteenth-century Romanticism, arguing that colour was not solely a physical phenomenon, existing only as a measurable property within light, but that it was a product of the harmonious mixture of light and dark. While the science behind Goethe's assertions is questionable, his theory that colour can impact and affect mood and emotion has influenced many artists, from J.M.W. Turner (1775–1851) to Olafur Eliasson (1967–).

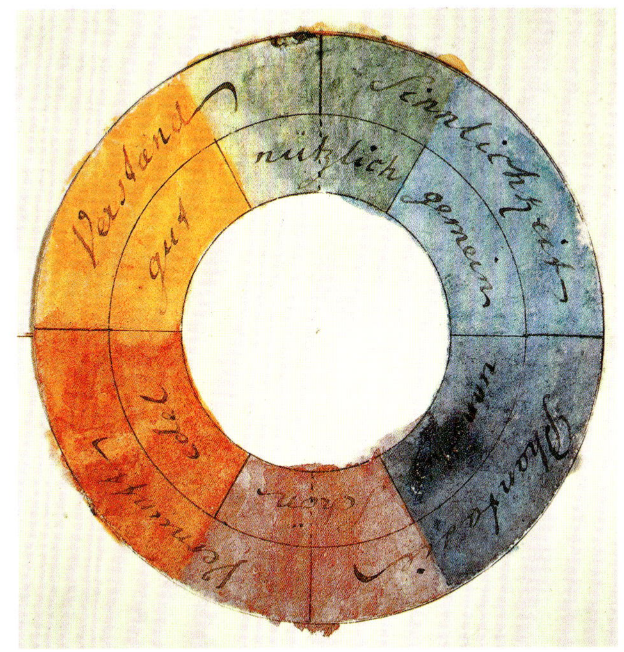

Divine Light

While artists engaged with these advances in physics and astronomy in the eighteenth century, Christianity remained the predominant power shaping European culture until the nineteenth century. Biblical texts, commentaries and mythical stories provided rich subject matter for artists, although visualising subjects ranging from creation and deliverance to visions experienced and miracles performed was not without its challenges.

Simon Mathurin Lantara (1729–78) in *The Spirit of God Moved Upon the Face of the Waters* 1751 (fig.4) abandoned the figural entirely in his attempt to visualise the events described in the Book of Genesis:

> In the beginning, when God created the universe, the earth was formless and desolate. The raging ocean that covered everything was engulfed in total darkness, and the Spirit of God was moving over the water. Then God commanded, 'Let there be light' – and light appeared. God was pleased with what he saw. Then he separated the light from the darkness, and he named the light 'Day' and the darkness 'Night.'

In this painting, the spirit of God is depicted emanating from a glowing triangular shape in the sky and reflecting on the crests of the waves below, presaging not only abstract iconography, but also the style of the Romantics, whose 'endless horizons symbolize the grandeur of creation'.[7]

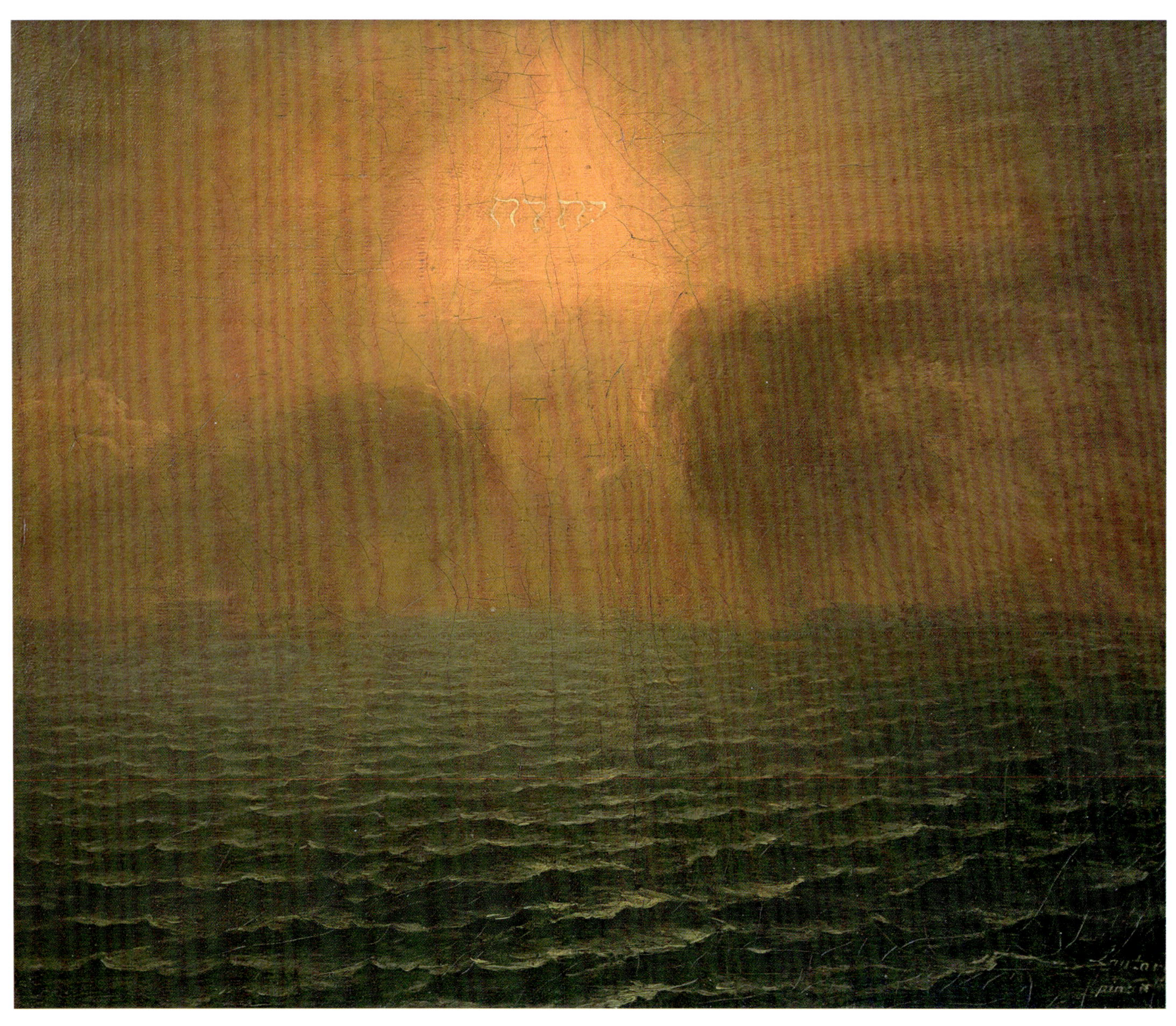

Fig. 4 Simon Mathurin Lantara *The Spirit of God Moved Upon the Face of the Waters* 1751
Oil paint on canvas 46.4 x 52.5
Musée de Grenoble, France

Eighteenth- and nineteenth-century European painting continued to borrow from the symbolism of the Old and New Testaments' association of light with goodness.[8] In Jacob More (1740–93) and J.M.W. Turner's paintings of the deluge from 1787 and c.1805 respectively (pp.40 and 44–5), light is both a guide and symbol of deliverance. The biblical story of the Great Flood, sent by God to return the earth to its pre-creation state before remaking it anew (Genesis 6:9–9:17), was a popular artistic subject in Britain in the eighteenth century. In More's painting, several people aboard a makeshift raft are depicted hunched over and vulnerable in the face of nature's immense power. Others in the water cling to the makeshift vessel, attempting to save themselves. In the centre of the composition, a silvery moon shines bright against a dark sky, casting light on the water and illuminating the wretched figures, the only light in an otherwise gloomy painting. While More's painting is largely monochrome and appears to depict the calm after the storm, Turner's painting shows the flood in full force; bodies struggling among raging waves beneath an ominous sky. The colours are vivid, and the strength of the wind is almost palpable. In the distance, dark clouds part to reveal a glowing orange sun on the horizon, which illuminates calm waters. Despite the artists' very different approaches to the same subject, they use light in exactly the same way, to represent hope.

Improvements in printing technologies in the early nineteenth century resulted in an explosion in publishing, and for the first time the Bible became a material object of everyday life throughout Europe and North America.[9] At the same time, studies of the scriptures as historical texts and scientific advances such as Charles Darwin's (1809–82) theory of evolution, formulated in his book *On the Origin of Species* 1859, cast doubt in the minds of educated people about the literal truth of the Bible. Some intellectuals queried the teachings of Christianity, and a substantial number of public figures for the first time openly declared that they had no religious beliefs.[10]

Working in this critical climate, the Pre-Raphaelite Brotherhood sought to articulate a new kind of painting, what Michaela Giebelhausen terms 'protestant biblical naturalism'.[11] William Holman Hunt (1827–1910), one of the founders of the Brotherhood, was especially committed to producing 'a historically acceptable and emotionally immediate image of Christ', which had been made more difficult by contemporary analyses of biblical texts.[12]

In the New Testament, Jesus describes himself as 'the light of the world', able to bring believers out from the darkness of ignorance and evil into the light of hope and redemption: 'Whoever follows me will never walk in darkness but will have the light of life.'[13] He told his disciples: 'You are the light of the world ... Let your light

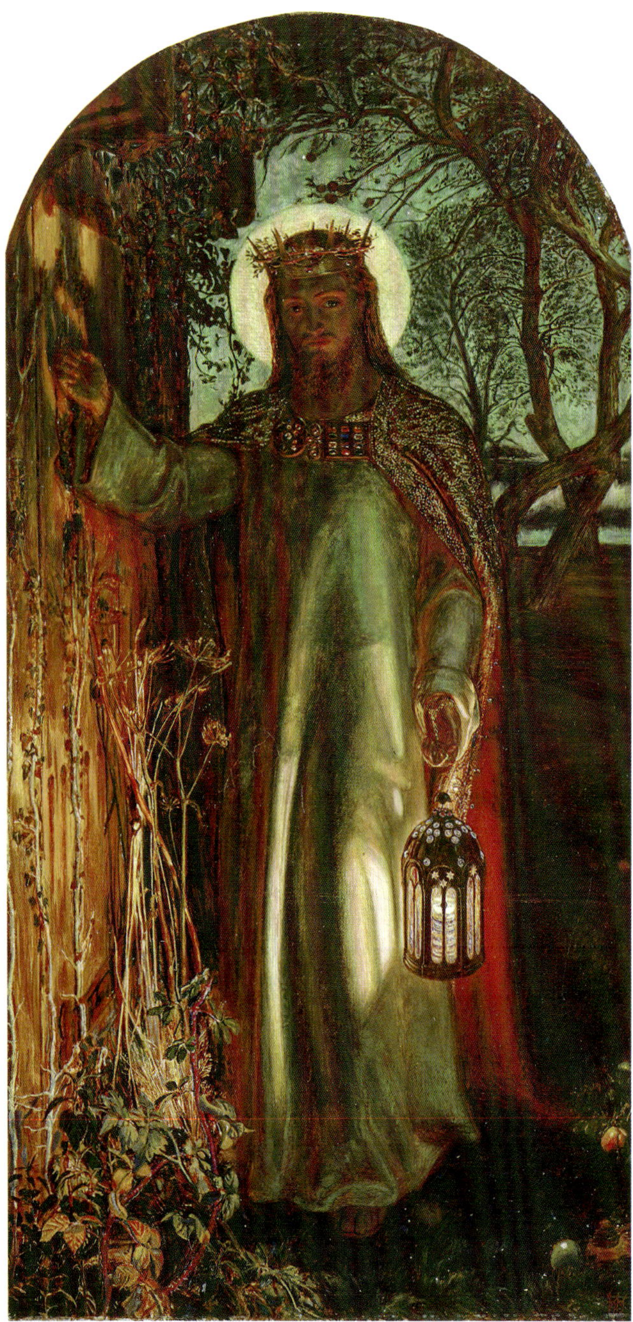

shine before men, that they may see your good deeds and praise your Father in heaven.'[14]

Hunt is best known for *The Light of the World* (fig.5), an image he painted three times, and which became a great Protestant icon.[15] Shaped like an arched doorway, this painting depicts Jesus facing forward and wearing a crown of thorns, which is illuminated by a halo that contrasts dramatically with the blue-tinged light among the trees in the orchard behind him. With his right hand, Jesus knocks at a disused wooden door overgrown with ivy and weeds. In his left hand he carries a lantern, which lights up his robes and the doorway, and casts a warm glow across his face and right hand.

While Hunt painted *The Light of the World* at night, he painted its material counterpart, *The Awakening Conscience* 1853, by day (p.105). To contemporary viewers, *The Awakening Conscience* may not appear to communicate a message of moral reform, but it is laden with symbolism that the Victorians would have easily decoded. The painting depicts a man and his mistress (known to be such due to the absence of a wedding ring) playing the piano and singing. Mid-song, the woman has a sudden revelation. Rising from her lover's lap, she gazes into the sunlit garden beyond, which is reflected in the mirror behind her. The cat playing with the broken-winged bird under the table, the discarded glove and the tangled skein of wool on the floor symbolise her vulnerable position. The ray of light in the foreground indicates that in spite of her loss of innocence, redemption is still possible.

Inspired by biblical scripture, these paintings emphasised the dichotomy between light and dark, reinforcing the idea that light signifies inspiration, power, truth and beauty, which had become entrenched during the Age of Enlightenment (1715–89).

Fig. 5 William Holman Hunt *The Light of the World* 1851–6
Oil paint on canvas 49.8 x 26.1
Manchester Art Gallery, UK

Fig. 6 J.M.W. Turner *Snow Storm: Hannibal and his Army Crossing the Alps* exh.1812
Oil paint on canvas 146 × 237.5
Tate. Accepted by the nation as part of the Turner Bequest 1856

Natural Light

By the early nineteenth century, and in the aftermath of the French Revolution of 1789, disillusionment with the Enlightenment values of reason and order had set in. With its emphasis on individualism and emotion, Romanticism emerged. Defined as an aesthetic in literary criticism around 1800, Romanticism gained momentum as an artistic movement in France and Britain in the early decades of the nineteenth century and flourished until mid-century. Romantic artists and their patrons yearned for a light that they believed to be pure, and it is this that drove many painters outside. There they created small studies of various weather conditions and transient light effects that served as a catalogue of elements for their subsequent compositions in the studio.

Born just a year apart, Turner and John Constable (1776–1837) revolutionised landscape painting of the nineteenth century, though their approaches were entirely distinct. Turner sought to depict high drama:

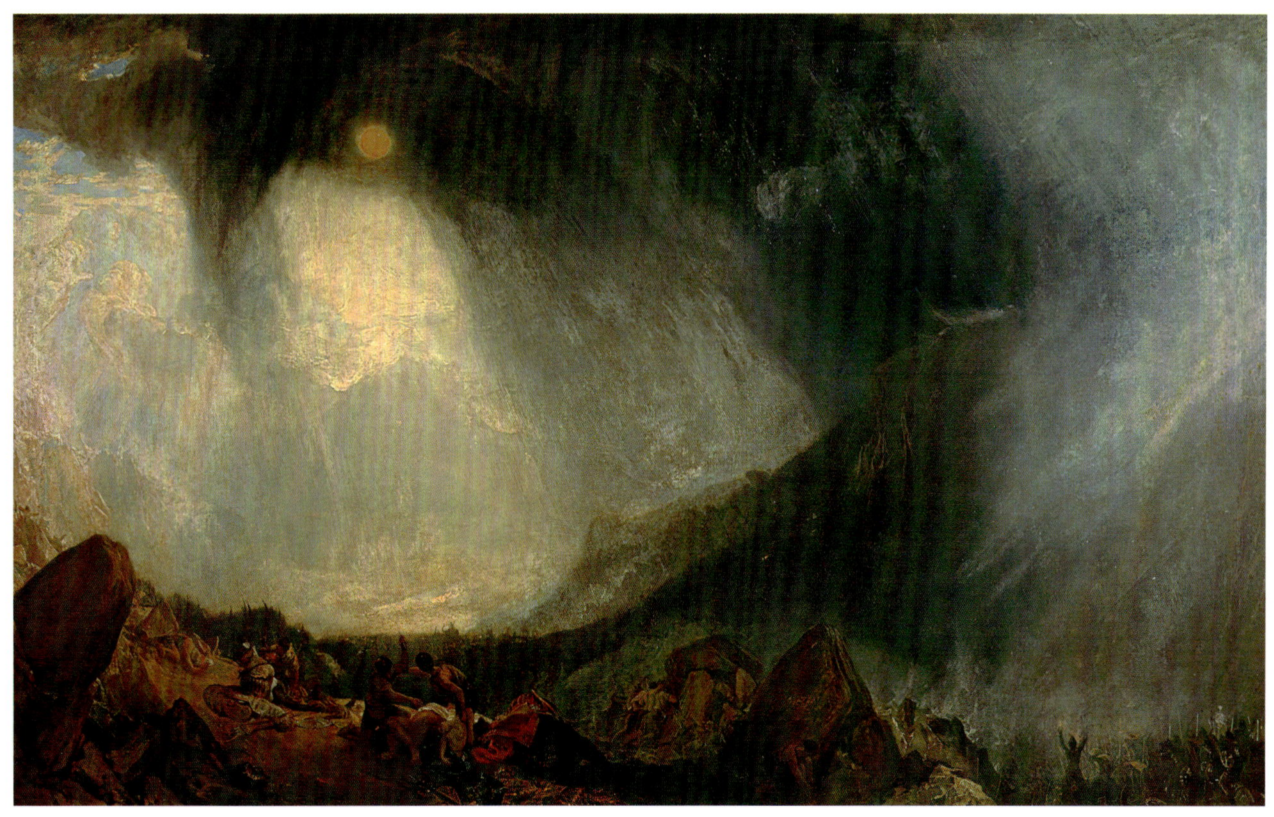

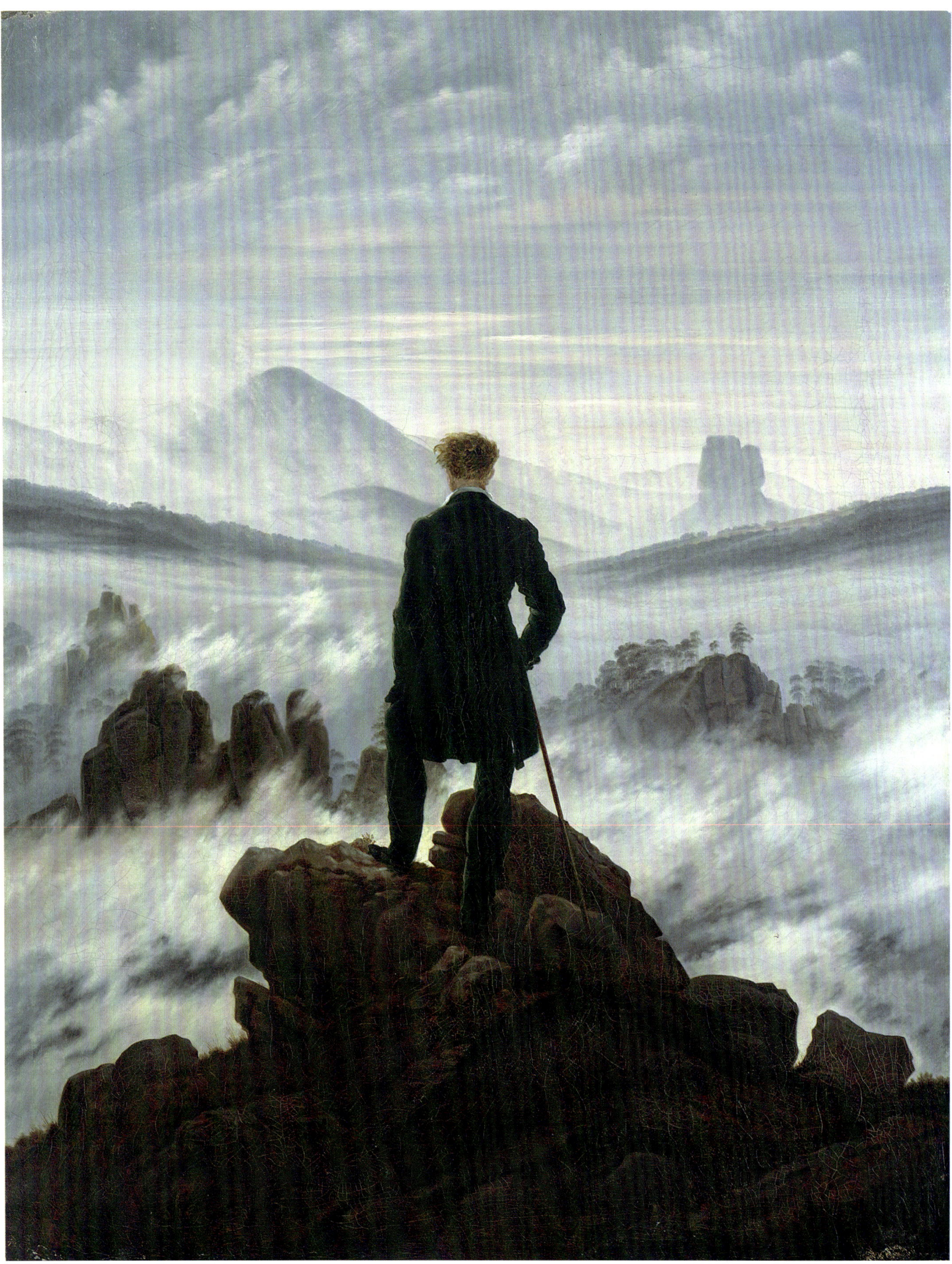

shipwrecks, storms, the horrors of the Napoleonic Wars and the impact of industrialisation, among other vivid scenes. His late paintings tend to be expressionistic, bordering on abstract, intent on capturing the unpredictability, uncontrollable power and beauty of nature (pp.47, 75–7).

Like Turner, Constable eschewed producing the highly idealised landscapes popular at the time. Instead, he sought to paint the everyday as truthfully as possible (pp.59–61 and 63–5). His realistic depictions of bucolic English landscapes might appear conservative in comparison to Turner's dramatic subjects and energetic brushwork, but they reveal a remarkable understanding of nature and the details of rural life. Constable's preparatory sketches, completed relatively quickly and often in oil paint outdoors in locations well known to him, allowed him to capture the effects of changing weather conditions on the countryside with spontaneity, which he was then able to transfer to his finished works. Between 1821 and 1822 Constable produced one hundred small-scale cloud studies, noting the season, time of day, wind direction and other weather conditions on the verso, a practice that suggests an interest in the emerging science of meteorology, and which he described as 'skying'.[16] Although none of his cloud studies are known to have been used directly in a more complete painting, they played an important role in informing his approach.[17]

While Constable invariably depicted rural landscapes in his native England, Turner and other Romantic artists like Caspar David Friedrich (1774–1840) and John Martin (1789–1854) favoured more dramatic scenery that enabled them to emphasise intense emotion as an authentic source of aesthetic experience. They believed a close connection with nature was mentally and morally healthy, and sought to convey apprehension, awe and horror in the face of its overwhelming power. For these artists, light was instrumental in contributing to the mood of the painting. In Friedrich's painting *Wanderer Above the Sea of Fog* c.1818 (fig.7), the fog envelops the valleys and diffuses the light, leaving only subtle tonal variations that suggest the expansiveness of the landscape that stretches out in front of the lone figure. By contrast the light source in Turner's *Snow Storm: Hannibal and his Army Crossing the Alps* exh.1812 (fig.6) is immediately apparent. Set in the upper third of the painting, high in the sky, the sun is a solid yolk-like yellow throwing light on to the soldiers below, who are struggling in the harsh mountainous conditions and are about to be besieged by a threatening storm.

The mood is even more ominous in John Martin's *The Destruction of Pompeii and Herculaneum* 1822 (pp.53–5). Mount Vesuvius is depicted in the early stages of the eruption, the magma blasting into the air, colouring the sky and billowing ash clouds vivid shades of red and orange. Survivors are shown fleeing in the foreground, but they are not the subject of the painting. Rather, Martin is concerned with portraying the power of nature, 'producing powerful contrasts by every reflection of light'.[18]

Vesuvius was considered one of the most spectacular instances of the 'natural sublime', and during the Romantic period became a metaphor for everything from poetic inspiration to political revolution.[19] The volcano was almost continuously active from the late seventeenth to late nineteenth century, and numerous artists visited it as part of their Grand Tour of Europe, invariably depicting it in a state of eruption whether they had witnessed this or not. Joseph Wright

Fig. 7 Caspar David Friedrich *Wanderer Above the Sea of Fog* c.1818
Oil paint on canvas 94.8 x 74.8
Kunsthalle Hamburg, Germany

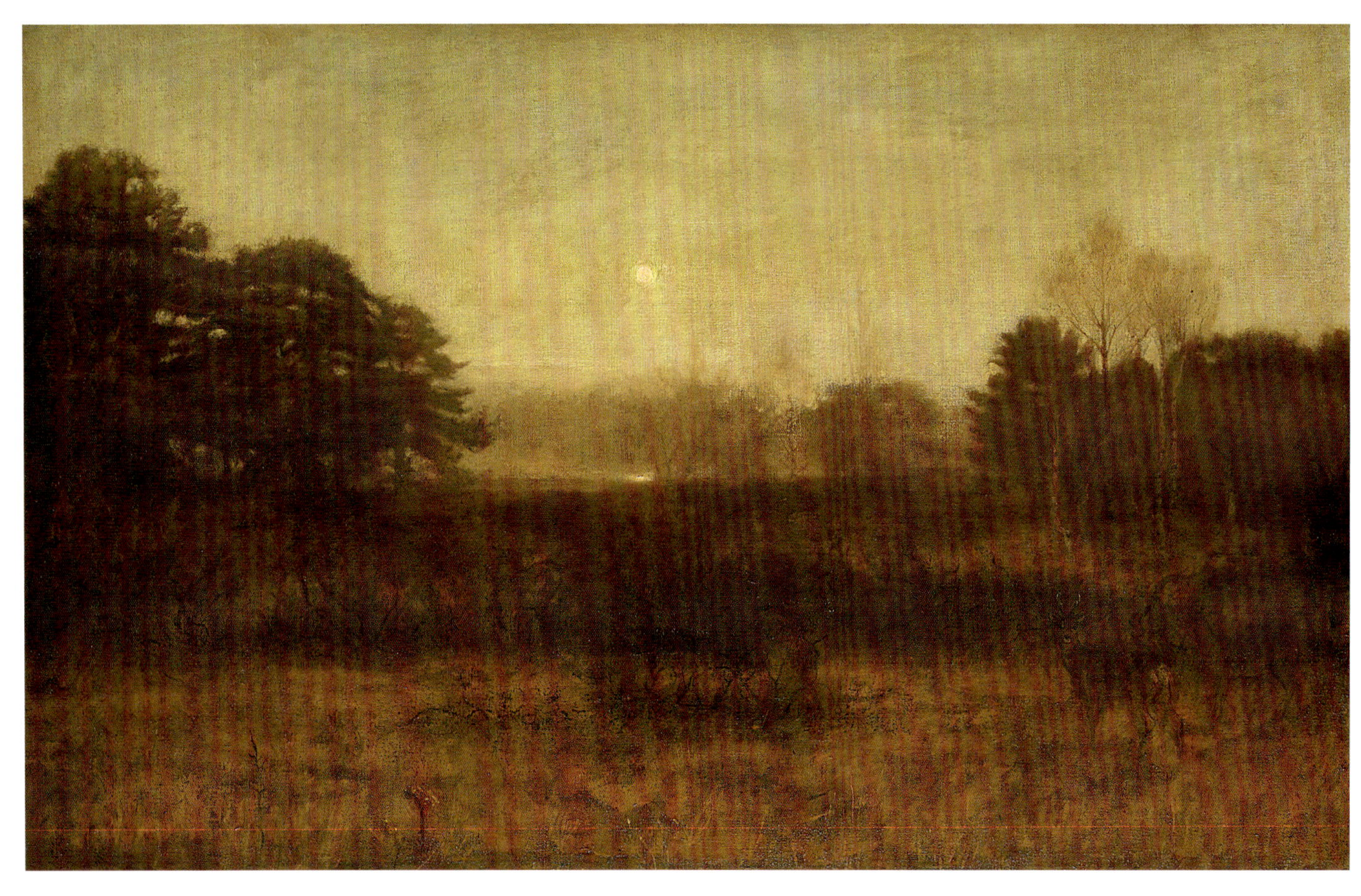

Fig. 8 John Everett Millais *'The Moon is Up, and Yet it is not Night'* 1890
Oil paint on canvas 104.1 × 168.9
Tate. Presented by Mrs H.S. Neilson 1946

of Derby (1734–97) is thought to have painted over thirty views of the exploding volcano.[20] Although he was a neoclassical artist, there are pre-Romantic influences in his work, and in most of his paintings the artist presents the two aspects of the sublime: beauty and danger. The light is mesmerising, but also potentially cataclysmic.

While the Romantic artists observed light effects outside and created sketches that informed the paintings they completed in their studios, the Pre-Raphaelite Brotherhood pioneered genuine *en plein air* (open air) painting in England during the 1850s and 1860s. *Ophelia* 1851–2 is arguably both John Everett Millais's (1829–96) masterpiece, and the most iconic work of the Pre-Raphaelite Brotherhood. Painted when he was only twenty-two years old, Millais worked for months outside, composing the background with painstaking detail before returning to his studio to add the figure of Ophelia (pp.81–3). The Pre-Raphaelites favoured bright, transparent colours, applying these in thin glazes on to a smooth, white ground, most often on canvas. It is this white background that gives these paintings their luminosity, while building up the colour through thin glazes imitates the effect of light falling on a subject and achieves a depth that cannot be obtained by using colours mixed on a palette. When painting interior scenes, the Pre-Raphaelites would often depict their subjects in relation to an open window or door left ajar, letting natural light into the painting, lending perspective and allowing the Brotherhood to demonstrate their skill in meticulously describing nature (pp.103 and 105).

While the Pre-Raphaelites' observations of nature and use of brilliant colour offered a powerful alternative to traditional academic painting formulas, Millais's later landscapes were not universally appreciated. The fault in Millais's landscapes was thought to lie with the artist's Pre-Raphaelite roots, which discouraged him from generalising. In a review of *'The Moon is Up, and Yet it is not Night'* 1890 (fig.8), a critic wrote: 'The drawback is still that he reproduces rather than ... interprets nature.'[21]

In France the practice of painting *en plein air* was pioneered in the early decades of the nineteenth century by the Realists, facilitated by the invention of metal tubes for storing oil paints, which extended their shelf life and made them easily transportable. At this time the Académie des Beaux-Arts still dominated French art, preserving traditional approaches to content and style. Paintings of historic subjects, religious themes and portraits rendered with carefully blended brushstrokes and restrained colour were highly valued. It was these paintings that tended to be accepted into the Académie's annual, juried art show, the Salon de Paris, an essential rite of passage for artists wishing to secure commissions and achieve recognition. The Salon jurists, however, tended to be conservative; they opposed any shifts away from traditional painting styles, and their decisions invariably reinforced the values of the Académie.

In the early 1860s, four young painters, Claude Monet (1840–1926), Pierre-Auguste Renoir (1841–1919), Alfred Sisley (1839–99) and Frédéric Bazille (1841–70), met while studying in Paris and discovered they shared an interest in painting landscapes and contemporary life rather than historical or mythological scenes. Together they would venture into the countryside to paint *en plein air*, not for the purpose of making sketches to be developed into carefully finished paintings in the studio, but to paint directly from nature, utilising the vivid colours of synthetic pigments to develop a lighter and brighter manner of painting.

In 1863, the Salon jury rejected an unusually large number of submissions, resulting in an outcry. In order to prove that the Salons were democratic, Napoleon III instituted the Salon des Refusés (Salon of the Refused), containing artworks the Salon had rejected that year. It opened on 17 May 1863, marking the birth of the French avant-garde and paving the way for the first impressionist exhibition a decade later. Organised by Monet, Renoir, Sisley, Camille Pissarro (1830–1903) and Edgar Degas (1834–1917), the 1874 exhibition presented 165 works by thirty artists, including Monet's *Impression, Sunrise* 1872 (fig.9), which gave the movement its name when the critic Louis Leroy derisively wrote in the satirical journal *Le Charivari*: 'Impression! Of course. There must be an impression somewhere in it. What freedom … what flexibility of style! Wallpaper in its early stages is much more finished than that.'[22]

Unlike their predecessors, the impressionists portrayed overall visual effects instead of details, using short, 'broken' brushstrokes of colour rather than gradations of shading to suggest both form and light. While the loose brushwork gives the impression of being spontaneous and effortless (or unfinished, as Leroy claimed), the impressionists' paintings were carefully composed, and the artists spent considerable time observing the effects of light before committing these to canvas. Today Monet is renowned for painting the same subjects – Rouen Cathedral, Poplars, Haystacks and Water Lilies among others – multiple times to show the different effects of light and atmosphere on a scene at varying times of the day, across the seasons and in a range of weather conditions (pp.85 and 87). In order to capture these fleeting effects, Monet would work on many paintings virtually simultaneously. Beginning at dawn, he would switch to sequentially later paintings as the light changed, sometimes working on as many as a dozen in a single day, each depicting a slightly different aspect of light, repeating the process over the course of days, weeks or months until the series was complete.[23]

A younger generation of French artists led by Georges Seurat (1859–91) renounced the spontaneity

Fig. 9 Claude Monet *Impression, Sunrise* 1872
Oil paint on canvas 48 x 63
Musée Marmottan Monet, Paris, France

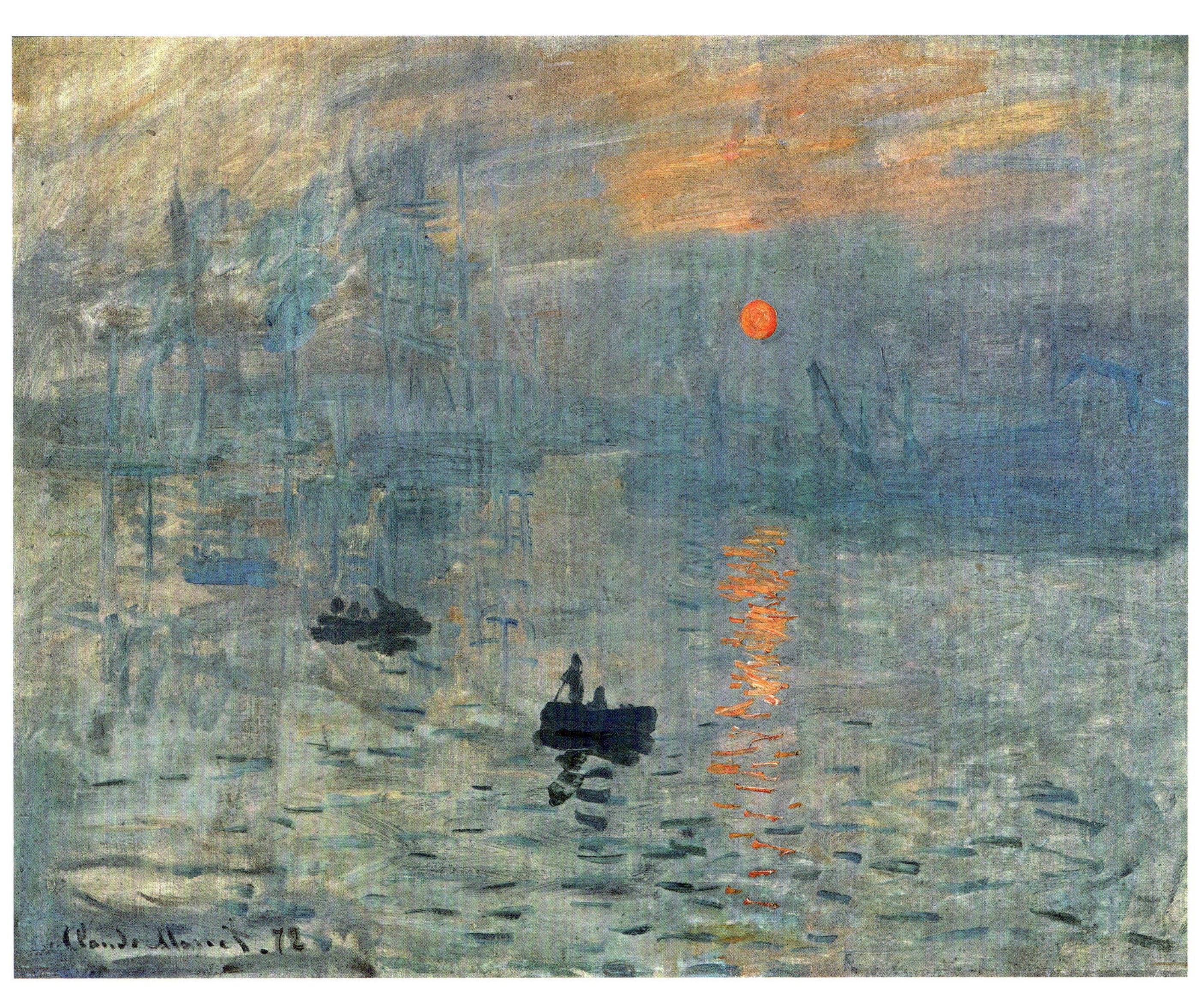

of impressionism in favour of a more systematic approach, grounded in the study of optics and scientifically based colour theories. They were particularly influenced by the scientific revelations of Charles Henry (1859–1926), who met Pissarro, Seurat and Paul Signac (1863–1935) during the last impressionist exhibition in 1886 and argued that the basic elements of art – line and colour – could be treated autonomously. The French chemist Michel Eugène Chevreul (1786–1889) was also an important influence. Building on Goethe's theories of colour, he noted during his tenure as director of a dye works in Paris that a colour could appear different in hue and intensity when presented in relation to another colour, an effect he called simultaneous contrast.[24] The American physicist Ogden Rood (1831–1902) meanwhile divided colour into three constants – purity, luminosity and hue – and suggested that small dots or lines of different colours, when viewed from a distance, would blend into a new colour.[25] Inspired by these contemporary writings on colour theory, the neo-impressionists came to believe that carefully positioned dabs of paint resulted in a greater vibrancy of colour and sensations of light and movement than could be achieved by the conventional mixing of pigments on a palette.

While Seurat made preparatory studies for *The Bridge at Courbevoie* 1886–7 (fig.10) from the bank of the River Seine, he tended to refine and develop his images in the studio.[26] This painstaking work involved analysing the colours of each form, and areas of light and shadow, and dividing these into their component parts before applying small brushstrokes of complementary colours to build up the image and create a luminous effect. Seurat referred to this process as 'chromoluminarism', a word he favoured for its suggestions of the effects of colour and light, but this term did not stick, and the technique became known instead as Pointillism.[27]

In 1959, Bridget Riley (1931–) painted a copy of Seurat's *Bridge at Courbevoie*, an exercise which provided her with a new understanding of colour, light and perception. Although grounded in nineteenth-century colour theory, the lessons Riley learned from Seurat 'emboldened her to strike out into the realm of pure abstraction'.[28] Since then, Riley has consistently used precise marks and chromatic variation to bring her paintings to life. In *Late Morning* 1967–8 (fig.11) she was particularly interested in the effects of the complementary cool and warm tones on the white ground, an interaction which 'creates an impression of light radiating from the centre of the canvas'.[29] In the seventy-odd years between Seurat and Riley, a major shift occurred which saw artists not only seek to represent light, but to manipulate and create it.

Fig. 10 Georges Seurat *The Bridge at Courbevoie* 1886–7
Oil paint on canvas 46.4 x 53.3
Courtauld Institute of Art, London, UK

Fig. 11 Bridget Riley *Late Morning* 1967–8
Polyvinyl acetate paint on canvas 226.1 × 359.4
Tate. Purchased 1968

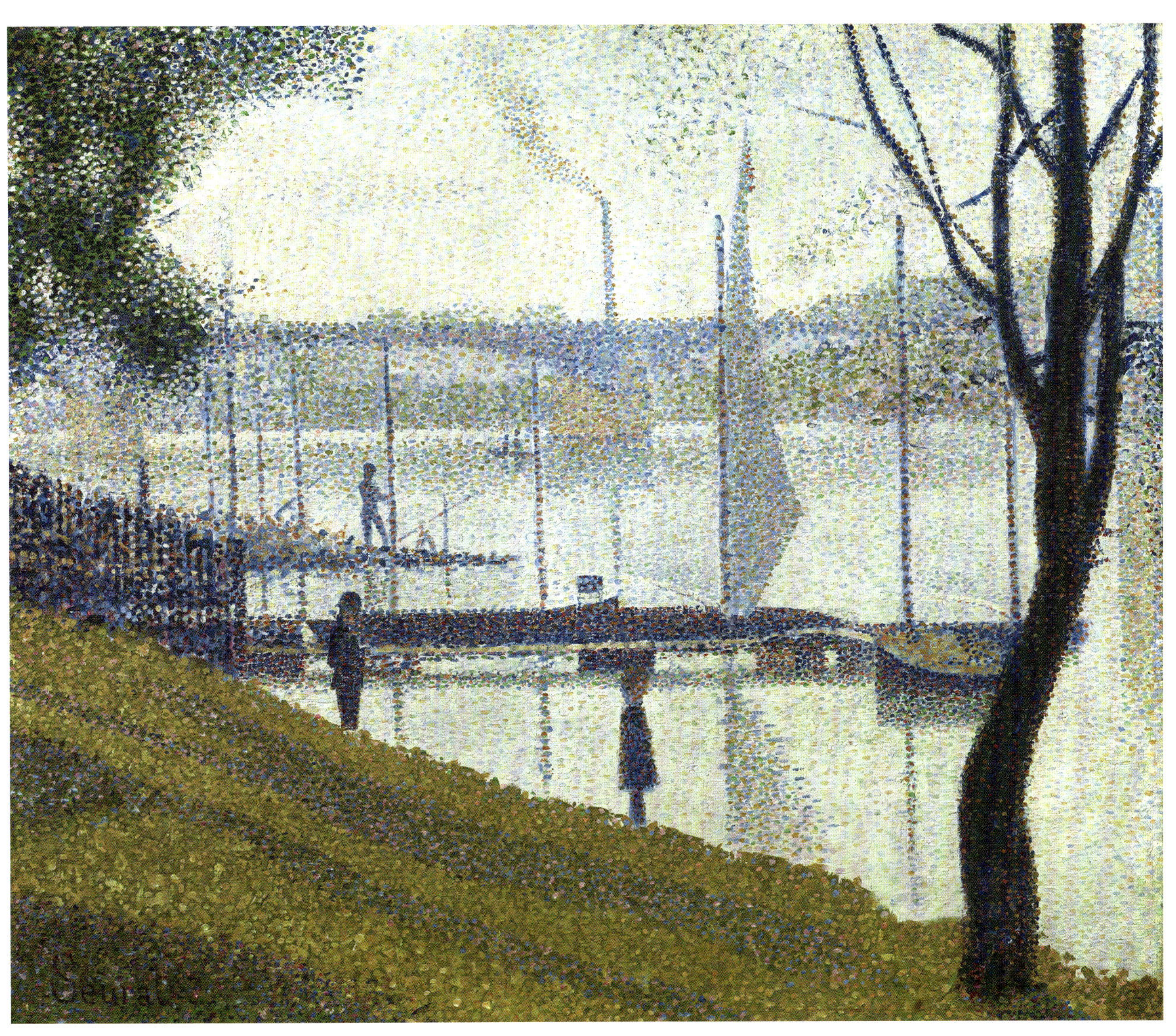

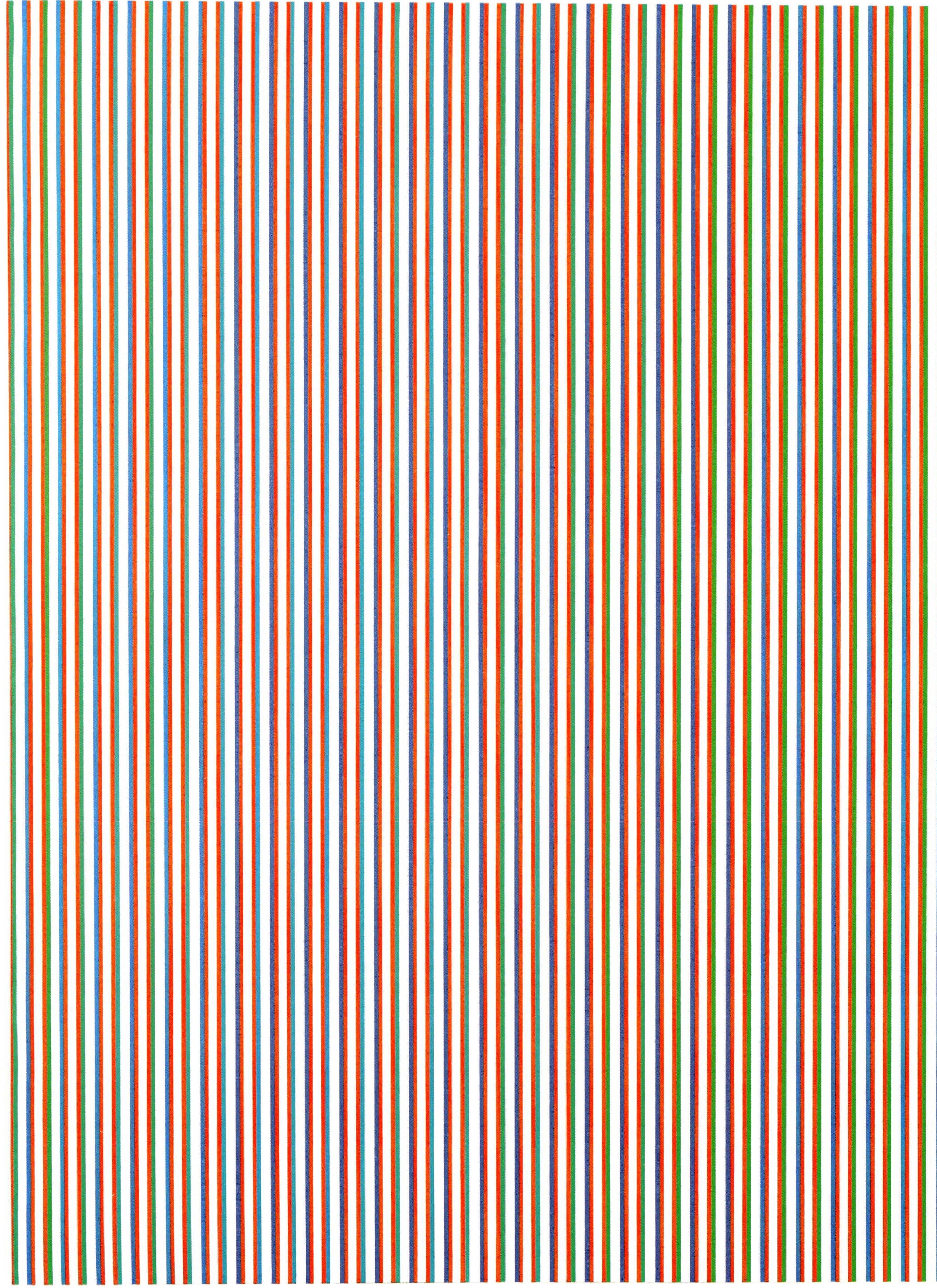

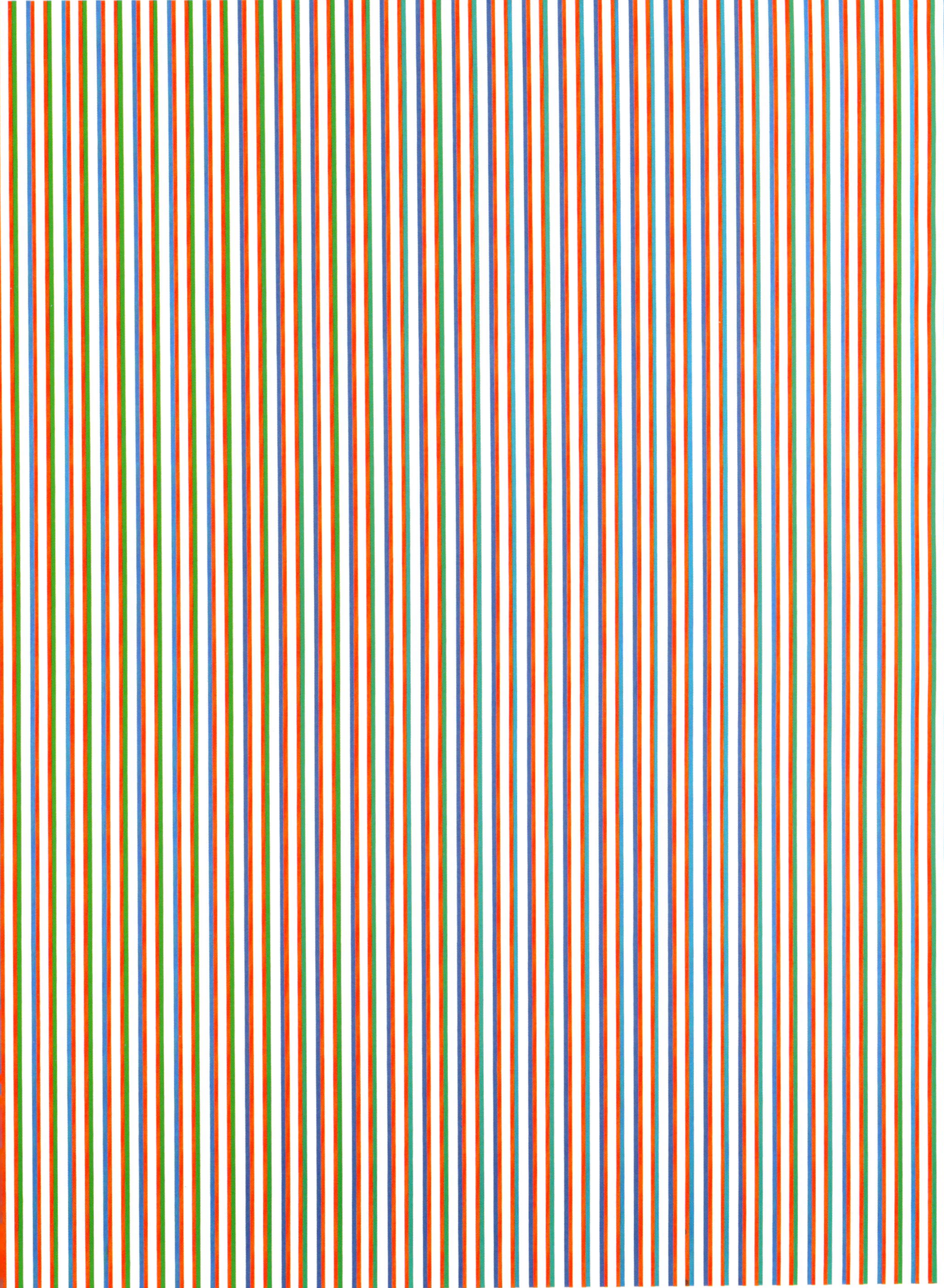

Artificial Light

In his book *Disenchanted Night* 1988, Wolfgang Schivelbusch recounts how artificial light developed in the nineteenth century, explaining how the technology of man-made illumination helped forge modern consciousness. With industrialisation from the mid-eighteenth century, cities expanded, becoming denser and increasingly urban in character. Oil lamps and gas burners became ubiquitous, first in Britain and then elsewhere. Photographic technologies gradually developed, with the daguerreotype, the first publicly available photographic process, becoming widely available during the 1840s.[30]

Some painters, like Joseph Wright of Derby, aligned

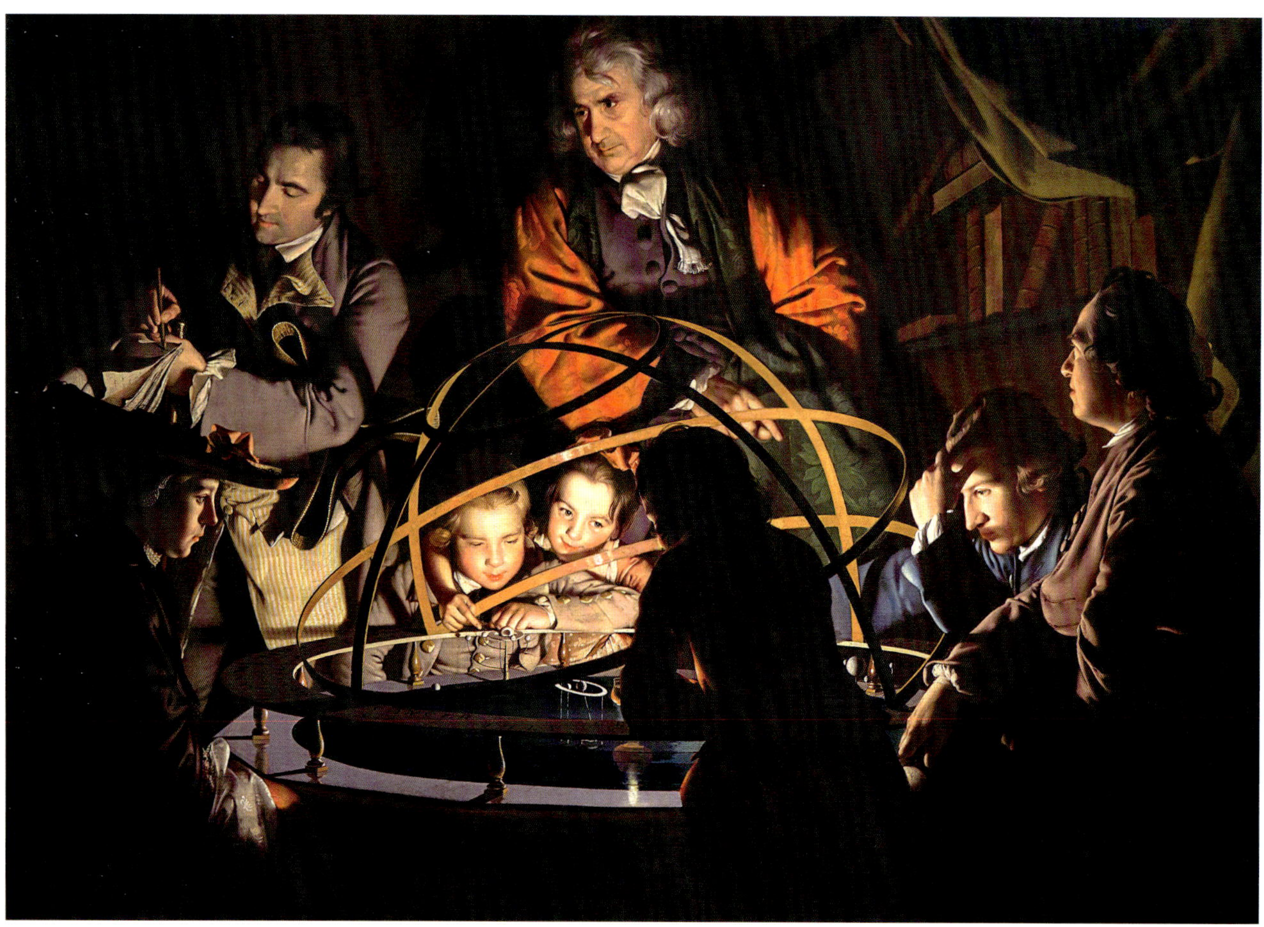

Fig. 12 Joseph Wright of Derby *A Philosopher Giving that Lecture on the Orrery, in which a Lamp is Put in Place of the Sun* 1764–6
Oil paint on canvas 147.3 x 203.2
Derby Museums and Art Gallery, Derby, UK

their art with the inventors of the Industrial Revolution (1760–1820/40). As scientists began to make sense of how light worked, artists reflected this. With paintings like *A Philosopher Giving that Lecture on the Orrery, in which a Lamp is Put in Place of the Sun* 1764–6 (fig.12), Wright used artificial light not only to heighten the drama, but to illustrate how our appreciation of the world could be enlightened by science. During the eighteenth century, a model of the solar system (an orrery) would have been used to demonstrate the relative positions and motions of the planets and moons to convey new understandings in astronomy, gravitation and mechanics to a wider public. In this painting, a lamp in the centre represents the sun and, while not visible, illuminates the faces of the audience, creating the strong light and deep shadows that give this painting its dramatic effect.

From 1800 onwards, various inventors began to devise different ways of generating electricity to create light, but it was not until Thomas Edison (1847–1931) patented the practical and inexpensive incandescent filament bulb in 1879 that electric light became widely accessible.[31] The popularisation of electric light from the 1880s onwards stimulated those involved in architecture, design, still photography, film, music and theatre to start working with light in new ways, and by 1893 Edison's kinetoscope had enabled the first public demonstration of the motion picture at the Brooklyn Institute of Arts and Sciences in New York.[32]

In 1919, architect Walter Gropius (1883–1969) established Staatliches Bauhaus, a school which advocated a return to craftsmanship, and aimed to abolish distinctions between artist and artisan.[33] The Bauhaus acted as a hub in post-First World War Germany for Europe's most experimental creatives, attracting well-known artists such as Josef Albers (1888–1976), Wassily Kandinsky (1866–1944) and Paul Klee (1879–1940) as faculty. At the Bauhaus, the instructors advocated for the centrality of the built environment and, among other things, evidenced a strong interest in exploring the creative possibilities of light.

Josef Albers believed the ability to accurately perceive differences in light needed to be trained. He gave his students at the Bauhaus and later at Black Mountain College in North Carolina, USA, various exercises to help them distinguish between different degrees of lightness and to recognise what he called the 'discrepancy between physical fact and psychic effect'.[34] Known for his *Homage to the Square* paintings (pp.153–5), created between 1950 and 1976 and comprising several coloured squares nesting within each other, Albers called colour the 'most relative medium in art', noting that what we perceive as colour is really light of different wavelengths and intensities.[35]

In the Bauhaus theatre workshop, Oskar Schlemmer (1888–1943) upgraded the role of light from basic illumination to an integral element of each production through the use of shadow play, film-projections and moving shapes of light and reflection (fig.13). The potential of light for 'sudden or blinding illumination, for flare effects, for phosphorescent effects, for bathing the auditorium in light synchronized with climaxes or with the total extinguishing of lights on the stage' was also recognised.[36]

While architecture, typography, carpentry, metalwork, weaving, sculpture, wall painting and theatre all had established workshops at the Bauhaus from early on, photography was not taught or even organised as an extra-curricular activity until a decade after the school was founded.[37] Nevertheless the medium attracted

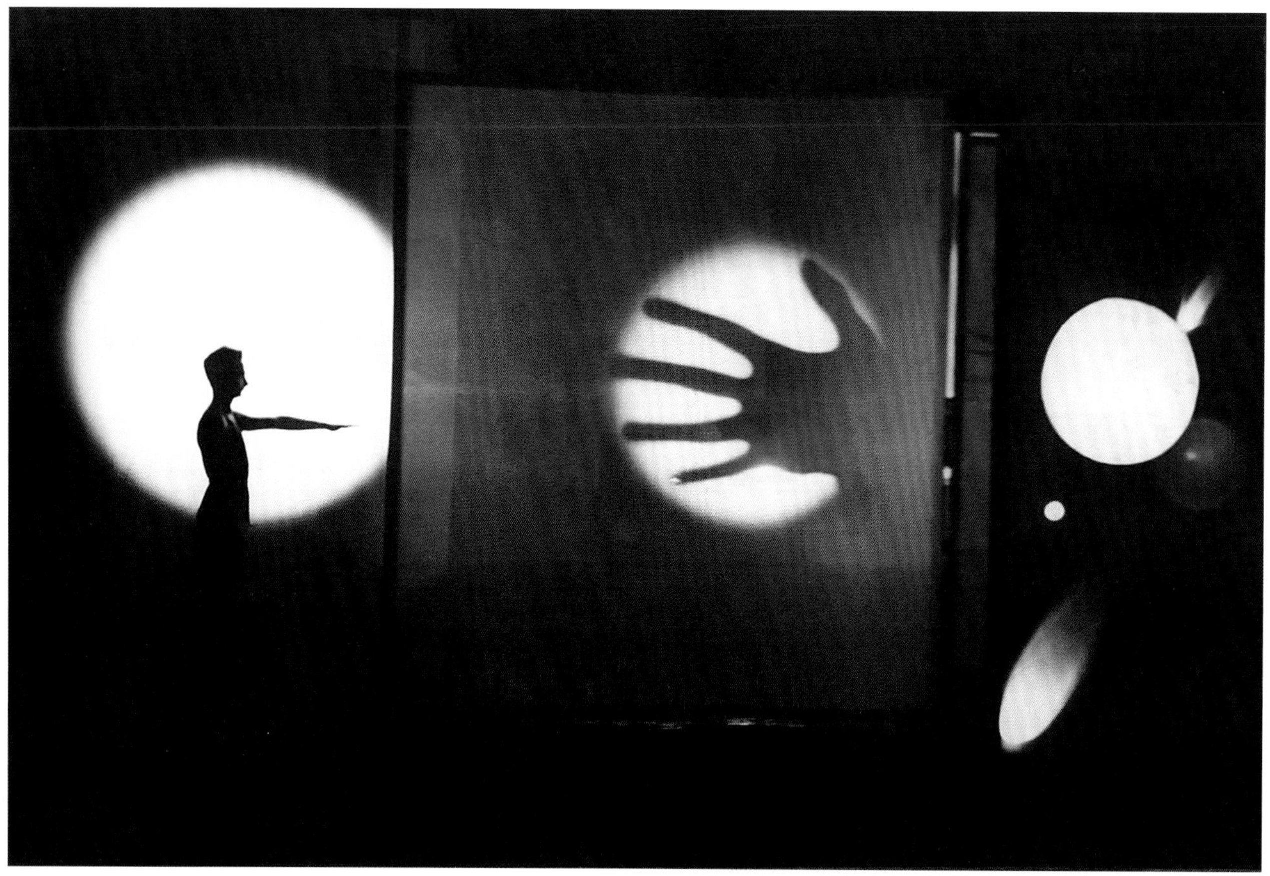

an enthusiastic following, particularly after the arrival of László Moholy-Nagy (1895–1946) and Lucia Moholy (1894–1989) in 1923. In the same way that traditional media and materials were subjected to intense reappraisal at the Bauhaus, Moholy-Nagy advocated unlimited experimentation with the photographic process, arguing that light would bring forth a new form of visual art.[38] Moholy-Nagy wrote articles and books on the subject, including his seminal *Malerei, Photographie, Film* (*Painting, Photography, Film*) 1925, illustrated with many of his own photographs, which are characterised by unusual perspectives and experimental compositions. His 'love of the camera was based on the fact that it demonstrated so persuasively that nothing was as it seemed'.[39] He believed that photography was capable not only of reproducing, but producing an entirely new art, an idea exemplified by his camera-less photographs

Fig. 13 T. Lux Feininger *Bauhaus Stage Dessau: 'Light Play' by Oskar Schlemmer with the Dancer and Pantomime Werner Siedhoff* 1928

Fig. 14 László Moholy-Nagy *Light Prop for an Electric Stage* 1930
Aluminium, steel, nickel-plated brass, other metals, plastic, wood and electric motor 151.1 × 69.9 × 69.9
Harvard Art Museums/Busch-Reisinger Museum, Cambridge, USA

created by placing objects on photographic paper and exposing them to light. This simple method, which became known as the photogram, was practised by photography's founders in the nineteenth century, but at the Bauhaus avant-garde artists revived the technique to explore the optical and expressive properties of light.[40]

Although many photographers were influenced by Moholy-Nagy (pp.127, 129, 131, 135, 137, 139 and 141–3), his most significant contribution is arguably the *Light Prop for an Electric Stage* 1930 (fig.14), a device with moving metal parts, which when correctly lit throws reflections and projects moving shadows on to nearby surfaces. Moholy-Nagy described this work as a 'light display machine, a potential stage prop and an apparatus for painting with light'.[41] It was the culmination of years of work and became the subject of experimental photographs and a film Moholy-Nagy made, titled *Lichtspiel Schwarz-Weiss-Grau* (*Lightplay Black-White-Grey*) 1930. *Light Prop for an Electric Stage* was so important to the artist that he took it with him to Chicago in 1937 and positioned it prominently in the New Bauhaus (later known as the Institute of Design). After his death, however, it fell into relative obscurity until the 1960s, when it was included in several important exhibitions including *Kunst-Licht-Kunst* at the Van Abbemuseum in the Netherlands in 1966, and featured on the cover of *Art in America* to illustrate an article on the subject of light art in 1967.[42] As a large number of artists began to use artificial light as their dominant medium of expression in the 1960s, Moholy-Nagy's position as a visionary was cemented.

In America, Dan Flavin (1933–96) was one of the pioneers of light art in the 1960s, working only with mass-produced, commercially available fluorescent

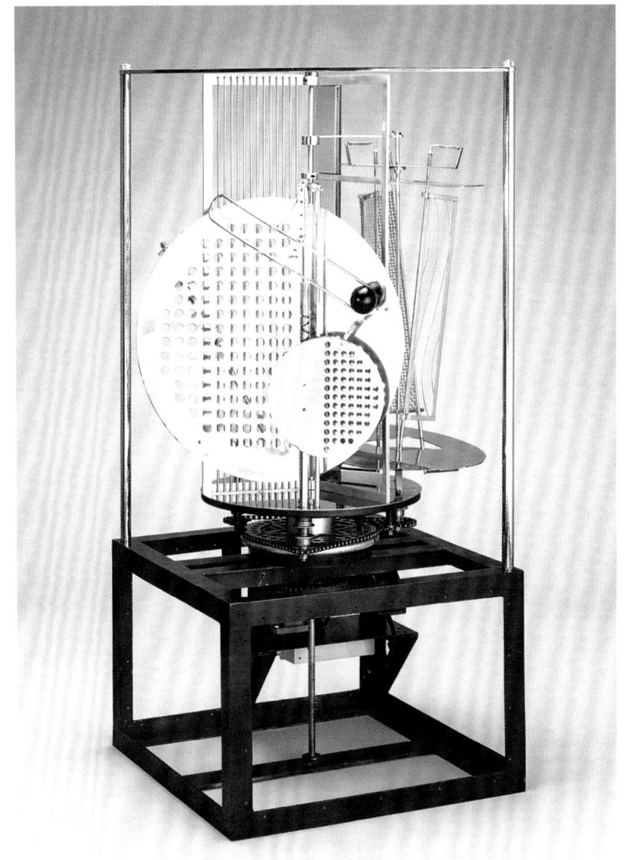

lamps (p.168). He confined himself to a limited palette (red, blue, green, pink, yellow, ultraviolet and four different whites) and form (straight two-, four-, six- and eight-foot tubes, and, beginning in 1972, circles), but despite these self-imposed restrictions he was able to create a seemingly endless number of combinations, transforming the surrounding space and architecture.[43]

Although many artists initially worked with light as they might have with paint, creating works of a

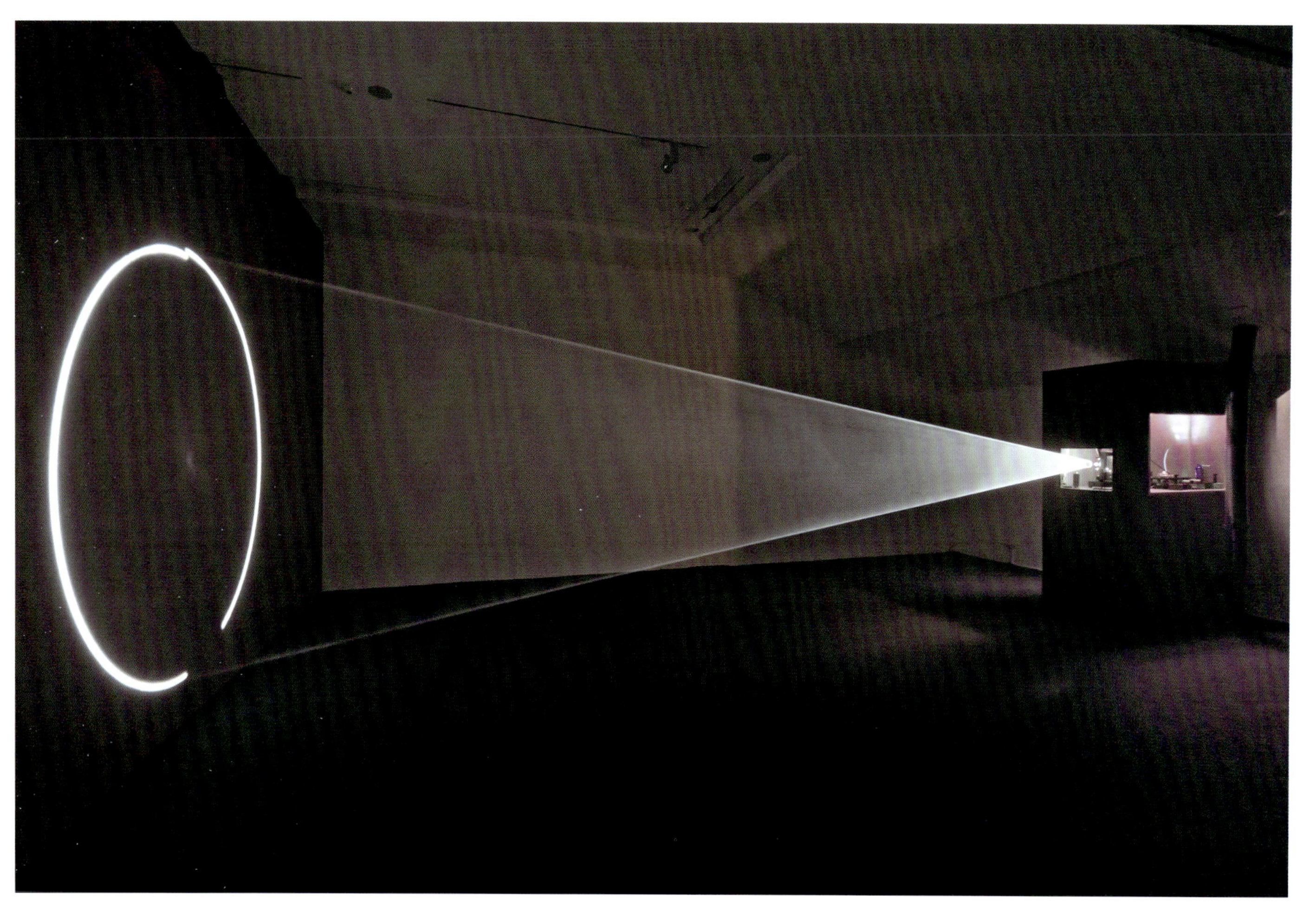

Fig. 15 Anthony McCall *Line Describing a Cone* 1973
Film; 16mm, projection. 30 min
Tate. Purchased 2005

predetermined size that were intended to be viewed frontally, the potential of light to produce new types of sculptural space developed rapidly, with light environments becoming the natural next step.[44] Artists like James Turrell (1943–) began to create highly controlled immersive spaces that emphasised the sensory aspects of light and often disoriented viewers by completely enveloping them in a coloured atmosphere (p.187). Decades later, Turrell's medium remains light – artificial and natural. He says, 'My work has no object, no image and no focus. With no object, no image and no focus, what are you looking at? You are looking at you looking. What is important to me is to create an experience of wordless thought.'[45]

While all filmmakers were completely dependent on projected light to show their films, only a handful began to use the medium in unconventional ways during the 1960s and 1970s. Anthony McCall (1946–) was one of those who exploited the potential of projected light in new ways, occupying a space between cinema, sculpture and drawing. McCall began his career as an experimental filmmaker in London, documenting performances involving natural elements, in particular fire. When he moved to New York in 1973 he developed a new body of work, beginning with *Line Describing a Cone* 1973 (fig.15), in which projections create the illusion of three-dimensional shapes, ellipses, waves and flat planes that gradually expand, contract or sweep through darkened, haze-filled rooms. Viewers are encouraged to move around the 'solid light films', challenging the motionless experience of viewing conventional cinema. This shift in emphasis from the viewer as passive observer to active participant is even more evident in *Light Music* 1975 (p.189), an intermedia installation by Lis Rhodes (1942–) which requires visitors to move through a space filled with sound and fog, interacting with the projections and altering the artwork and experience for both themselves and other viewers.

In 2000 Martin Creed (1968–) made a work that may have signalled an end point for light art, though artists continue to employ light in myriad ways. Creed's *Work No. 227: The lights going on and off* consists of an empty room which is illuminated for five seconds and then plunged into darkness for five seconds, a pattern that is repeated ad infinitum. The content of this work is almost nothing: an empty room with lighting that appears to be misbehaving. With economy of means Creed controls the fundamental conditions of visibility within the gallery, confounding viewers' expectations. With traditional art, one knows what one is looking at. According to Creed, with this work 'you can look at a floor, or the ceiling, or the walls. They're all equal; they're all just as important, or just as unimportant. The work's everywhere.'[46]

Given the history of light is essentially the history of human perception, it is no wonder that light and its effects have preoccupied scientists and artists for centuries. Although our understanding of light and our ability to produce and control it have developed tremendously over the centuries, this has not diminished its allure or capacity to elicit a wide range of responses. Light remains beautiful but impermanent, visible but intangible.

Kerryn Greenberg

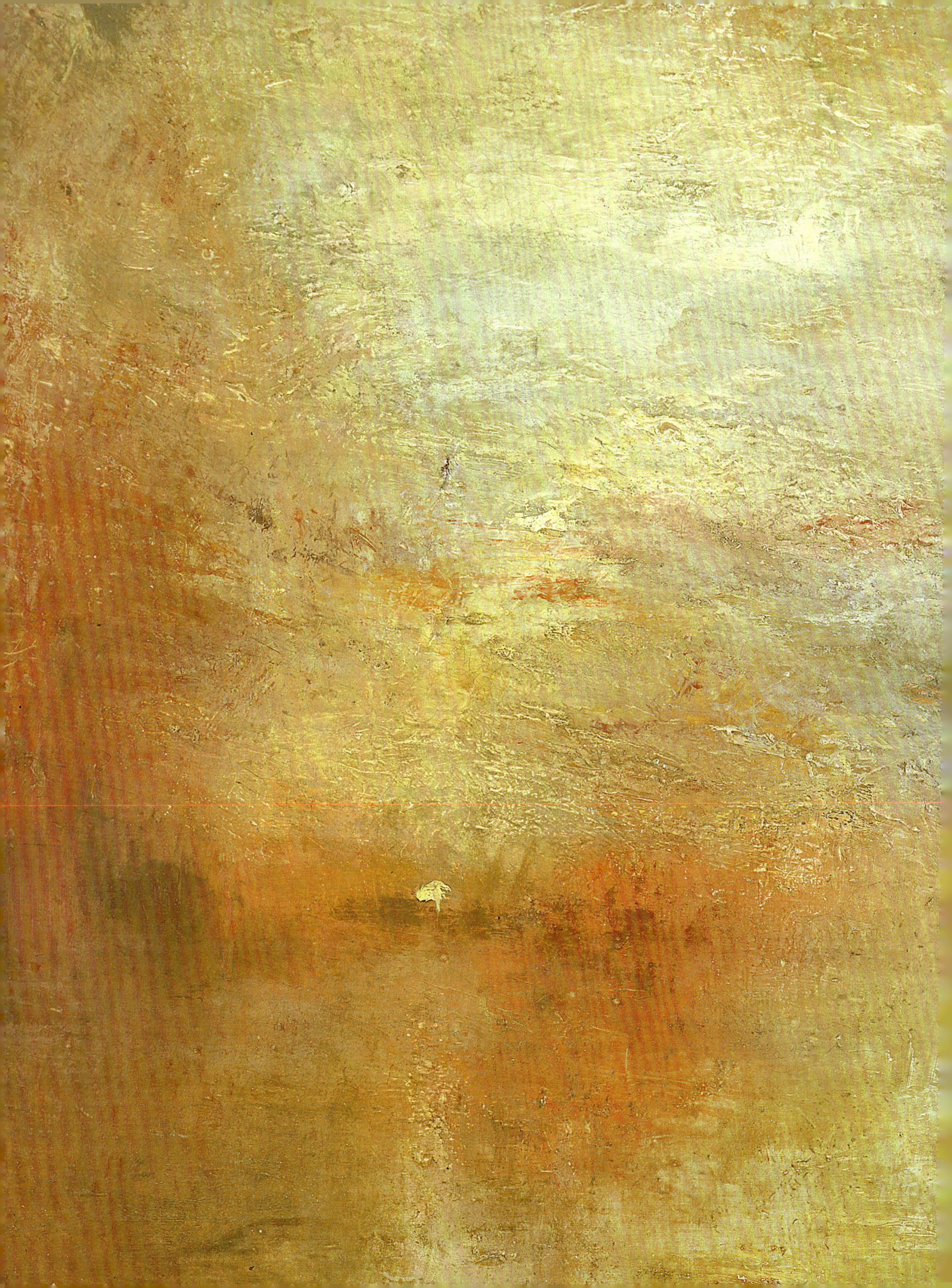

Spiritual and Sublime Light

According to the book of Genesis, God's first act was the creation of light. Across the Old and New Testaments, light represents goodness, truth and purity, while darkness signifies evil and destruction. As religious subjects became popular in British art in the late eighteenth and early nineteenth century, artists started drawing on this symbolism and using the interplay of light and dark in their paintings to express spiritual themes. In depictions of biblical scenes, light signifies divine power, with painted flickers of illumination in the gloom suggesting hope amid suffering. During the seventeenth and eighteenth centuries there was an intense period of scientific, philosophical and technological activity in Europe, known as the 'Age of Enlightenment'. Many artists responded by addressing new scientific and technological subjects while promoting reason and order. By the end of the eighteenth century, artists had begun to challenge these values, emphasising instead the role of emotion in understanding the world. Artists associated with Romanticism made use of the dramatic effects of light and dark to portray nature's immense power and unpredictability, aiming to evoke feelings of awe in the viewer. While religious and enlightenment motivations faded over time, the spiritual significance of light continues to inspire artists, who use the interplay of light and colour to provoke physical and emotional responses.

George Richmond 1809–96

George Richmond enrolled as a student at the Royal Academy in London in 1825, joining the circle of young artists who gradually gathered around William Blake (1757–1827) and Samuel Palmer (1805–81) and later became known as 'The Ancients'. This was a formative period for Richmond, who was inspired by Blake's and Palmer's interest in illustrating subjects from the Bible. Richmond also used the same paint medium as Blake did for his temperas, and a similar range of pigments. *The Creation of Light* refers to the description of the fourth day of Creation in Genesis, Chapter 1, which includes the words 'And God made two great lights' (Verse 16). This painting was submitted to the Royal Academy exhibition in London in 1826, but was rejected, probably due to the controversial subject matter. Even if inspired by Michelangelo's (1475–1564) fresco *The Creation of Adam* c.1508–12 on the ceiling of the Sistine Chapel, depictions of the 'Supreme Being' were frowned on in early nineteenth-century Britain. Richmond's daring could be attributed in part to the example of Blake, who was largely unrecognised during his lifetime but is now considered a seminal figure in the history of the poetry and visual arts of the Romantic Age. Certain features of *The Creation of Light* owe an obvious debt to Blake's work of this period: the naked, muscular figure of God, and the manner of depicting billowing clouds, flames shooting up from the sun and the effect of waves on the sea all have prototypes in, for example, Blake's tempera *Satan Smiting Job* c.1826 and the watercolours for Dante's *Divine Comedy*, which Blake was working on at the time. However, Richmond departed from Blake in his greater use of intense greens and the application of many transparent layers of paint.

The Creation of Light 1826
Tempera, gold and silver on mahogany
48 × 41.7

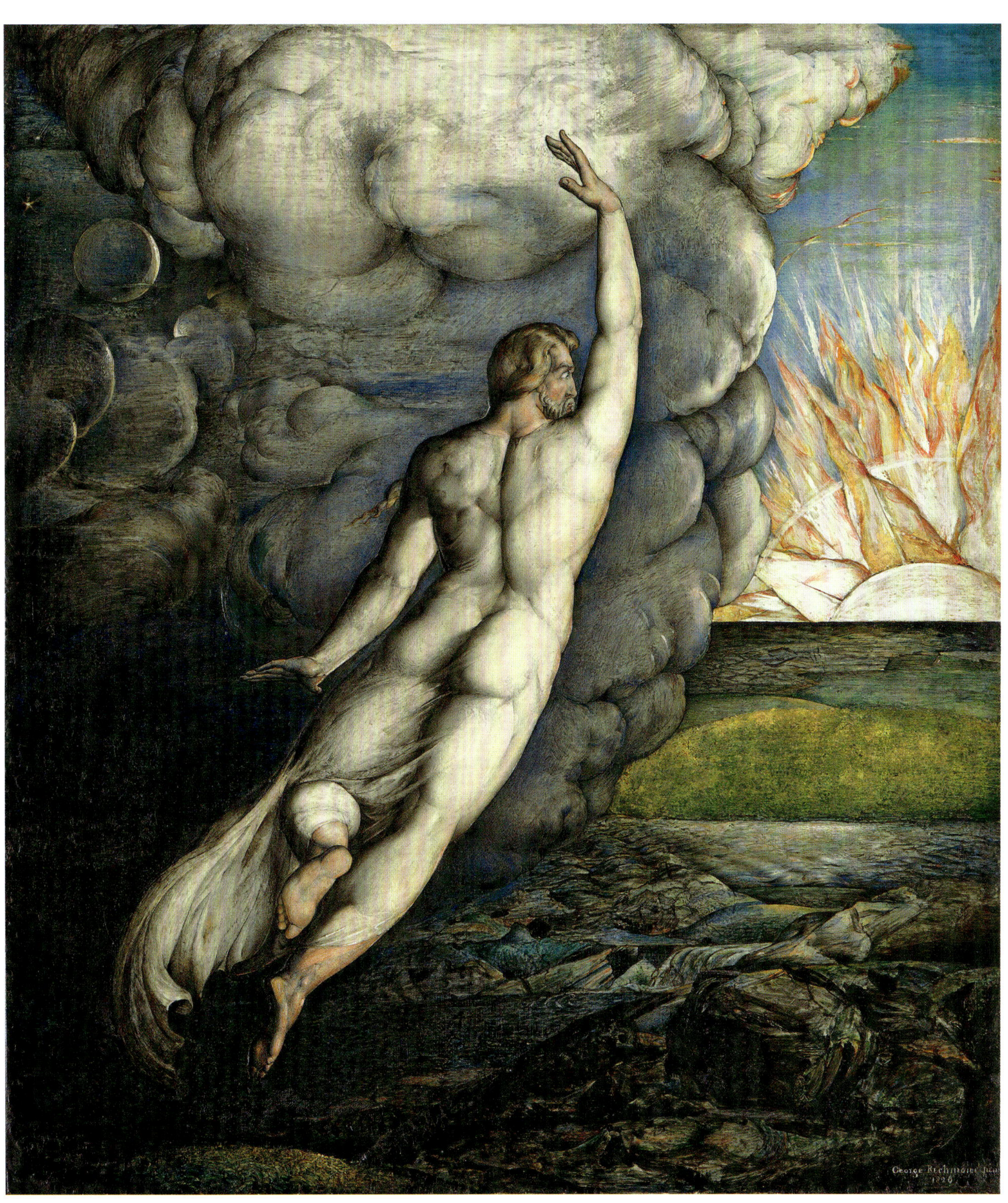

William Blake 1757–1827

William Blake was a poet, painter and printmaker. Largely unrecognised during his lifetime, Blake is now considered a seminal figure in the history of the poetry and visual arts of the Romantic Age, which peaked around 1800–50. In *God Judging Adam*, Blake's figure of God resembles Urizen, a tyrannical law-maker in the artist's mythology. The design reflects Blake's negative attitude in the mid-1790s to the God of the Old Testament. The stern embodiment of unyielding justice imposes his laws on the stooping figure of Adam, who is shown transformed into God's own image. Much of the imagery, especially the book on God's lap, and the flames, is paralleled in the verses of Blake's book *Urizen* 1794, in which Urizen is heard declaiming 'But no light from the fires: all was darkness.'[1] In its depiction of the perverted energy of fire, *God Judging Adam* can be seen as a counterpart to *The Good and Evil Angels*, where the fire represents energy as 'the only Life'.[2] Here light is positive, even if the scene shows a stage in the breaking-up of humankind into separate elements. The two works condemn the uniformity imposed by Urizen's law, and the frustration of energy resulting from the opposition of the two angels. In constructing his figures, Blake drew on eighteenth-century racist stereotypes described by Swiss pseudoscientist Johann Lavater.[3] The fair hair and light skin of the 'good' angel were associated with prejudiced ideas of physical and intellectual perfection. Blake was attempting to illustrate, in his view, the error of dividing humankind into the different elements of a 'body' and 'soul', which he considered to be indivisible.

Above: *God Judging Adam* 1795
Relief etching, ink and watercolour on paper
43.2 × 53.5

Below: *The Good and Evil Angels* 1795–c.1805
Colour print, ink and watercolour on paper
44.5 × 59.4

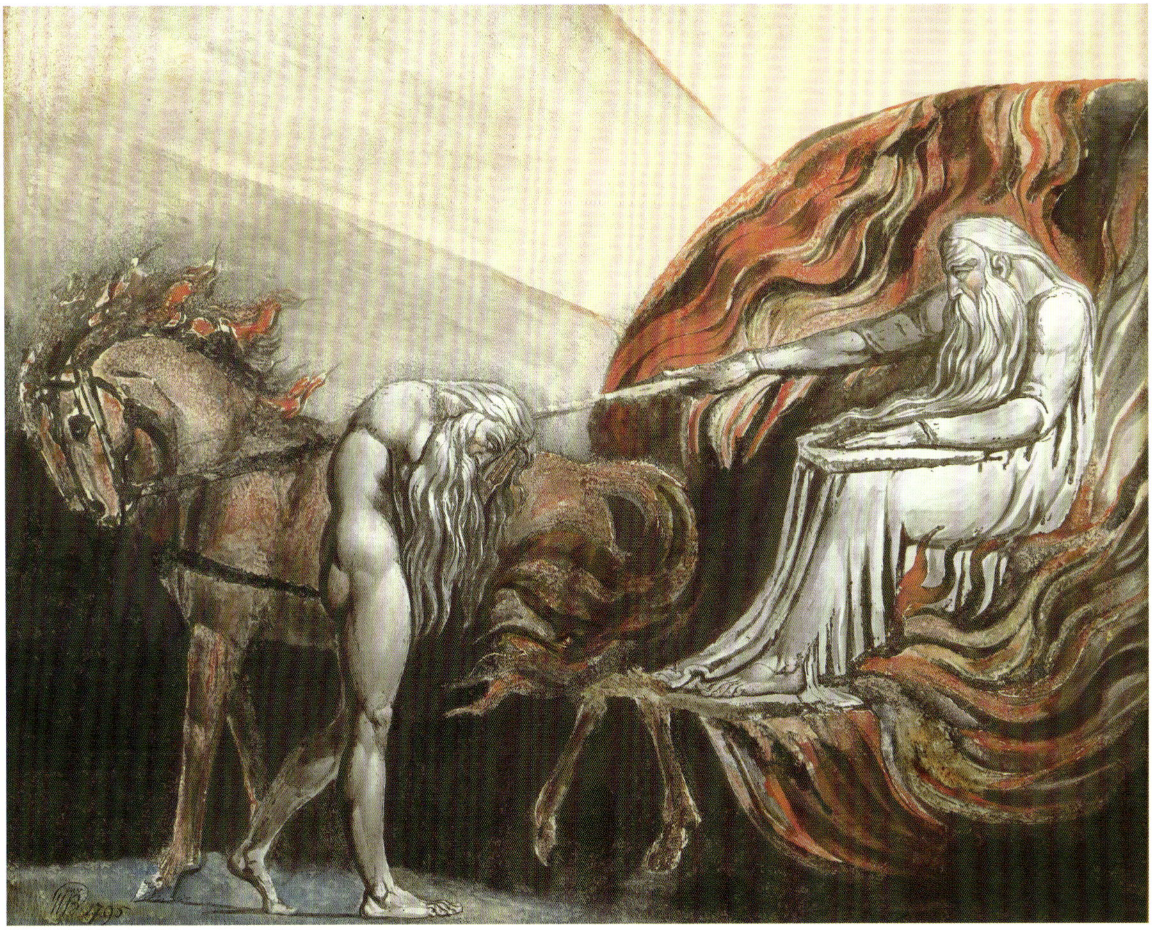

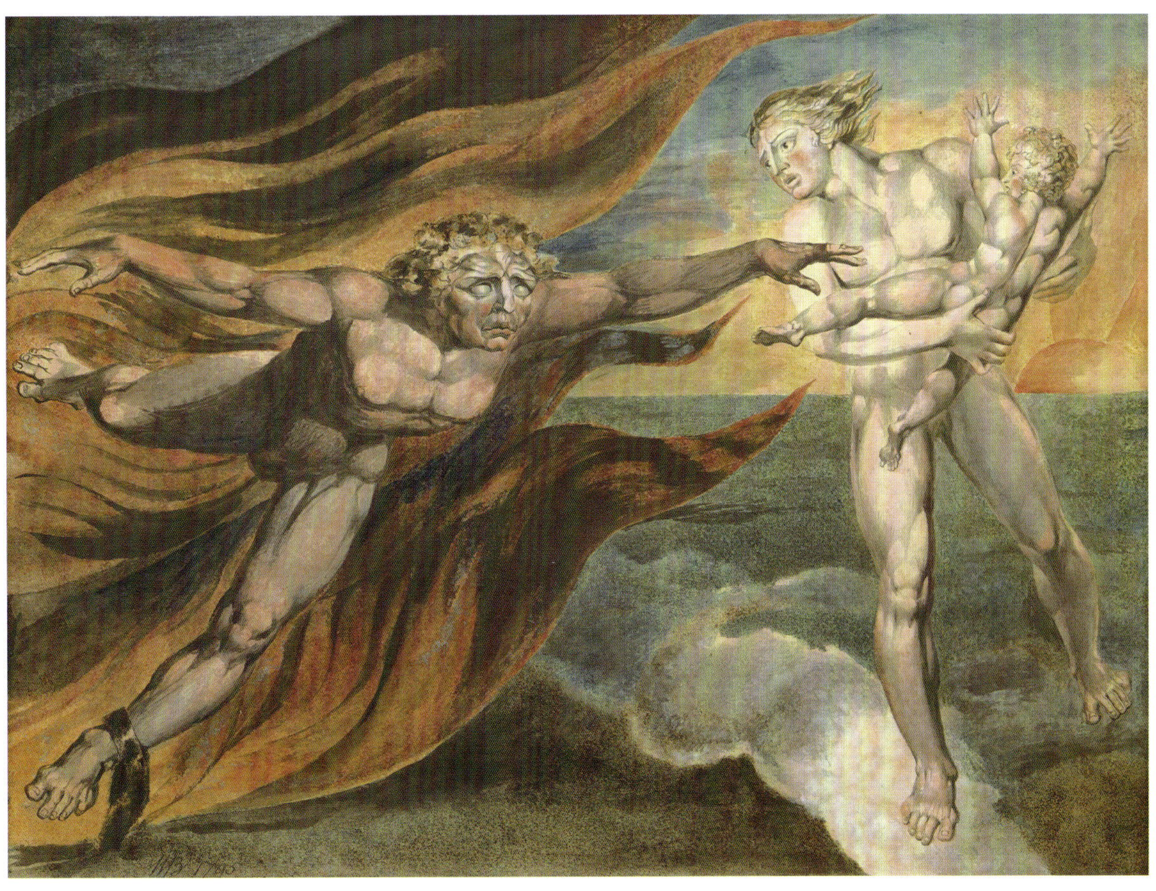

Jacob More 1740–93

Jacob More was Scottish but spent much of his career in Italy, pursuing the classical ideal in landscape painting. In the year that he painted *The Deluge*, More was visited by the German writer and statesman Johann Wolfgang von Goethe (1749–1832), whose thoughts on colour and light later inspired J.M.W. Turner (1775–1851), among others. More's *Self-Portrait* 1783 depicts the artist sitting under a large tree, canvas in hand, and attests to his love of nature, but also prefaces the developments of Turner and the impressionists, who preferred to paint in the open air directly from nature. More's contemporaries admired his use of general atmospheric effects, appealing to the spirit of a place, rather than attempting to perfectly copy nature. Joshua Reynolds (1723–92), one of the leading portrait painters in England at the time and President of the Royal Academy in London, called More 'the best painter of air since Claude' [Lorrain (1600–82)].[4] It is More's ability to capture the beauty and power of nature that is evident in *The Deluge*, which is based on the biblical story of the flood that God purportedly unleashed on the earth to rid it of evil before creating it anew. According to the Bible, God instructed Noah to build an ark in which he, his sons and their wives, together with one male and one female of all living creatures, would be saved from the waters. It is this sense of hope in the face of great calamity that More depicts in the painting here. The light radiating from the centre of the composition illuminates the figures in the foreground and suggests that all is not lost.

The Deluge 1787
Oil paint on canvas
150.4 × 204.6

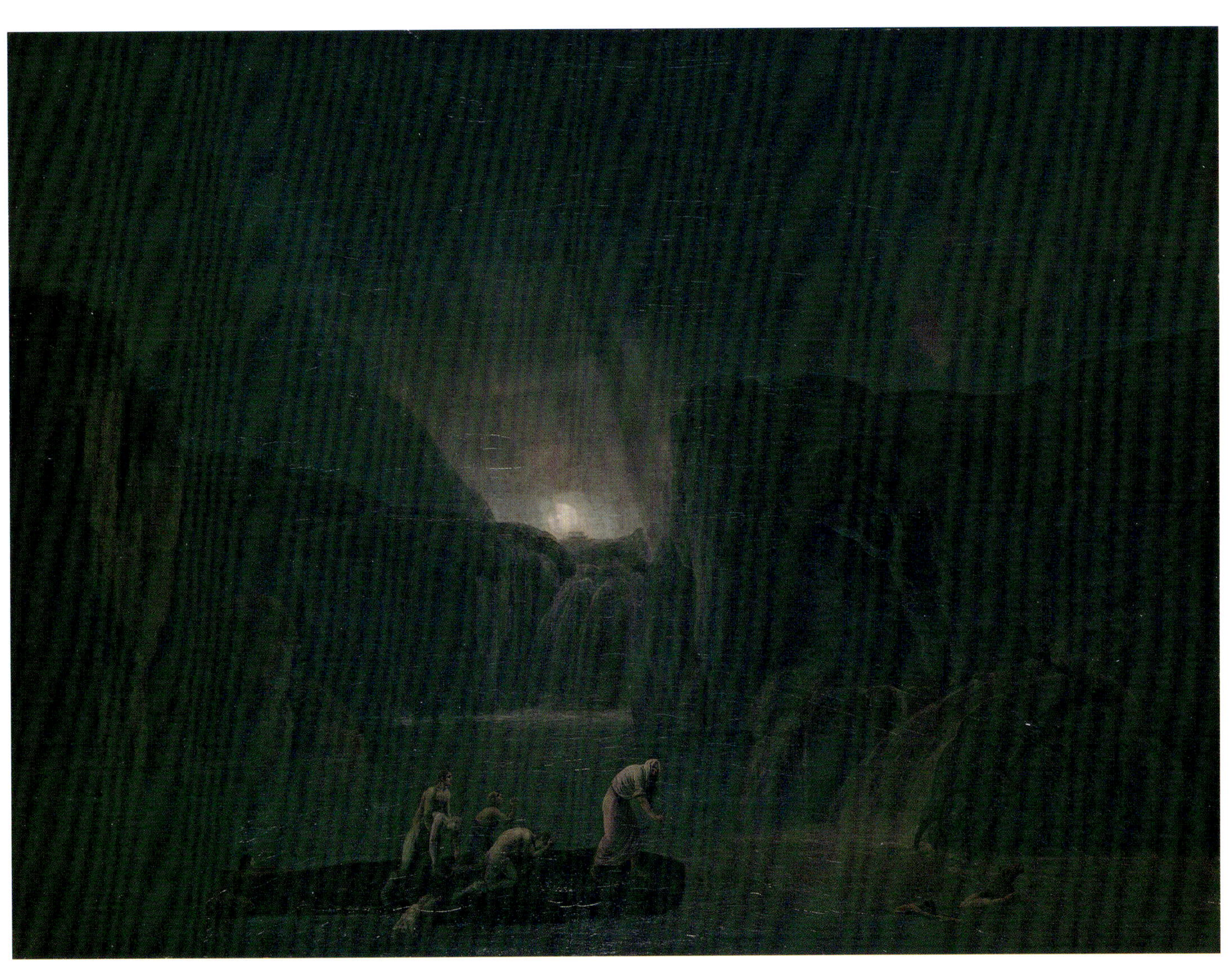

Anish Kapoor 1954–

Throughout his career, Anish Kapoor has challenged the boundaries of sculpture. Polarities such as darkness and light, substance and emptiness have been central to his work and are expressed through a wide spectrum of materials. His powder pigment-coated sculptural groups of the 1980s were followed by works that explored the void, either as freestanding objects or as architectural interventions in the museum space. These enigmatic forms combine saturated colours and contrasting materials, encouraging in the viewer a heightened awareness of their own presence and perceptions through the interplay of light, colour and texture. Kapoor exploits the contrasts between convex and concave forms and matt and polished surfaces, referencing ancient art and boldly exploring ideas of abstraction. In *Ishi's Light* the egg-shaped outer shell is pale and rough, contrasting sharply with the smooth and glossy dark-red core, in which viewers find themselves reflected upside down, creating a sense of being enveloped within the sculpture. Its curved sides produce a central column of light. This light is integral to the sculpture. 'It's a physical object,' Kapoor has said. 'It isn't simply on the surface.' This sculpture is named after Kapoor's son, Ishan, but also refers to *Anna's Light* 1968, a monumental colour field painting by the American artist Barnett Newman (1905–70).

Ishi's Light 2003
Fibreglass, resin and lacquer
315 × 250 × 224

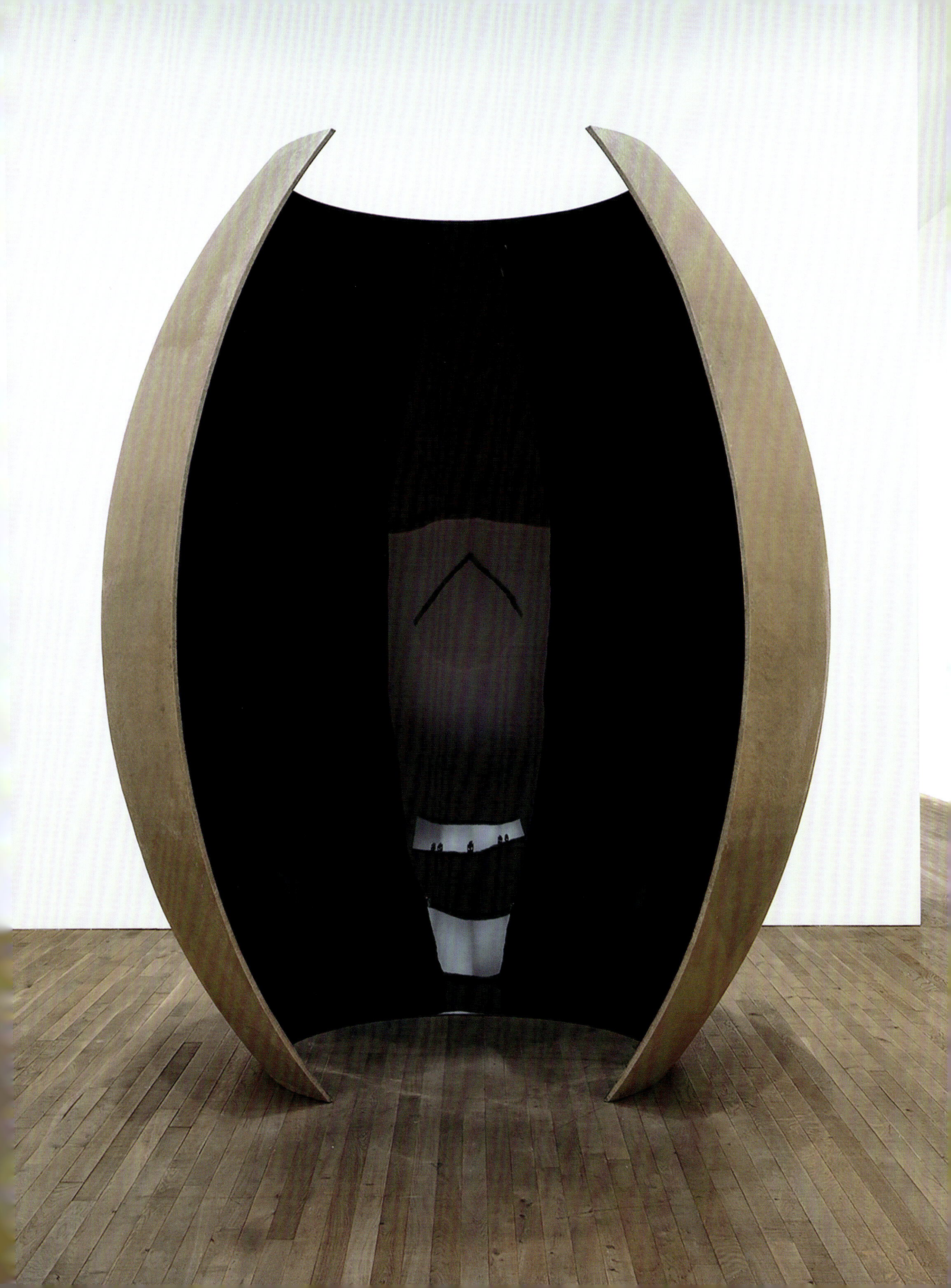

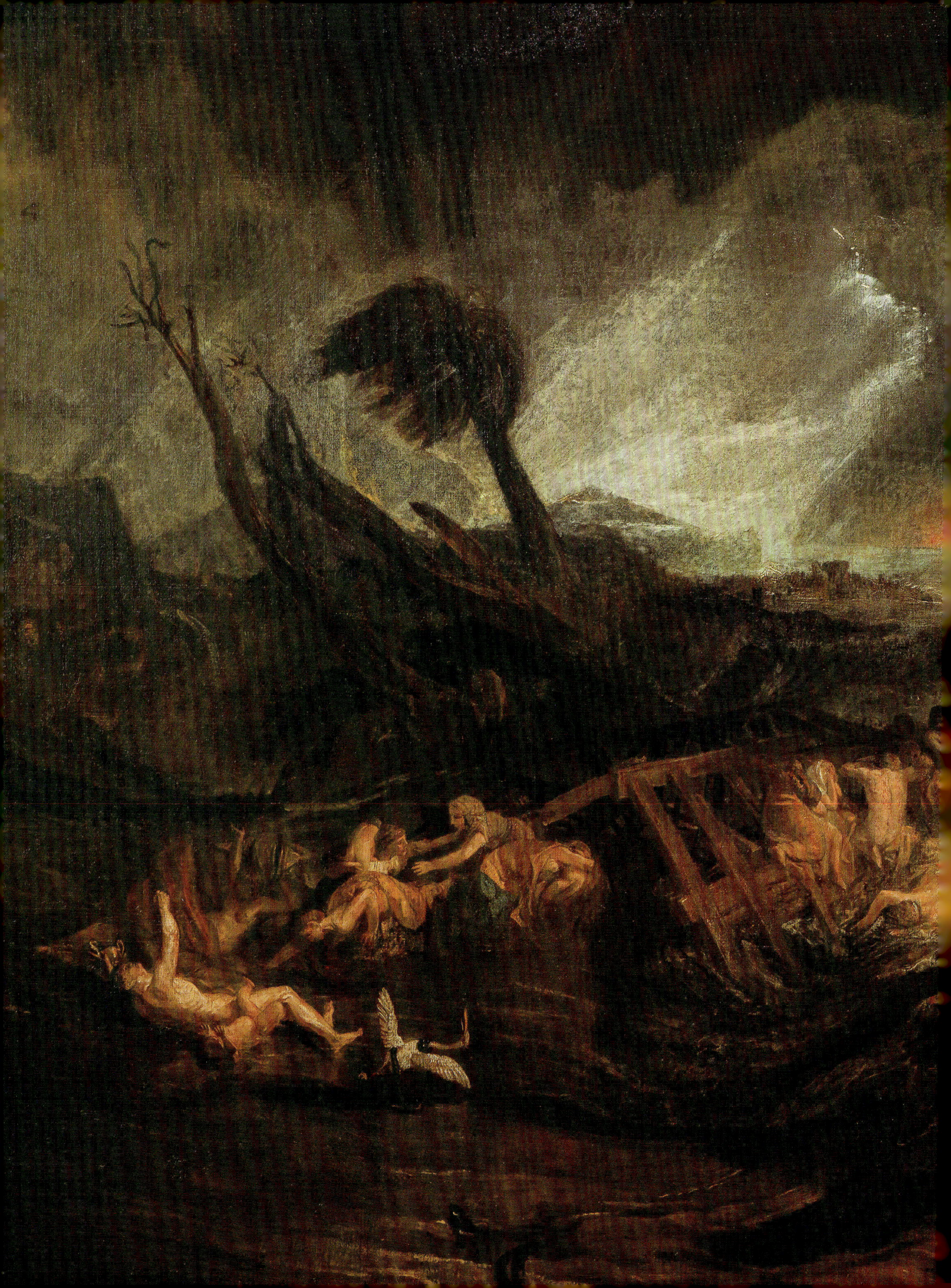

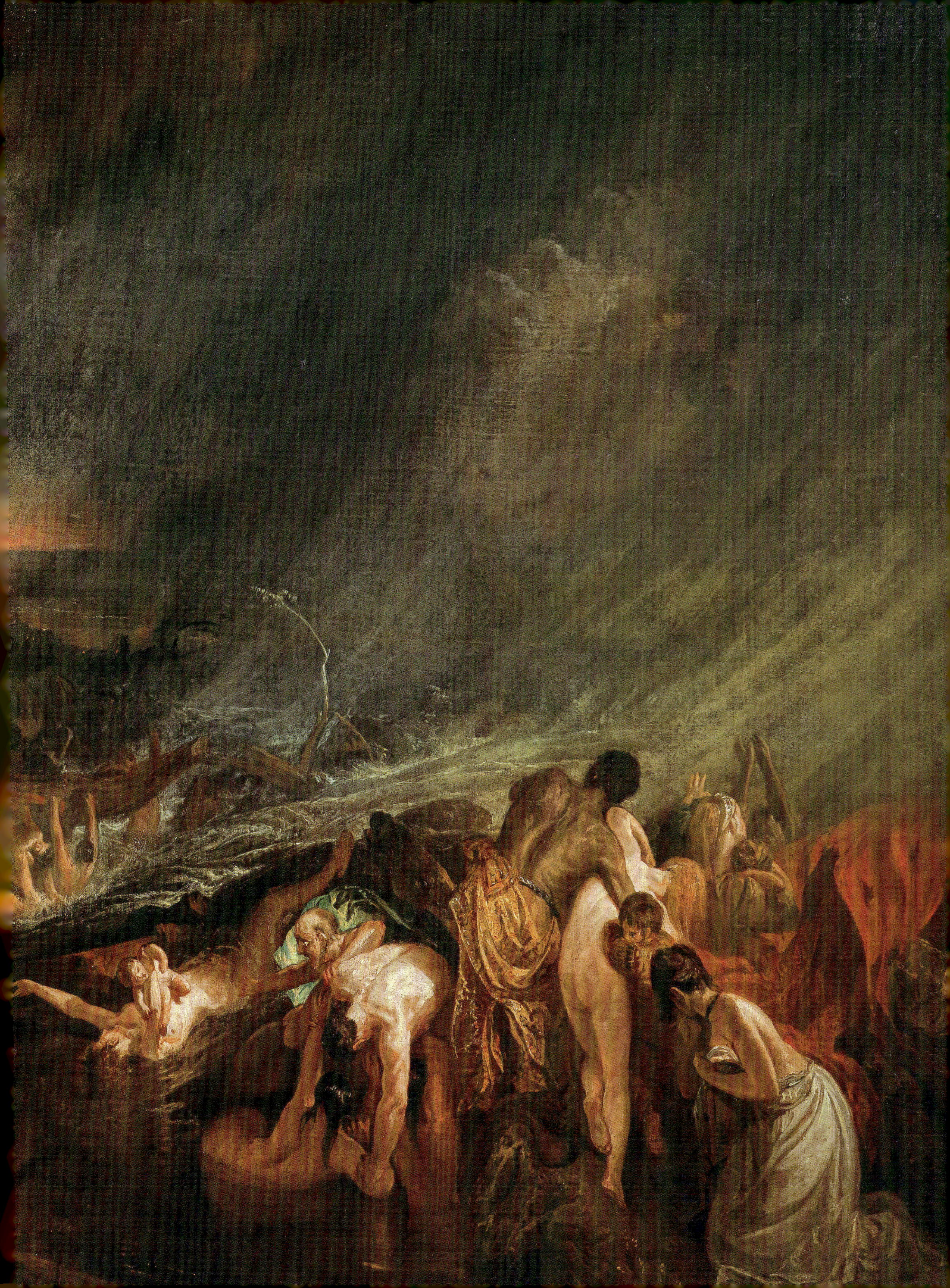

Joseph Mallord William Turner 1775–1851

J.M.W Turner related *The Deluge* (previous pages) to a passage from the epic poem *Paradise Lost* 1667 by John Milton (1608–74), a poet of the sublime movement who advocated for artistic effects designed to produce the strongest emotion the mind is capable of feeling. In *The Deluge*, we see scenes of desperation and suffering in the face of the flood, which God unleashed upon the earth to restore the goodness of his creation, as described in the book of Genesis, chapters 6–9. Turner's depiction of a powerful Black man rescuing a drowning white woman illustrates the free will of all people to act independently. When a print of this picture was made in 1828, it was dedicated to Lord Carysfort, a prominent advocate for the abolition of slavery, indicating Turner's sympathies. In the later painting *The Angel Standing in the Sun*, Turner emphasised the atmospheric effects of light, and his biblical theme is more sombre. The Archangel Michael is heralded by a rainbow, standing for truth and justice, on the Day of Judgement, while scenes from the Old Testament of murder and betrayal unfold in the foreground. Adam and Eve weep over the body of Abel to the left, as Judith stands over the headless body of Holofernes to the right. Turner became increasingly pessimistic in later life, as criticism of his progressive style increased. In this painting he appears to suggest not only that there is death and suffering in life, but that his own life and art would soon be judged.[5]

Previous pages: *The Deluge* ?exh.1805
Oil paint on canvas
142.9 × 235.6

Opposite: *The Angel Standing in the Sun* exh.1846
Oil paint on canvas
78.7 × 78.7

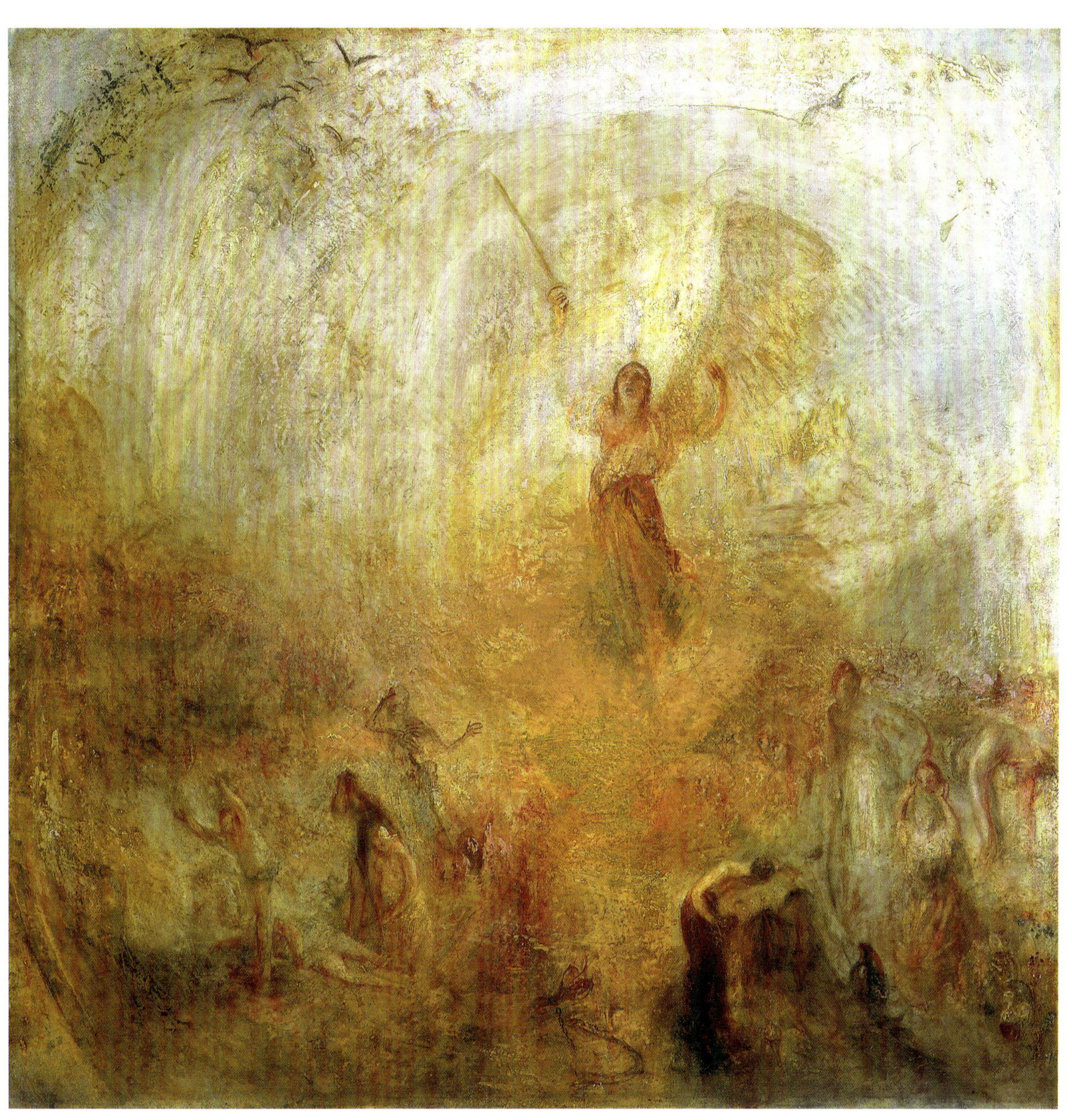

Joseph Wright of Derby 1734–97

Joseph Wright's close contact with pioneering English industrialists and progressive figures of the British Enlightenment spurred a preoccupation with scientific and technological subjects largely considered unfit for depiction in painting at the time. Despite his varied interests, Wright applied the same heroic treatment to themes from common life as he did the natural world. He was fixated with pronounced light effects and dramatic compositions, employing strong contrasting effects of light and dark known as *chiaroscuro*. Wright toured Italy once between 1773 and 1775, but drew on the experience for the rest of his career. Although he did not witness a major eruption at Mount Vesuvius, his imagination was gripped by the power of the place and he returned repeatedly to the subject, producing over thirty views of the volcano. His work *Vesuvius in Eruption, with a View over the Islands in the Bay of Naples* emphasises the drama of the erupting volcano through contrasts: 'between the tranquillity of the sea and the violence of the volcano, the cool light reflected from the moon and clouds with the hellish spewing of fire and lava'.[6] In comparison to the volatile power of the volcano, the tiny figures in the foreground emphasise humanity's insignificance and vulnerability in relation to the sublime power of nature. *A Moonlight with a Lighthouse, Coast of Tuscany* (pp.50–1) is an imagined scene created by Wright years later in England. This scene gave the artist a context in which to compare the differing effects of natural and artificial light sources that had so long fascinated him. In this painting, the luminosity of the moonlight in the night sky is contrasted with the hazy beam of the lighthouse and its reflection in the water. The looming dark mass of the cliff and portentous-looking rocks in the lower left create a sense of melodrama.

Vesuvius in Eruption, with a View over the Islands in the Bay of Naples c.1776–80
Oil paint on canvas
122 × 176.4

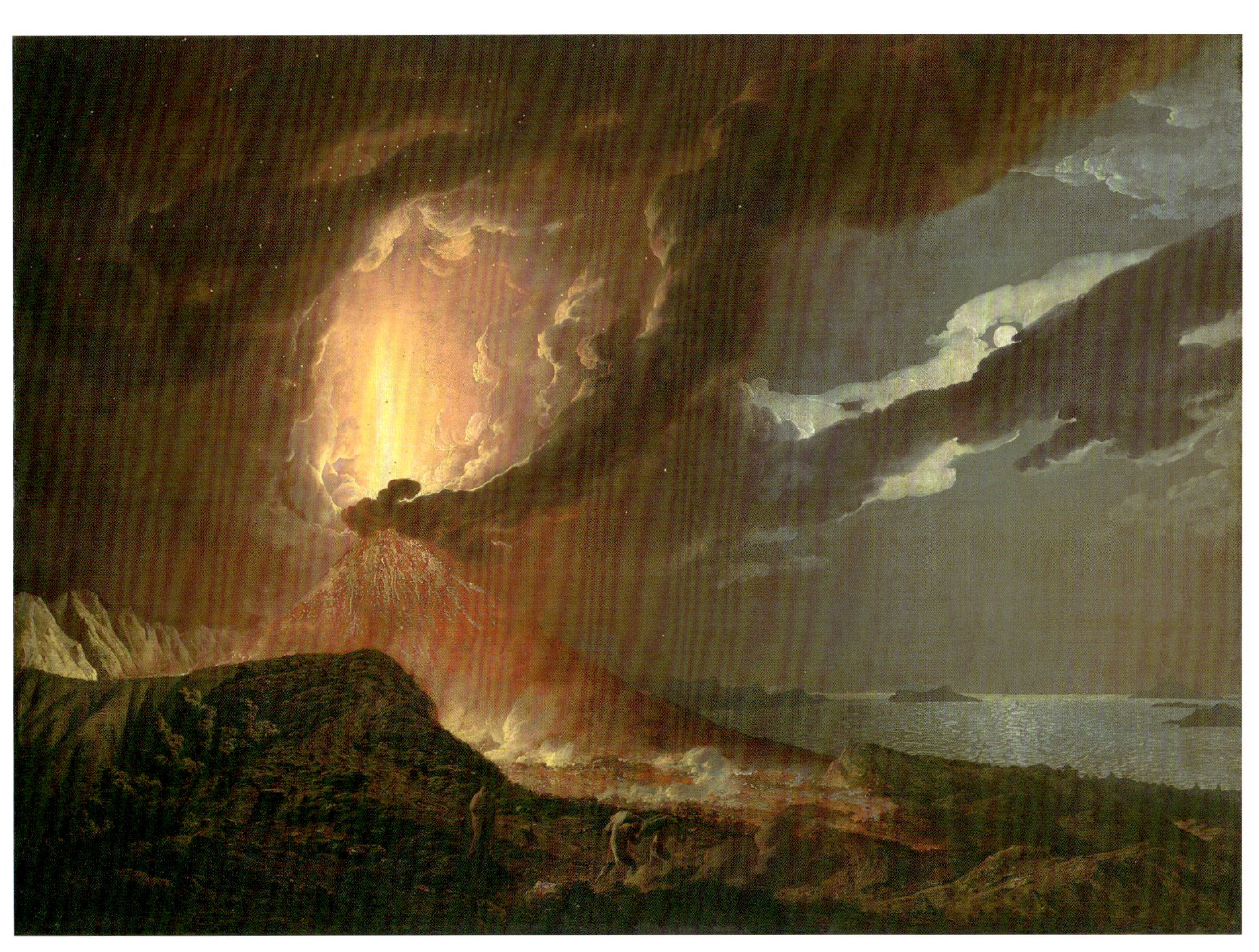

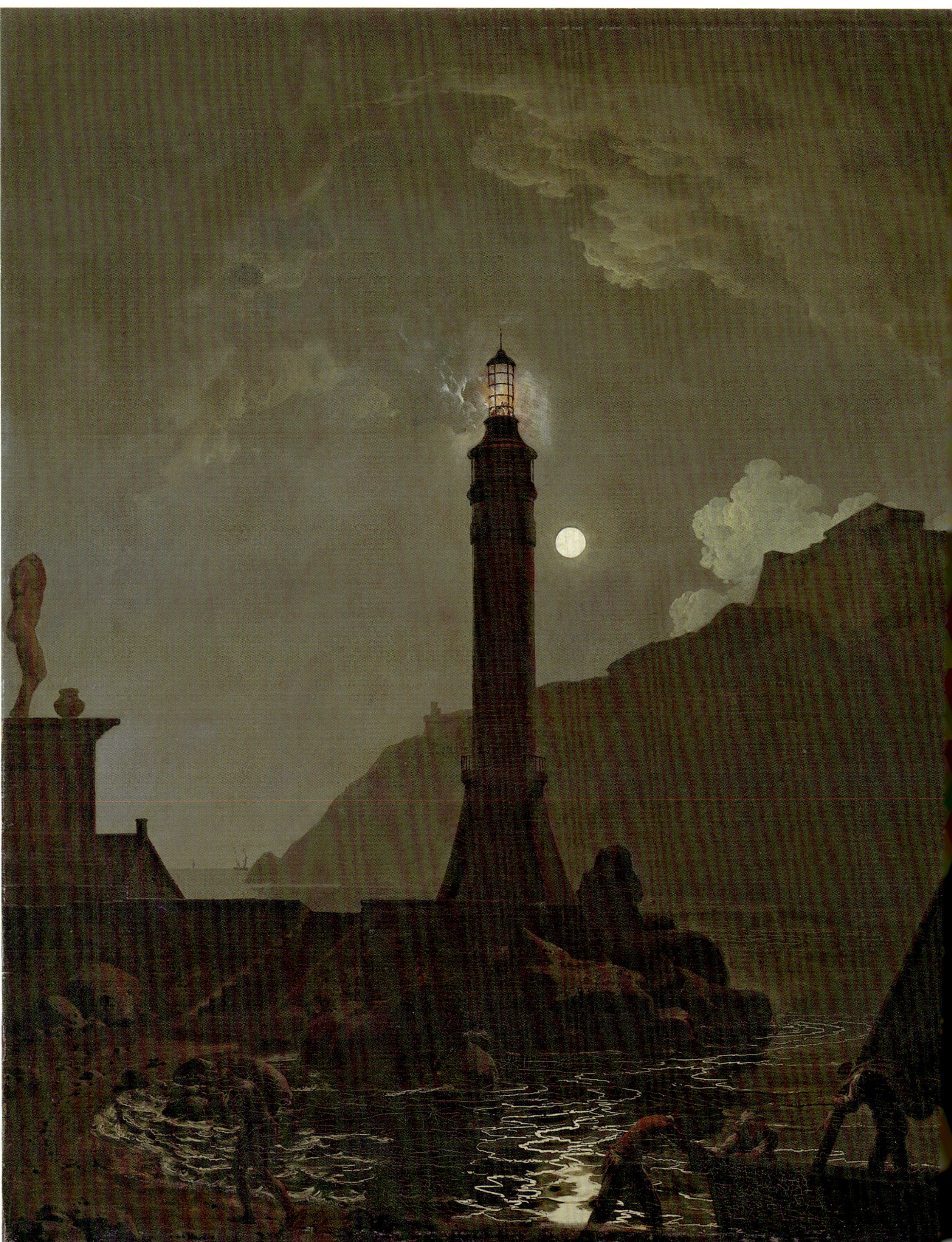

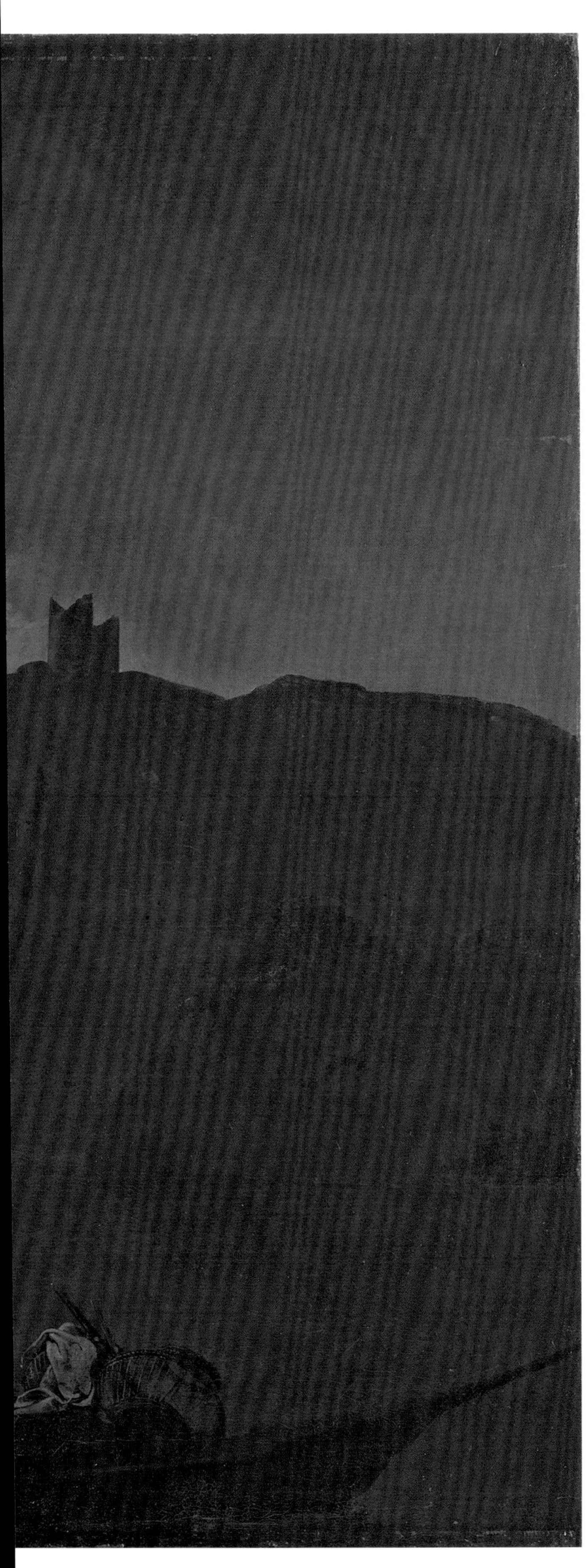

A Moonlight with a Lighthouse, Coast of Tuscany exh.1789
Oil paint on canvas
101.6 × 127.6

John Martin 1789–1854

In London, John Martin exhibited at the Royal Academy from 1811, designed various urban improvements and painted landscapes of the Thames Valley. His large-scale paintings, depicting dramatic natural events and religious subjects, were popular spectacles in their own day, and directly inspired the treatment of such themes in theatrical presentations and early cinema.[7] This vividly coloured, detailed painting imagines the extent of the calamity that famously beset the sister cities of Pompeii and Herculaneum, on the Italian peninsula, when Mount Vesuvius erupted in 79 CE. Taking as its vantage point the shores of the town of Stabiae, on the opposite side of the Bay of Naples, this painting shows a multitude of tiny figures fleeing in the foreground. Herculaneum is in the distance to the left, smothered with lava; Pompeii is laid out in sufficient detail for us to be able to identify specific buildings, most prominently the circular 'Great Theatre' and the Basilica. Mount Vesuvius is shown in the early stages of the eruption, the glow of lava colouring the whole landscape a vivid red, while the sky is convulsed by billowing ash clouds and shredded by lightning. This painting was first exhibited as the centrepiece of Martin's solo exhibition in 1822. Although some critics derided his paintings as sensationalist entertainment rather than serious art, this exhibition affirmed Martin's reputation among the general public. Given his commercial success, it is perhaps unsurprising that some of his contemporaries began to pursue similar highly Romantic subjects, expressing the sublime, apocalyptic forces of nature and the helplessness of humanity to combat God's will. Similarities in style and subject resulted in paintings by other artists, such as *The Fallen Angels Entering Pandemonium, from 'Paradise Lost', Book 1* ?exh.1841, being incorrectly attributed to Martin.

The Destruction of Pompeii and Herculaneum 1822
Oil paint on canvas
161.6 × 253

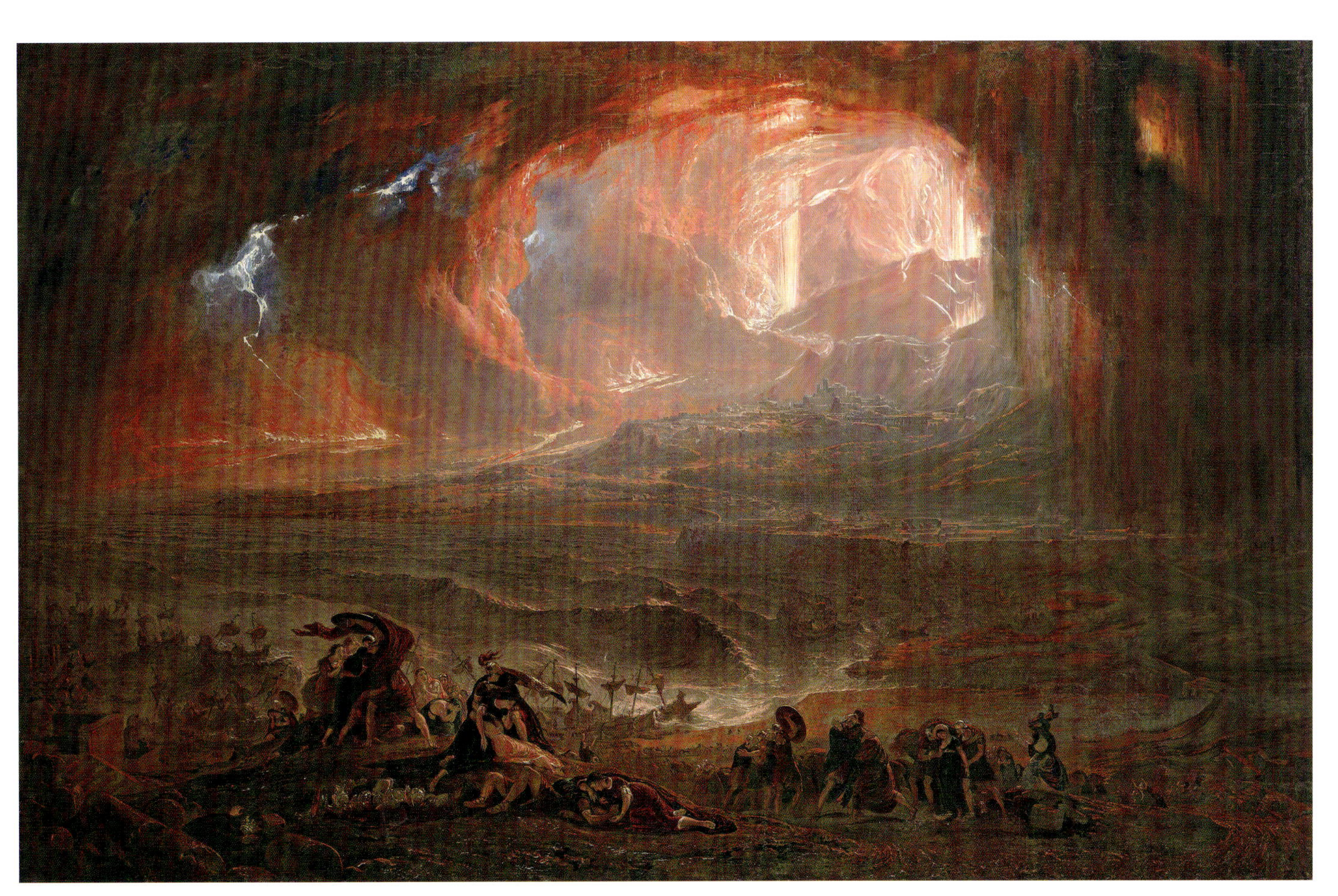

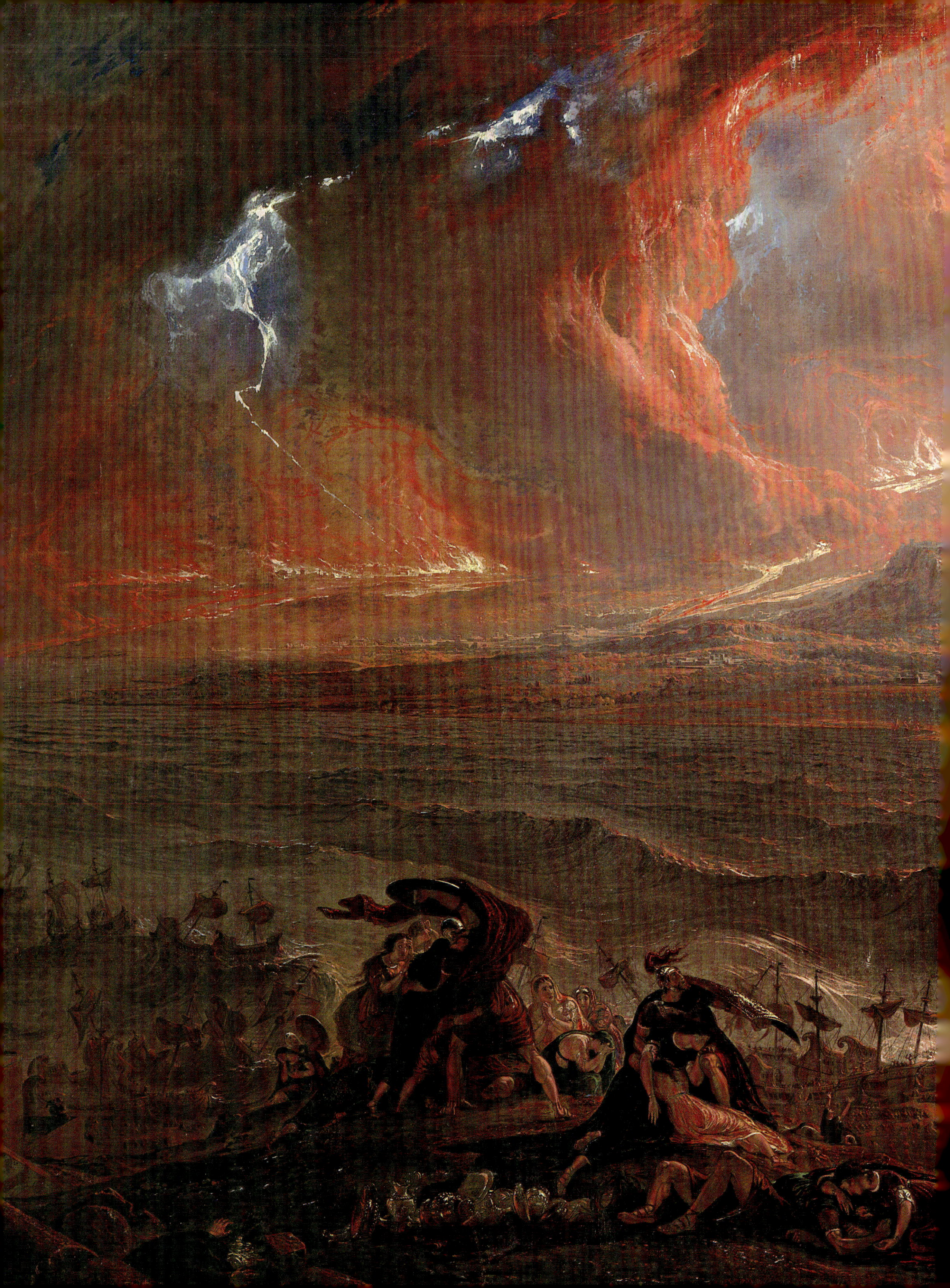

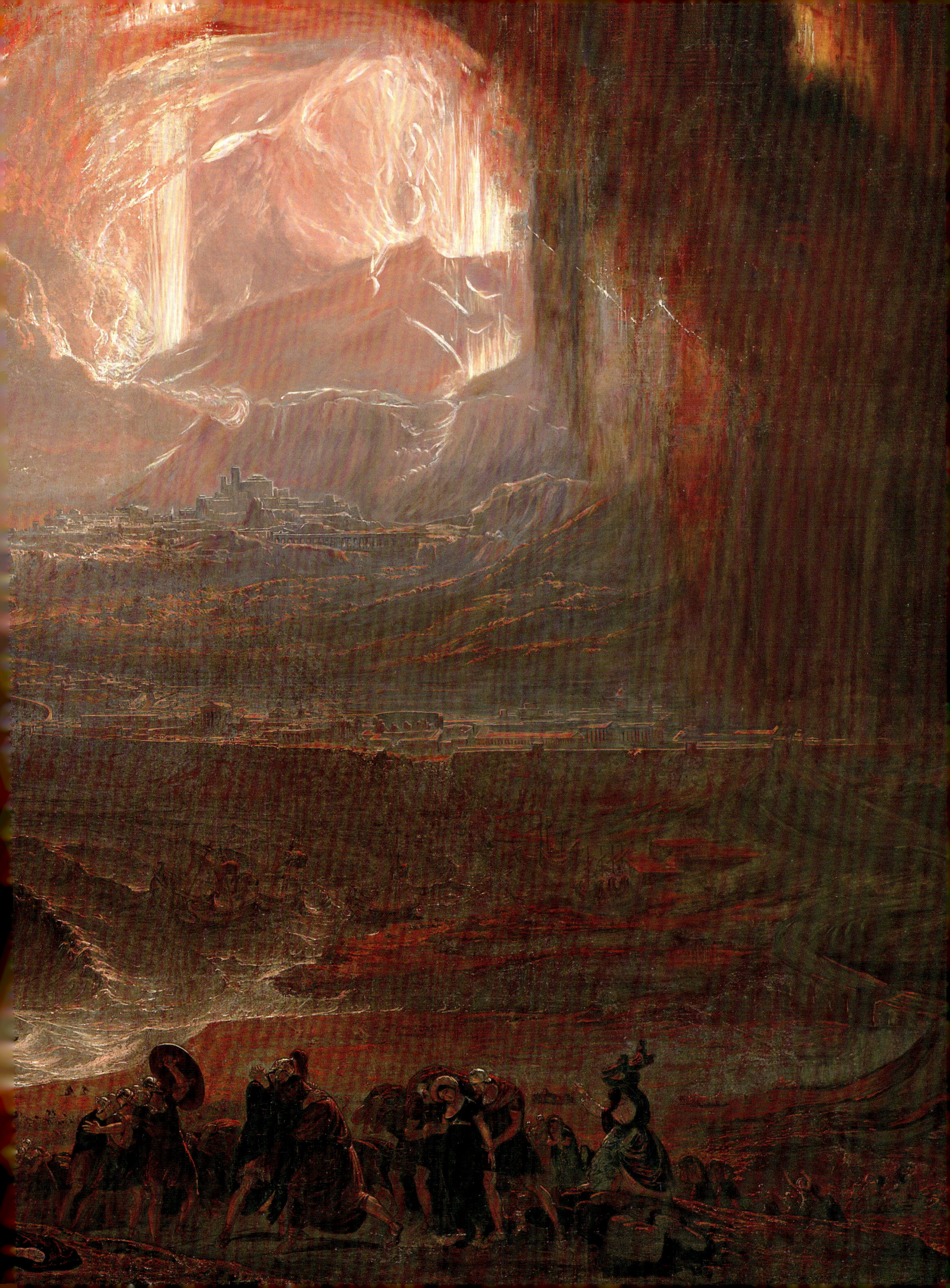

Natural Light

Dramatic weather, shifting skies and the effects of light on the landscape have inspired artists for centuries. Many have been fascinated by the transience of natural light, depicting brooding clouds and piercing sun rays, amid various shades of sky. The weather proved to be a fruitful subject for exploration, especially for J.M.W. Turner, who focused on the subtle effects of light and colour to create dramatic and atmospheric landscapes and seascapes. In later nineteenth-century Europe, many artists reacted to the rapid technological and societal changes of industrialisation with a renewed interest in the natural world. Some captured the effects and emotive qualities of light in depictions of the land and the sea, while others considered light as a subject in itself. In France, Claude Monet (1840–1926) and other Paris-based artists, together known as the impressionists, worked outside, recording the transitory effects of light on both the natural and man-made world. For these artists, subject matter became increasingly subservient to paint's formal qualities; by emphasising the surface of their canvases, they revolutionised painting in Europe and North America and anticipated the abstract and non-objective art that emerged in the twentieth century.

John Constable 1776–1837

Alongside J.M.W. Turner (1775–1851), John Constable was one of the most important and influential landscape painters of the nineteenth century. His pictures, which aimed for truthful rather than idealised representations of nature, revolutionised landscape painting. Seeking to capture fleeting meteorological phenomena, he produced numerous preparatory oil sketches directly from nature, which later informed the canvases painted in his studio. A single drawing made on location in the port of Harwich, Essex, in the south-east of England, provided the starting point for the small coastal scene *Harwich Lighthouse*, one of at least three versions the artist made of the subject. In this masterful study of light and shadow, the wooden lighthouse and its environs are bathed in bright sunlight as the dark shadows cast by overhead clouds blow inland. Flecks of white oil paint map the play of light on the sea – a distinctive technical device that Constable regularly employed to create the illusion of light hitting water (disparagingly referred to as 'Constable's snow' by critics). A similar effect is seen in *Branch Hill Pond, Hampstead Heath, with a Boy Sitting on a Bank*, one of many paintings of this location that Constable produced between 1819 and 1836. Presenting a view to the west and south-west over the pond, the painting shows a young boy sitting on a bank, surveying the windswept landscape with its wide, expansive sky; his brilliant red costume draws the viewer's eye to the rays of light that stream from behind the dark rain clouds, falling onto the pond's surface below.

Above: *Harwich Lighthouse* ?exh.1820
Oil paint on canvas
32.7 × 50.2

Below: *Branch Hill Pond, Hampstead Heath, with a Boy Sitting on a Bank* c.1825
Oil paint on canvas
33.3 × 50.2

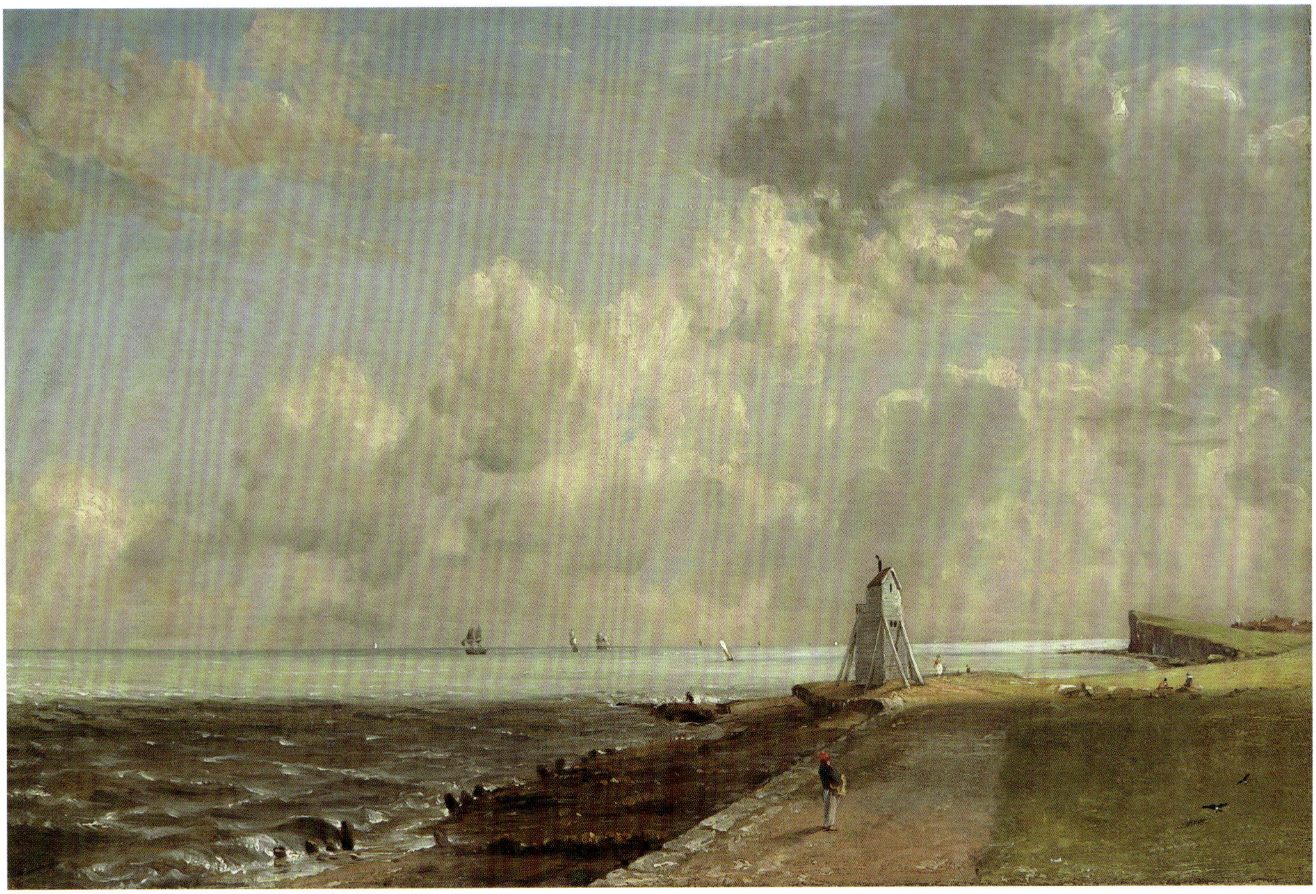

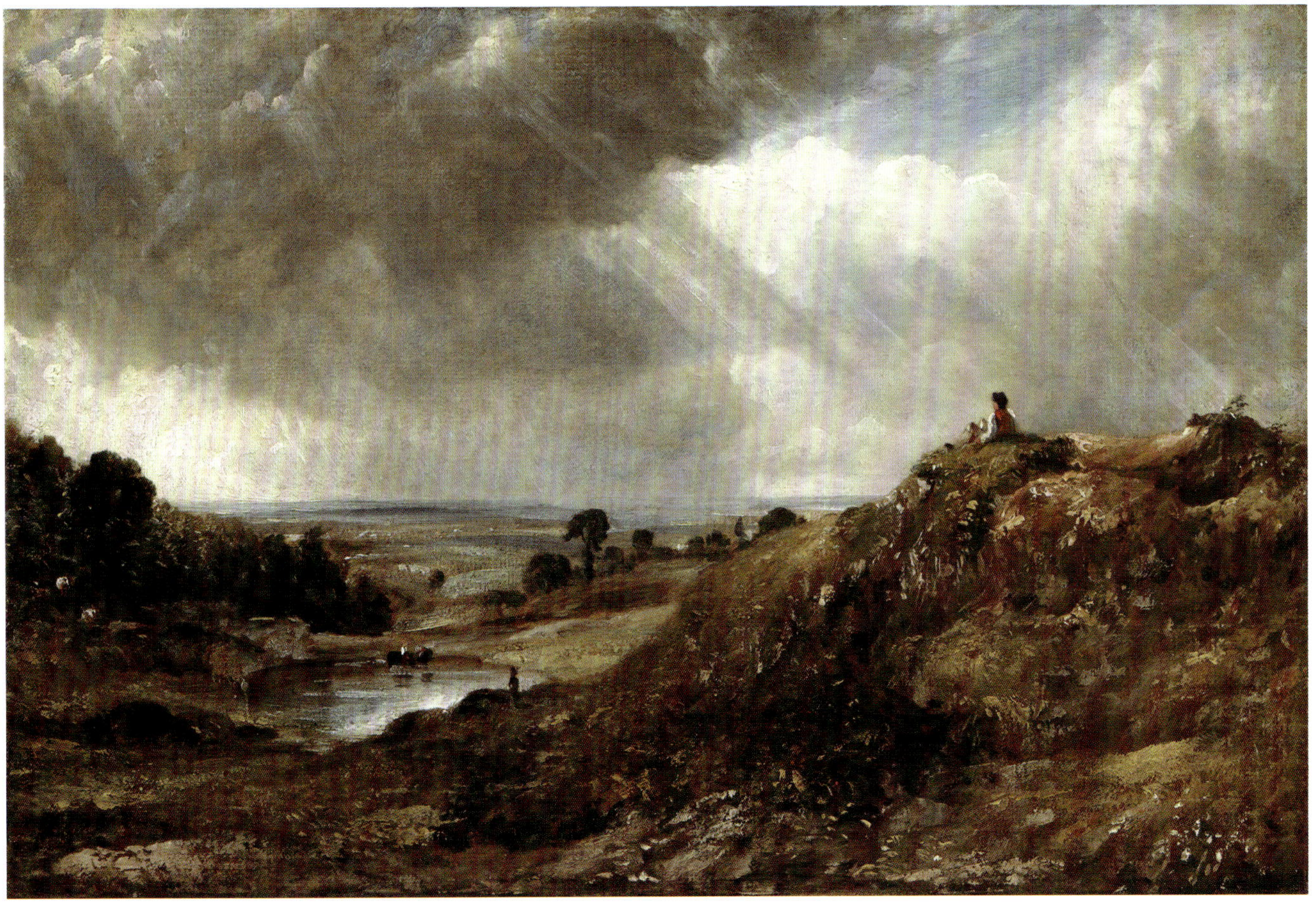

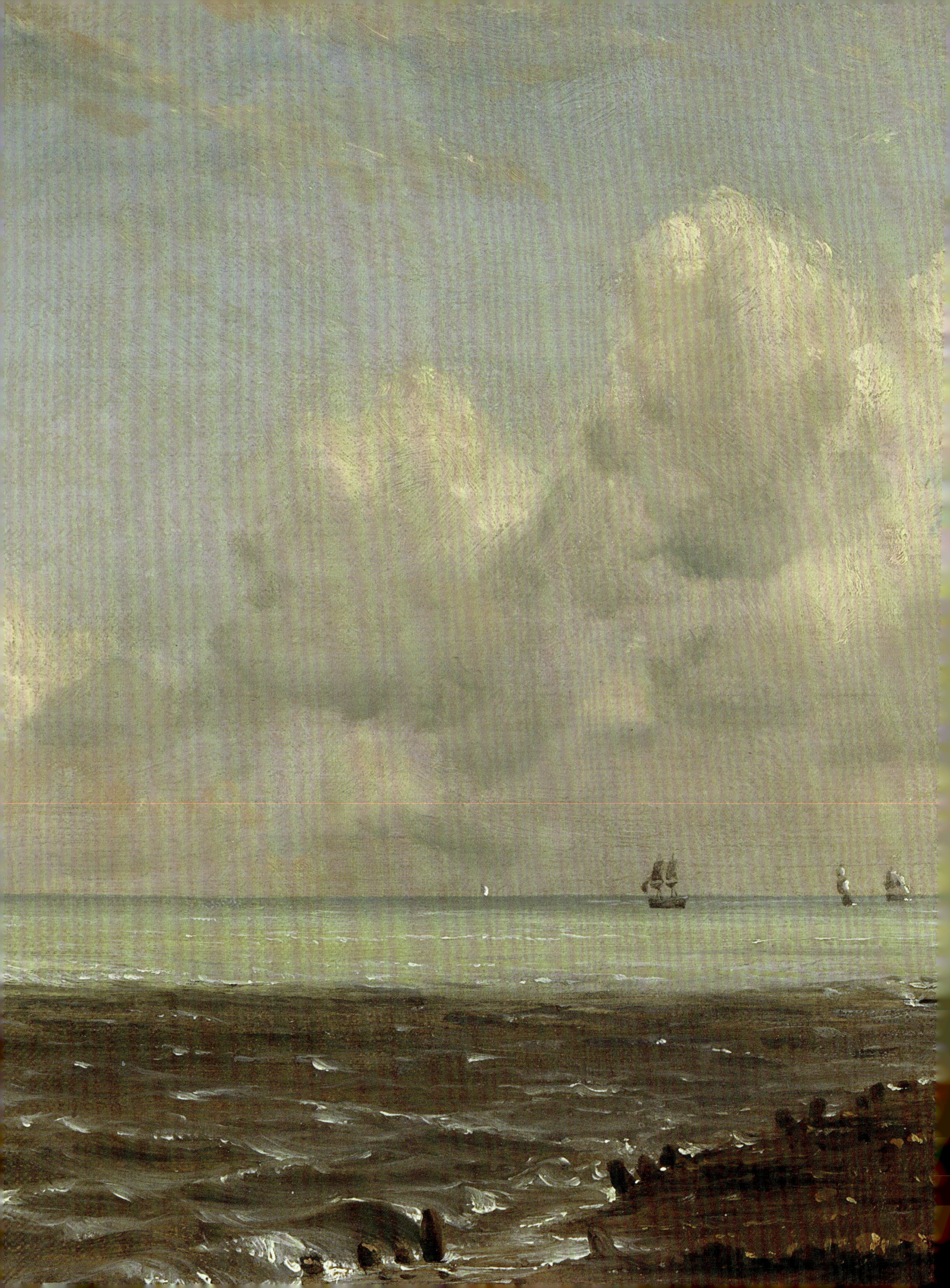

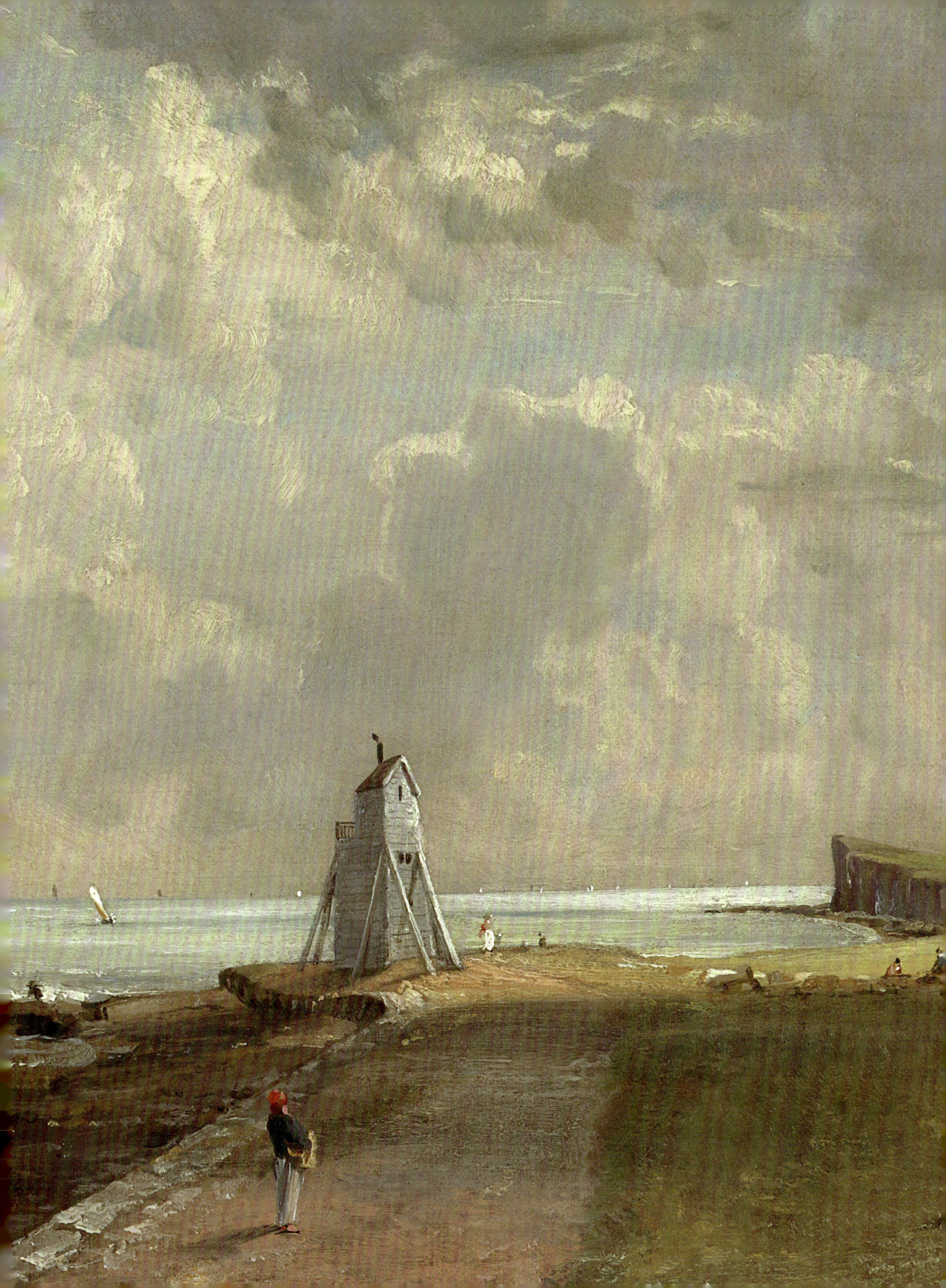

John Constable 1776–1837

After abandoning the small canvases of his youth, it was John Constable's monumental paintings, such as *Salisbury Cathedral from the Meadows*, that sealed his reputation as one of Britain's greatest landscape artists. Following the sudden death of his wife, Maria, in 1828, the artist received great emotional support from his friend and patron the Archdeacon John Fisher (1788–1832), who suggested this architectural subject. Begun in 1830, the painting shows the gothic cathedral from the north-west, surrounded by billowing storm clouds. Illuminated by the returning sun, its famous spire points heavenwards, drawing attention to patches of blue sky. In the foreground, horses pull a cart across a shimmering river, while on the far right, cattle graze in a sun-dappled meadow. Constable's varied paint handling ranges from thick, textured passages to thin, almost translucent areas, as well as his signature white flecks, used here to suggest glistening raindrops. It is thought that the majestic rainbow was added later, since its appearance is not consistent with the lighting conditions seen in the rest of the painting. Having studied the physics of rainbows, Constable knew that the sun must be directly behind the observer in order for one to be visible. Here, however, the sun's rays emerge from the right of the composition. Moreover, the rainbow – a Christian symbol of peace and hope – comes to rest on Leadenhall, the Archdeacon's home in the Cathedral Close, where Constable often visited. The painting can thus be understood as a tribute to Fisher and an expression of gratitude for his friendship in a time of grief.

Salisbury Cathedral from the Meadows exh.1831
Oil paint on canvas
153.7 × 192

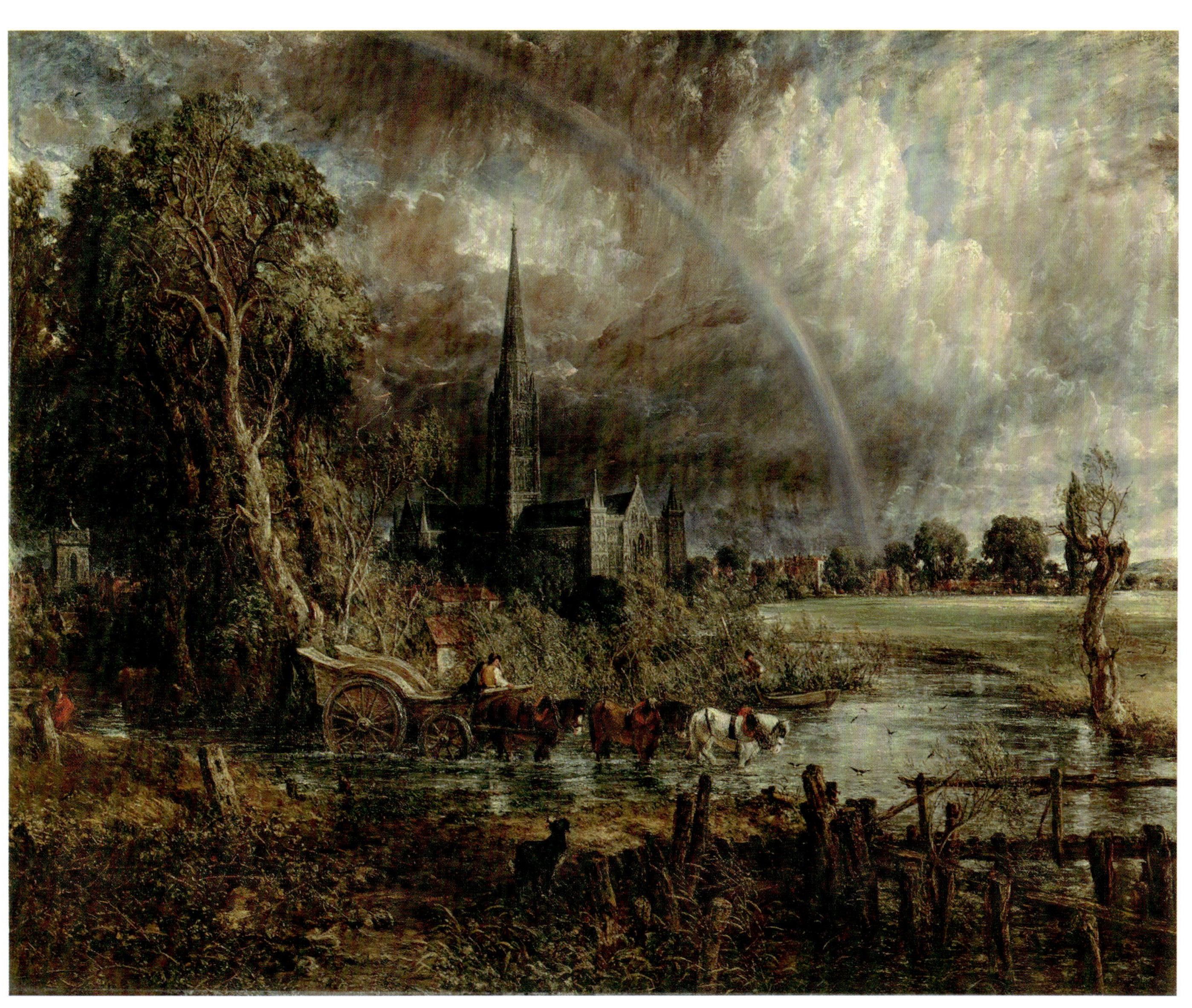

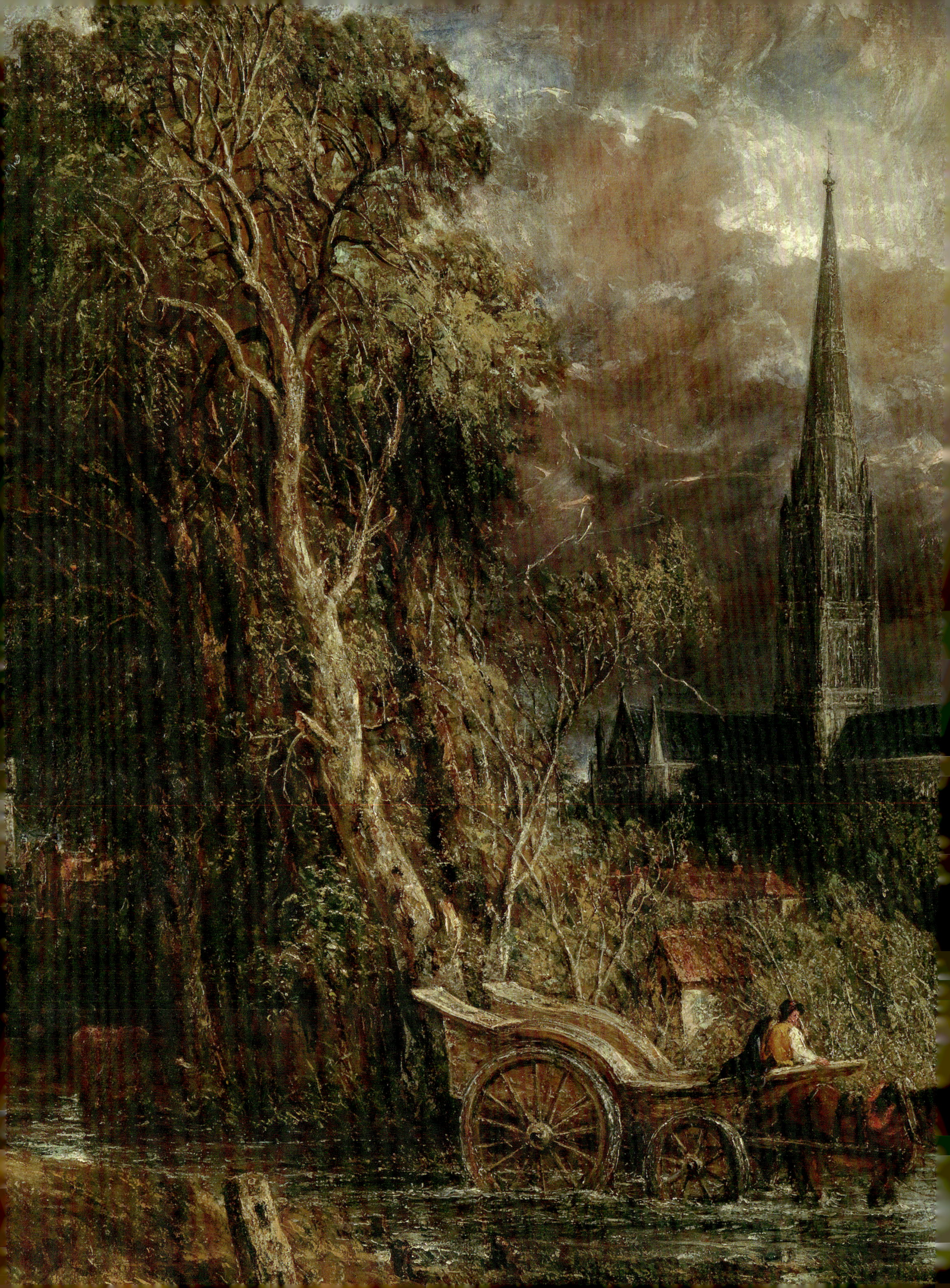

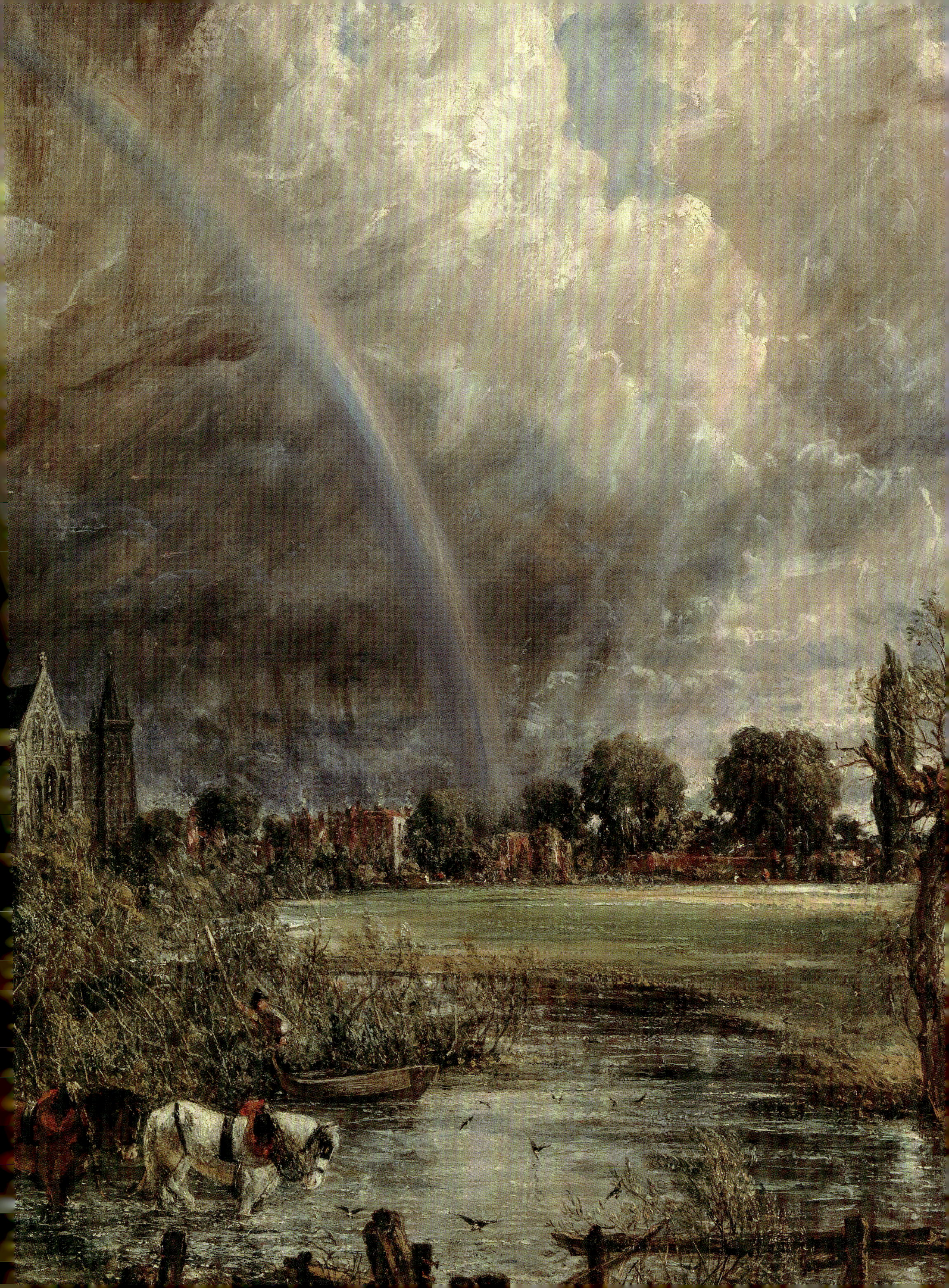

John Constable 1776–1837 and David Lucas 1802–81

John Constable was fascinated by the drama of the British weather and the changing effects of light on the landscape. His bucolic canvases sought to accurately capture the light and atmosphere of the English countryside as well as its topography. From 1829 until his death in 1837, he devoted considerable time and energy to printmaking. Intended to encapsulate his life's work, the series *Various Subjects of Landscape, Characteristic of English Scenery ('English Landscape')*, comprising twenty-two prints, was originally published in five parts between June 1830 and July 1832. Constable chose the engraving technique of mezzotint for its rich, velvety blacks and soft gradations of tone. Working with the professional printmaker David Lucas, he explored extreme contrasts of light and dark, depicting the dramatic effects of changing light on the landscape in unprecedented ways.

The subjects, many of which are familiar from Constable's canvases and oil sketches, were selected primarily for their inclement weather: the bright light which frames a windmill on the hillside contrasts dramatically with receding dark clouds around the church steeple in *Summer, Afternoon – After a Shower*, while the looming rainstorm in *A Heath* (p.68) casts a sudden patchwork of shadows across the shining heathland. In *River Stour, Suffolk* (p.68) the artist's favourite cumulus and nimbus clouds are pierced by rays of bright sunlight, causing the sinuous river below to glisten. Another sky with large hail clouds characterises *Spring* (p.69), which depicts a ploughing scene in the artist's birthplace of East Bergholt in Suffolk in the east of England. It was here, while working in his father's windmill as a youth, that Constable's abiding interest in what he termed 'the natural history of the skies' was sparked.

Summer, Afternoon – After a Shower published 1831
Part of *Various Subjects of Landscape, Characteristic of English Scenery ('English Landscape')*
Mezzotint on paper
14.3 × 19

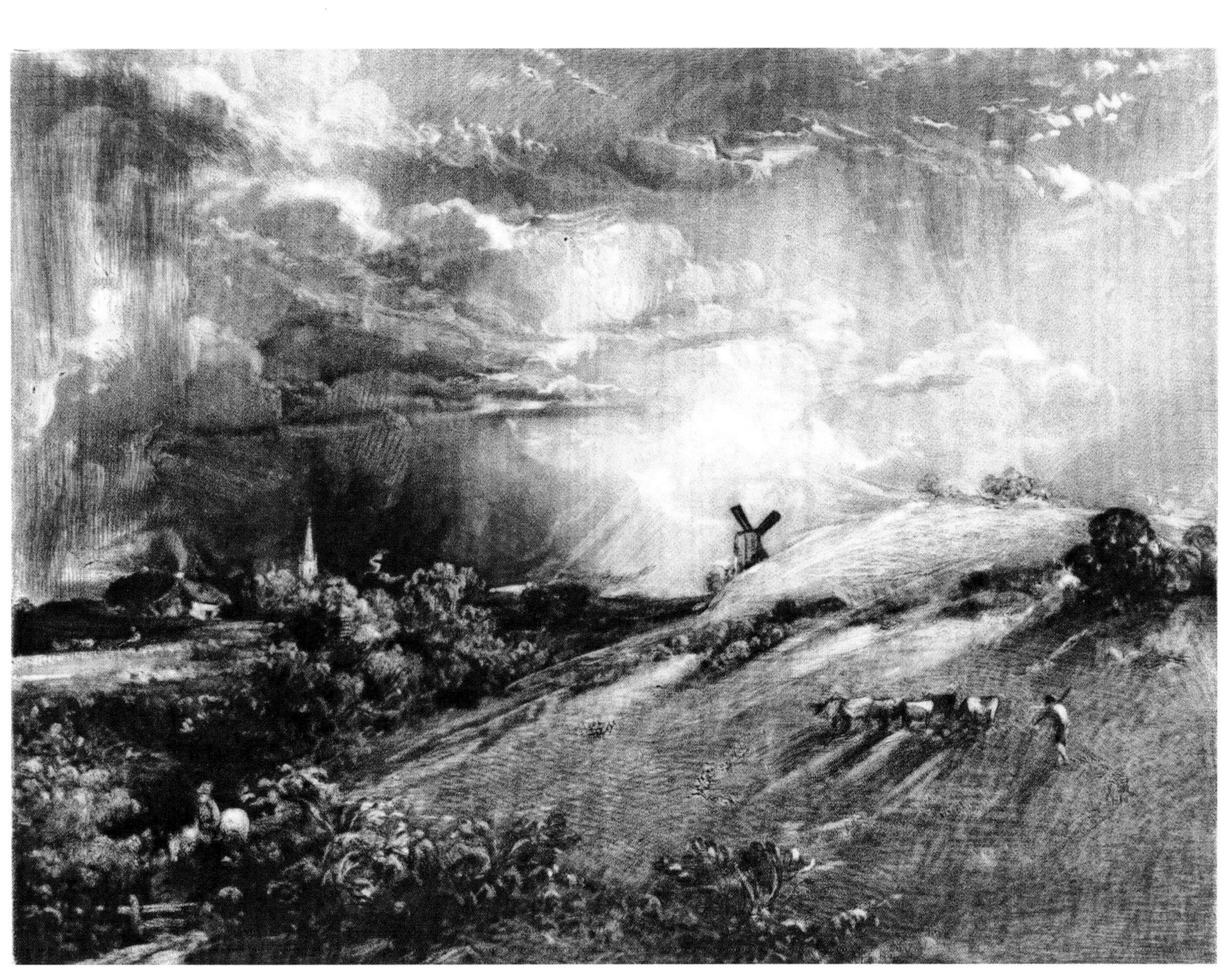

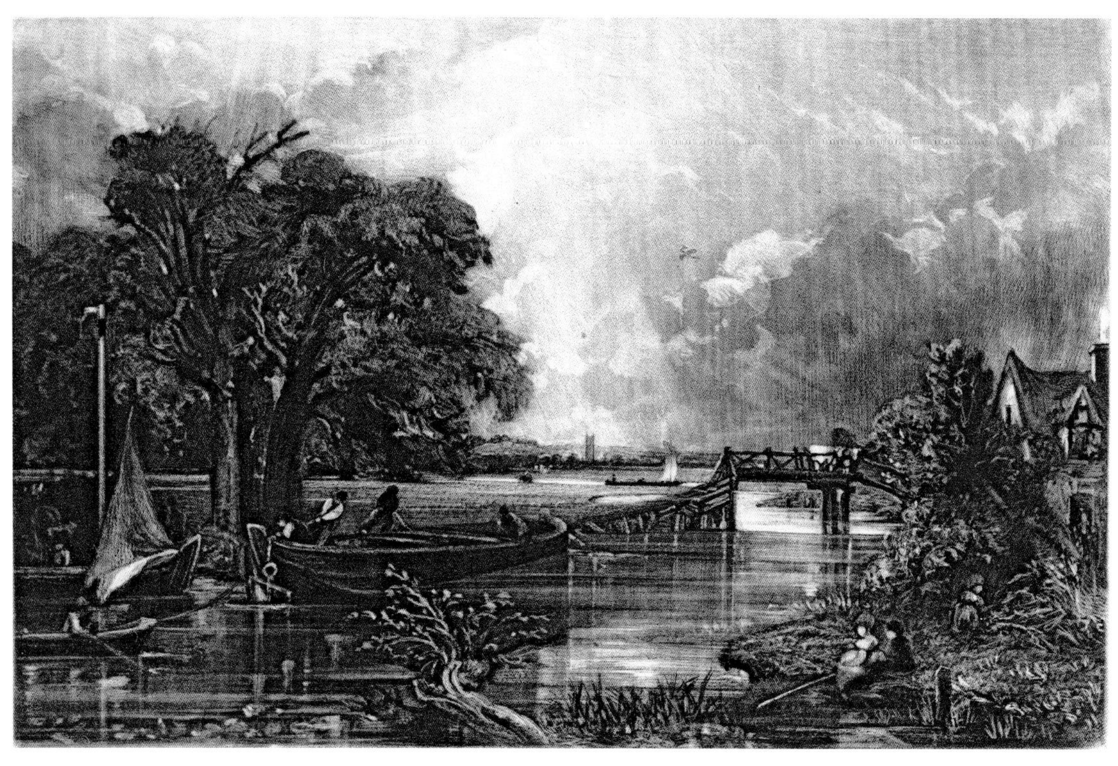

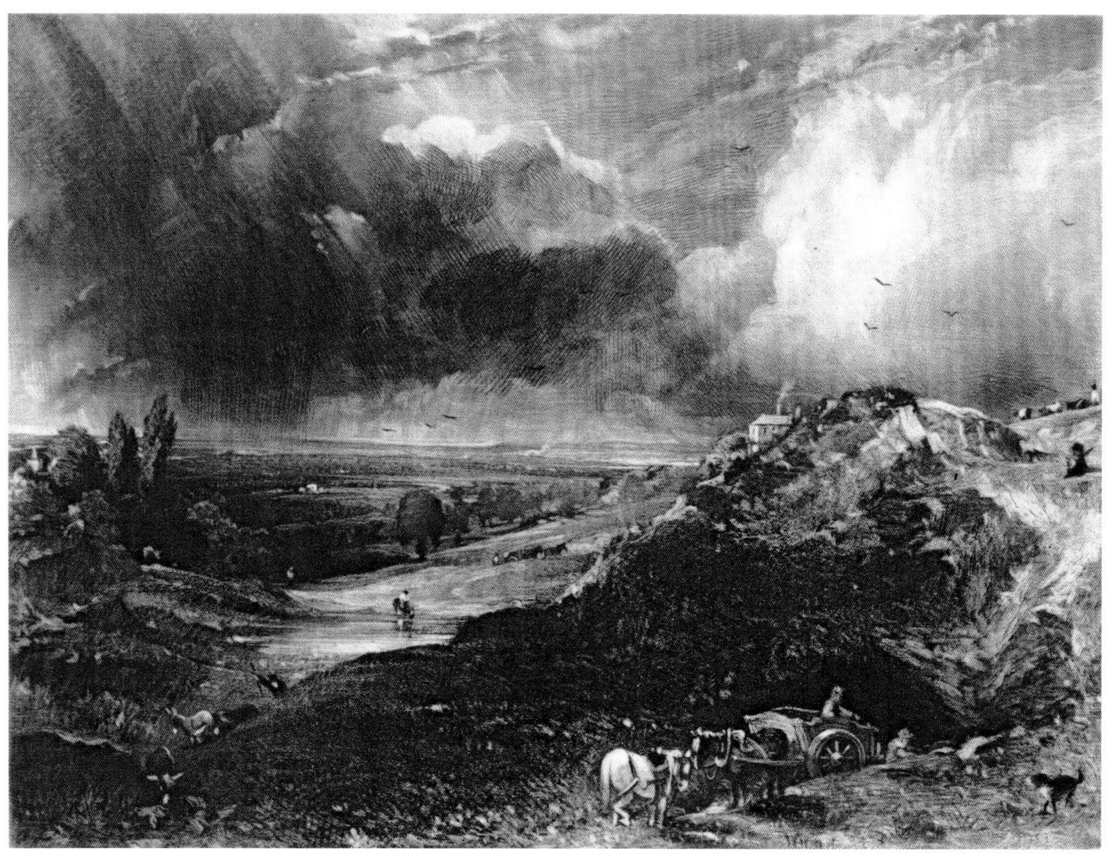

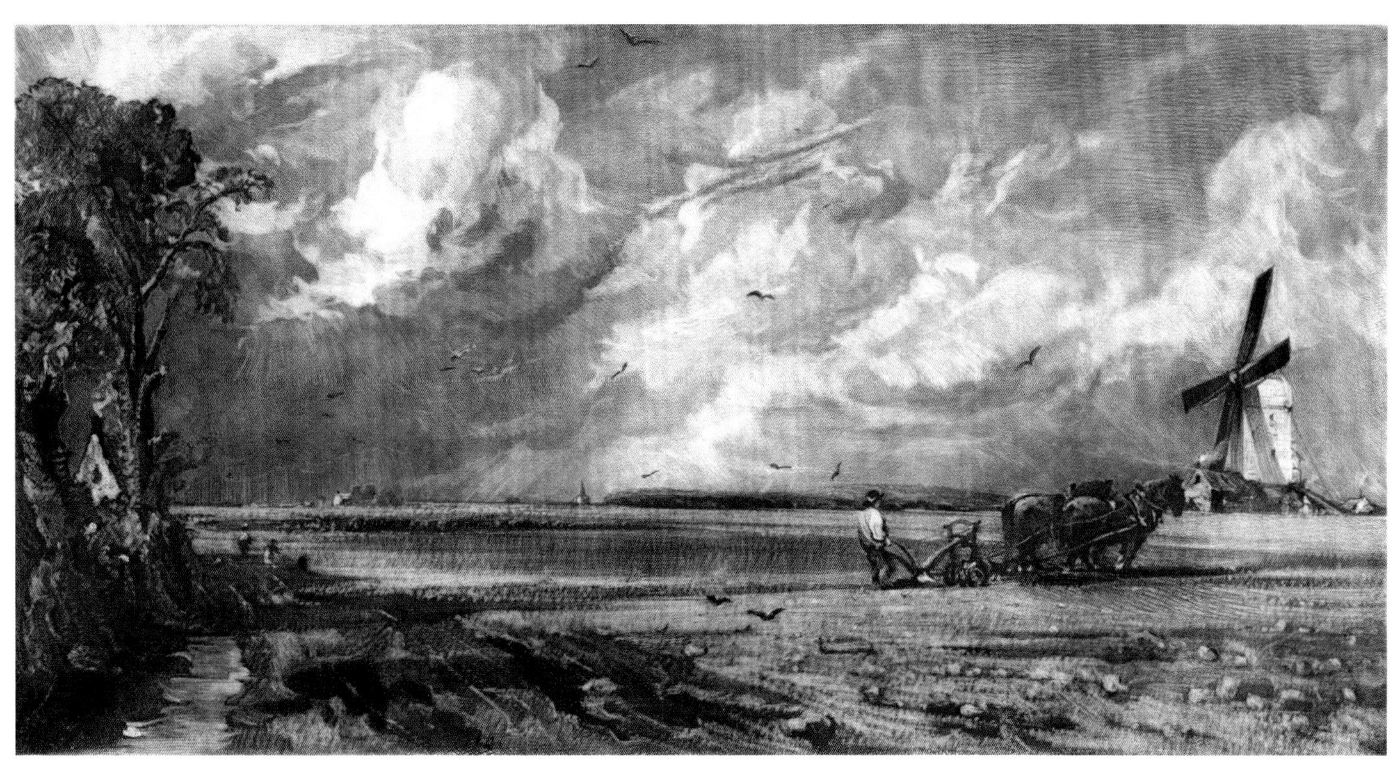

Opposite, above: *River Stour, Suffolk* published 1831
Part of *Various Subjects of Landscape,*
Characteristic of English Scenery ('English Landscape')
Mezzotint on paper
14.5 × 22.2

Opposite, below: *A Heath* published 1831
Part of *Various Subjects of Landscape,*
Characteristic of English Scenery ('English Landscape')
Mezzotint on paper
14.1 x 19

Above: *Spring* published 1830
Part of *Various Subjects of Landscape,*
Characteristic of English Scenery ('English Landscape')
Mezzotint on paper
12.7 × 24.5

John Linnell 1792–1882

John Linnell was a prolific landscape painter, and one of the nineteenth century's most commercially successful artists. As a pioneer of the new observational landscape painting that emerged in Britain in the early 1800s, he sought to record the world around him as accurately as possible, following the advice of his teacher John Varley (1778–1842) to 'go to nature for everything'. For the painting *Kensington Gravel Pits*, Linnell produced a series of carefully observed watercolour studies made on location at the gravel quarries close to present-day Notting Hill Gate in west London. Innovative for its date, this highly detailed work departed from the European picturesque landscape tradition of the time, presenting instead a naturalistic depiction of toiling labourers in a working landscape. Paying careful attention to the effect of light on different surfaces and textures, Linnell shows the striking contrast and definition that the bright sunlight and strong shadows bring to the piles of gravel and spoil, as well as the pit workers. The contrast between light and shade is used similarly in *Landscape (The Windmill)* (pp.72–3). Here, Linnell shows sunlight hitting a bank of cumulonimbus clouds, illuminating their billowing white forms; below, their dark, brooding undersides threaten rain, covering the fields and hills to the rear of the scene with a blanket of shadow. A windmill leads the viewer's eye down the gently sloping bank to a herd of cattle drinking from a pool, where light hitting the water is painted with brushy white highlights, recalling the painting techniques of his rival John Constable (1776–1837).

Kensington Gravel Pits 1811–12
Oil paint on canvas
71.1 × 106.7

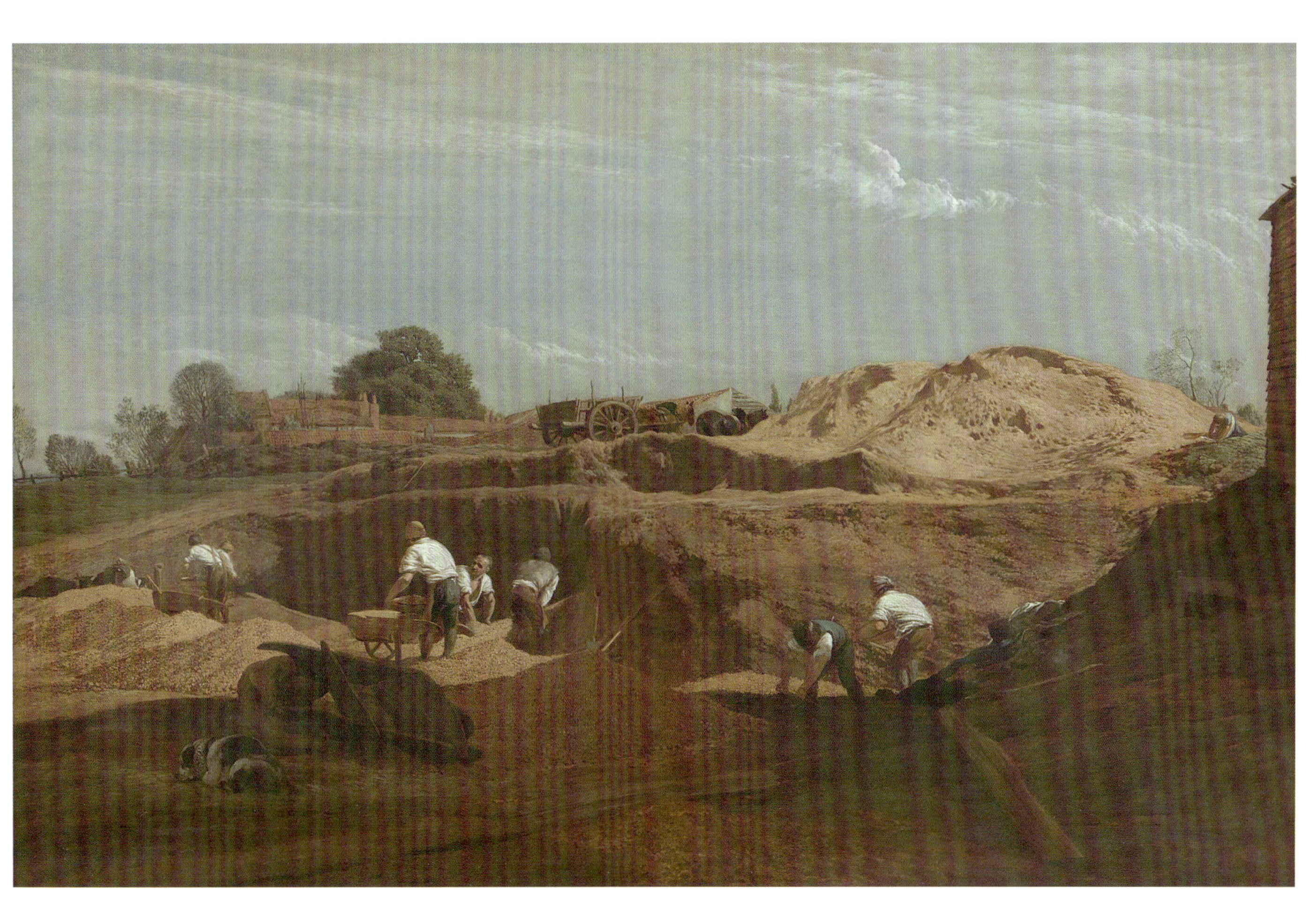

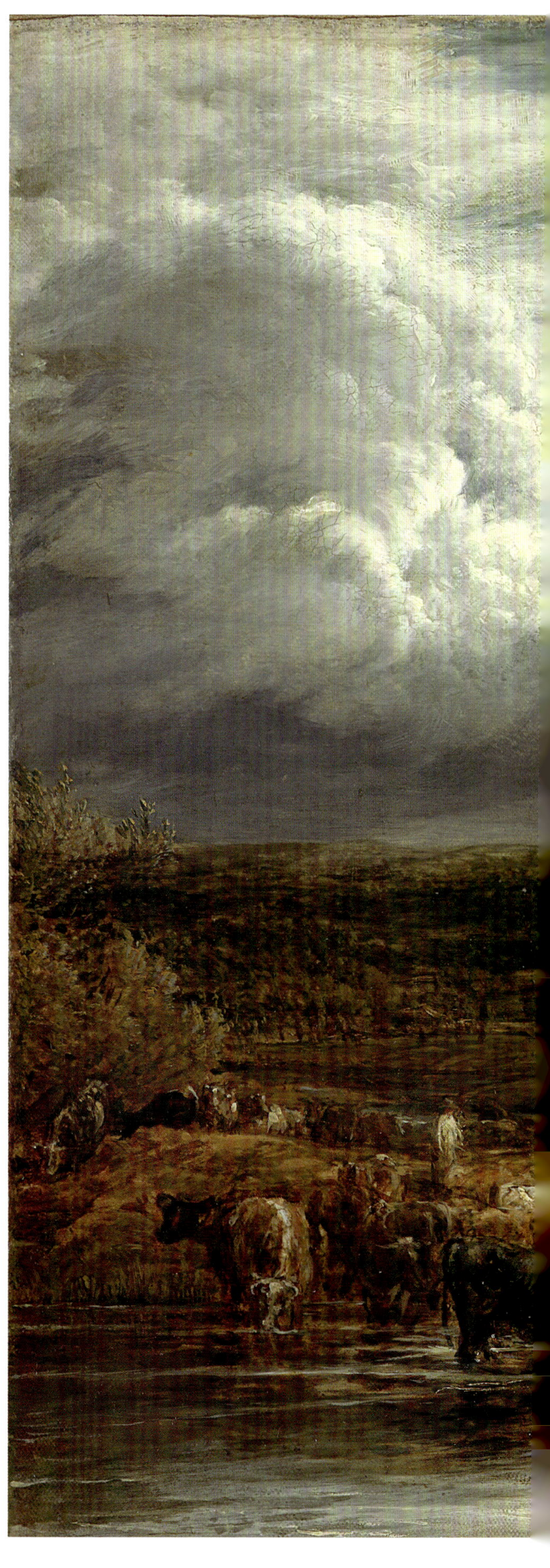

Landscape (The Windmill) 1844–5
Oil paint on canvas
38.1 × 45.7

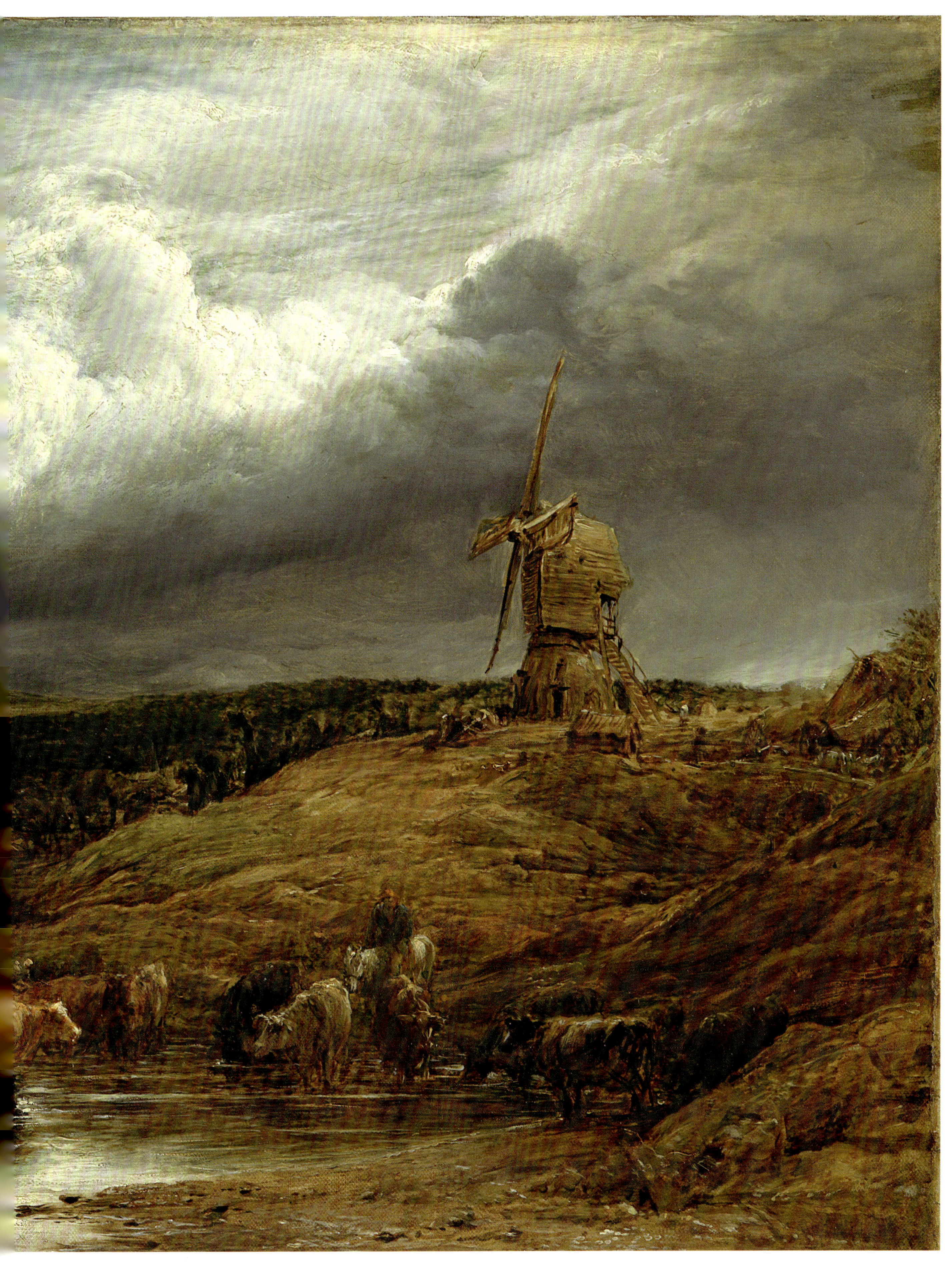

Joseph Mallord William Turner 1775–1851

Turner refined his techniques during the latter stages of his career, applying oils in transparent glazes and using warm-toned colours to depict pure light. *Sun Setting over a Lake* is emblematic of his series of late, and largely unfinished Sea Pieces from the 1830s and 1840s. During this period, Turner became more eccentric and withdrawn. He had few close friends other than his father, the loss of whom in 1829 had a deep and lasting effect on him. While the topographical details of this painting are hazy and indistinct, the sunset is vividly depicted, lighting up the sky in vibrant reds and oranges, reflected across the water.

Although Turner was preoccupied with depicting nature throughout his life, as his career progressed he began to pay less attention to the details and focused more on capturing the effects of light and colour. *Shade and Darkness – the Evening of the Deluge* (p.76) and the companion work *Light and Colour (Goethe's Theory) – the Morning after the Deluge – Moses Writing the Book of Genesis* (p.77) are two of Turner's last and most inspired statements on a natural atmospheric vortex. In *Shade and Darkness – the Evening of the Deluge*, Turner explores the emotional associations of light and colour espoused by Johann Wolfgang von Goethe (1749–1832) in *Zur Farbenlehre* (*Theory of Colours*) 1810, returning to notions of the sublime he had mastered in earlier paintings.[8] In order to depict the greatness of nature and inspire awe in the viewer, Turner also drew from literary works, exhibiting the paintings alongside suspenseful accounts of humanity's relation to nature.[9] *Light and Colour (Goethe's Theory) – the Morning after the Deluge – Moses Writing the Book of Genesis* is a triumphant explosion of warm hues from Goethe's colour circle. Turner intended this as a celebration of God's covenant with humanity after the Great Flood.

Turner's commitment to depicting ephemeral atmospheric conditions placed him at the forefront of progressive European painting, inspiring future generations of artists. The impressionists particularly admired his late works, chiefly Claude Monet (1840–1926), who studied Turner's techniques closely.

Sun Setting over a Lake c.1840
Oil paint on canvas
91.1 × 122.6

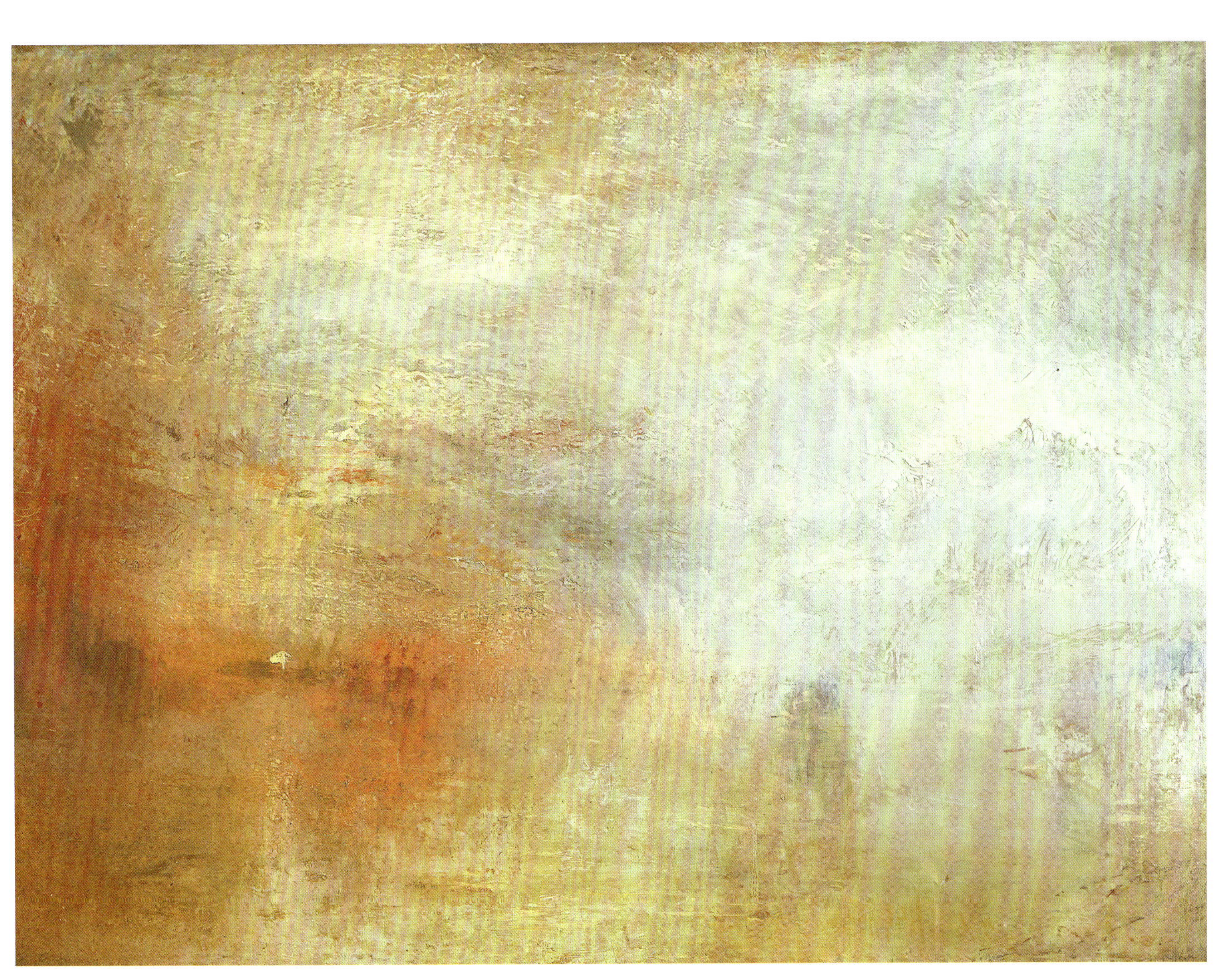

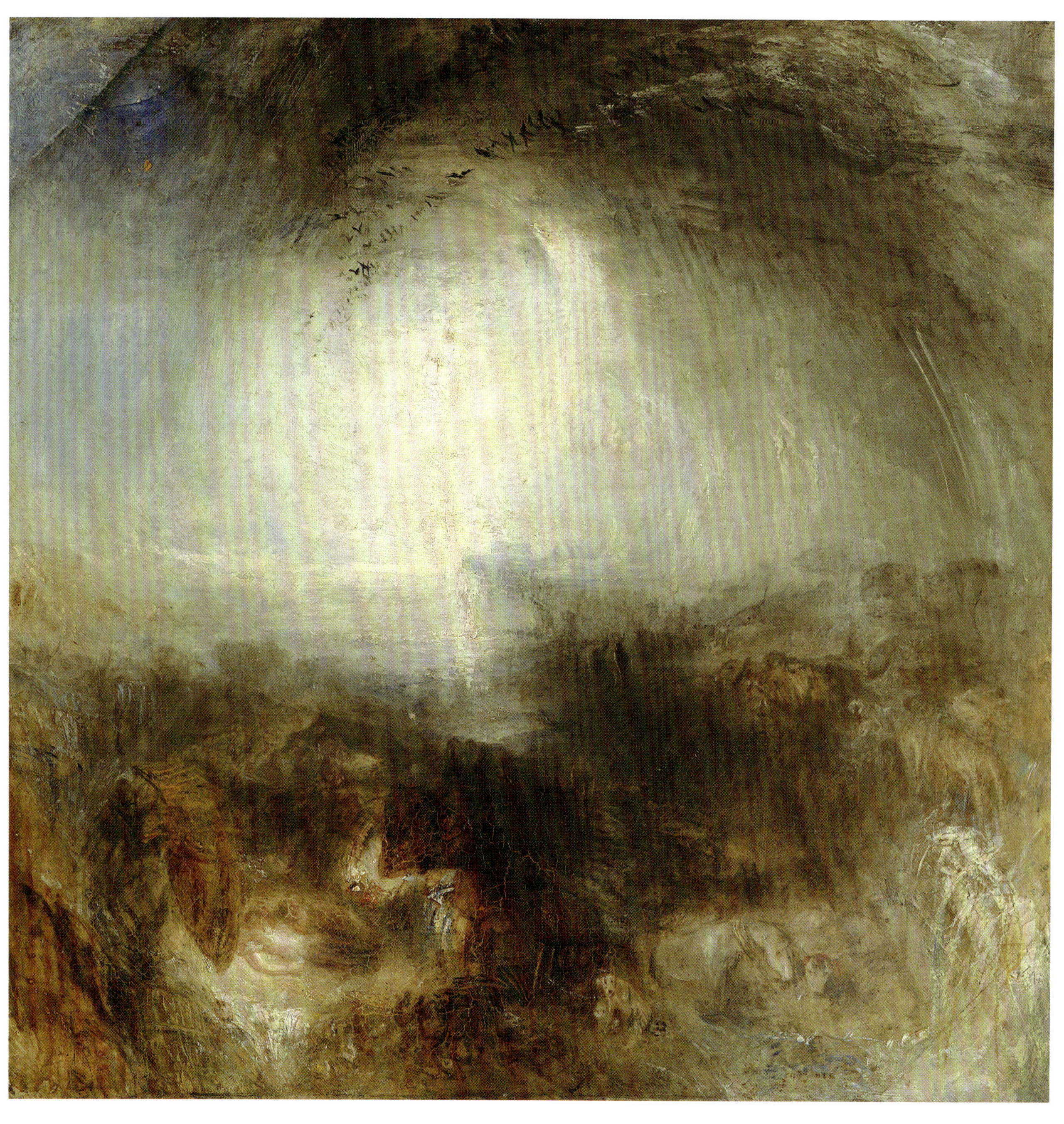

Shade and Darkness – the Evening of the Deluge exh.1843
Oil paint on canvas
78.7 × 78.1

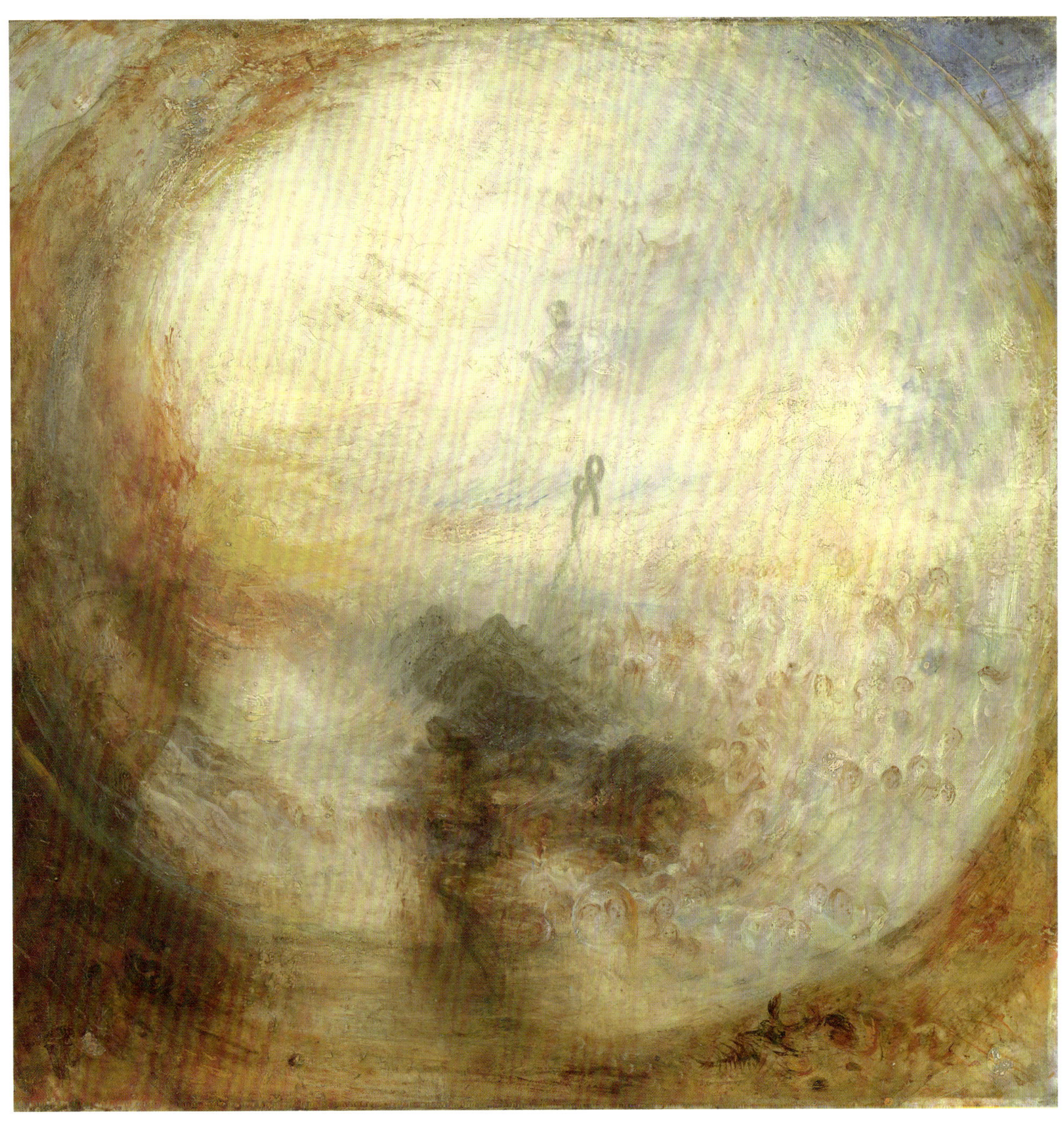

Light and Colour (Goethe's Theory) – the Morning after the Deluge – Moses Writing the Book of Genesis exh.1843
Oil paint on canvas
78.7 × 78.7

John Brett 1831–1902

In his early career, John Brett established himself as a painter of brightly lit, highly detailed landscapes. For a time, he was associated with the Pre-Raphaelite Brotherhood and, under the influence of the art critic John Ruskin (1819–1900), infused his early work with moral and religious significance. In later years, Brett turned his attention to seascapes and coastal views, subjects he had come to know well due to his many sailing expeditions aboard his schooner *Viking*, a large vessel requiring a crew of twelve. Inspired by the paintings of John Constable (1776–1837), Brett became increasingly interested in the transitory effects of weather and light and approached his subjects with a scientific rigour (he established relationships with several well-known scientists and even gained a reputation for himself as an astronomer). His large painting *The British Channel Seen from the Dorsetshire Cliffs* is based on detailed notes, sketches and studies made while sailing round England's south-west coast in the summer of 1870. Though the precise location of this view is not known, it is probably from the cliffs above Lulworth Cove in Dorset. The painting's subject is the effect of light on the open channel; the richly coloured, almost Mediterranean blue water reflects the soft rays emanating from the unseen sun as fluffy cumulus clouds cast patchy shadows. Brett took great care in his study of the sky and sea in order to reproduce them as faithfully as possible. However, when this painting was exhibited at the Royal Academy in London, some viewers complained that his colour choices, especially the blues used for the sea, seemed to them unnaturally vivid.

The British Channel Seen from the Dorsetshire Cliffs 1871
Oil paint on canvas
106 × 212.7

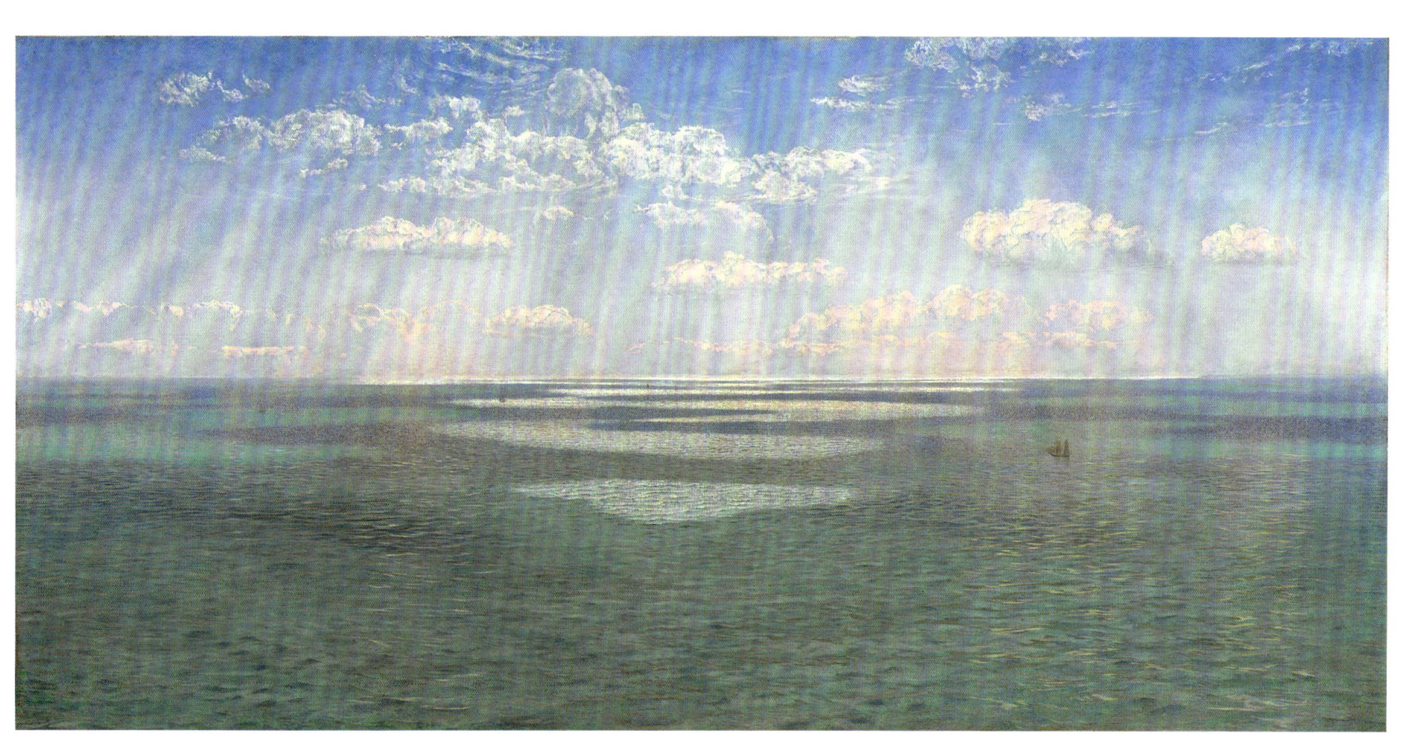

John Everett Millais 1829–96

Born to a prosperous family, John Everett Millais was a child prodigy who was sent to Sass's Art School in London and won a silver medal at the Society of Arts at the age of nine. In 1840 he was then admitted to the Royal Academy Schools as their youngest ever student, winning a silver medal in 1843 and gold in 1847. There he became friendly with fellow students William Holman Hunt (1827–1910) and Dante Gabriel Rossetti (1828–82). In 1848 the three artists formed the Pre-Raphaelite Brotherhood, a loose association which advocated for a close study of nature and used these techniques to express Christian ideals, particularly relating to themes of love and death. William Shakespeare (1564–1616) was a popular source of inspiration for Victorian painters such as Millais. This painting depicts the death of Ophelia from Act IV, Scene vii, in Shakespeare's play *Hamlet* 1609.

Overwhelmed by grief when Hamlet murders her father, Ophelia unwittingly falls into a stream and drowns. The flowers she holds are symbolic: the poppy signifies death, daisies innocence and pansies thoughts. When it was painted, it was regarded as one of the most accurate studies of nature ever made, more detailed than photographs of the day. Millais painted the background from life by the Hogsmill River in Surrey in south-east England. Artist, poet and model Elizabeth Siddall (1829–62) posed for *Ophelia* in a bath of water at Millais's London studio. The water was kept warm by lamps underneath, although this did not prevent her falling ill for a short period due to the cold. Millais used lead white paint as an underpainting. He then painted a layer of zinc white to make the canvas even brighter. In order to make the most of the bright white surface, he would mix colours as little as possible so that they remained pure. Paint was then applied thinly in little hatches and dabs with fine brushes to exploit the reflective properties of the white ground. It is this technique that gives his paintings their luminosity.

Ophelia 1851–2
Oil paint on canvas
76.2 × 111.8

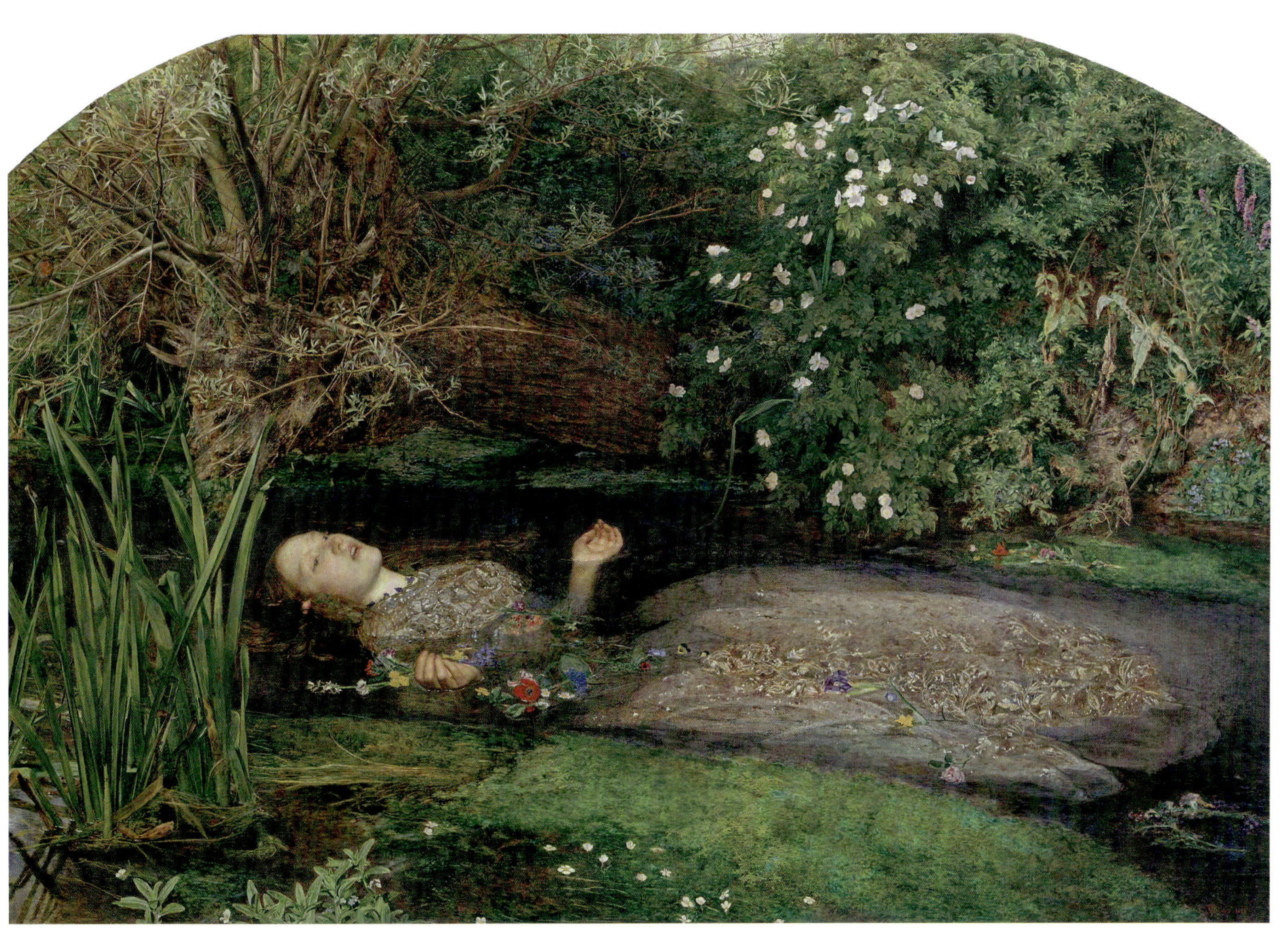

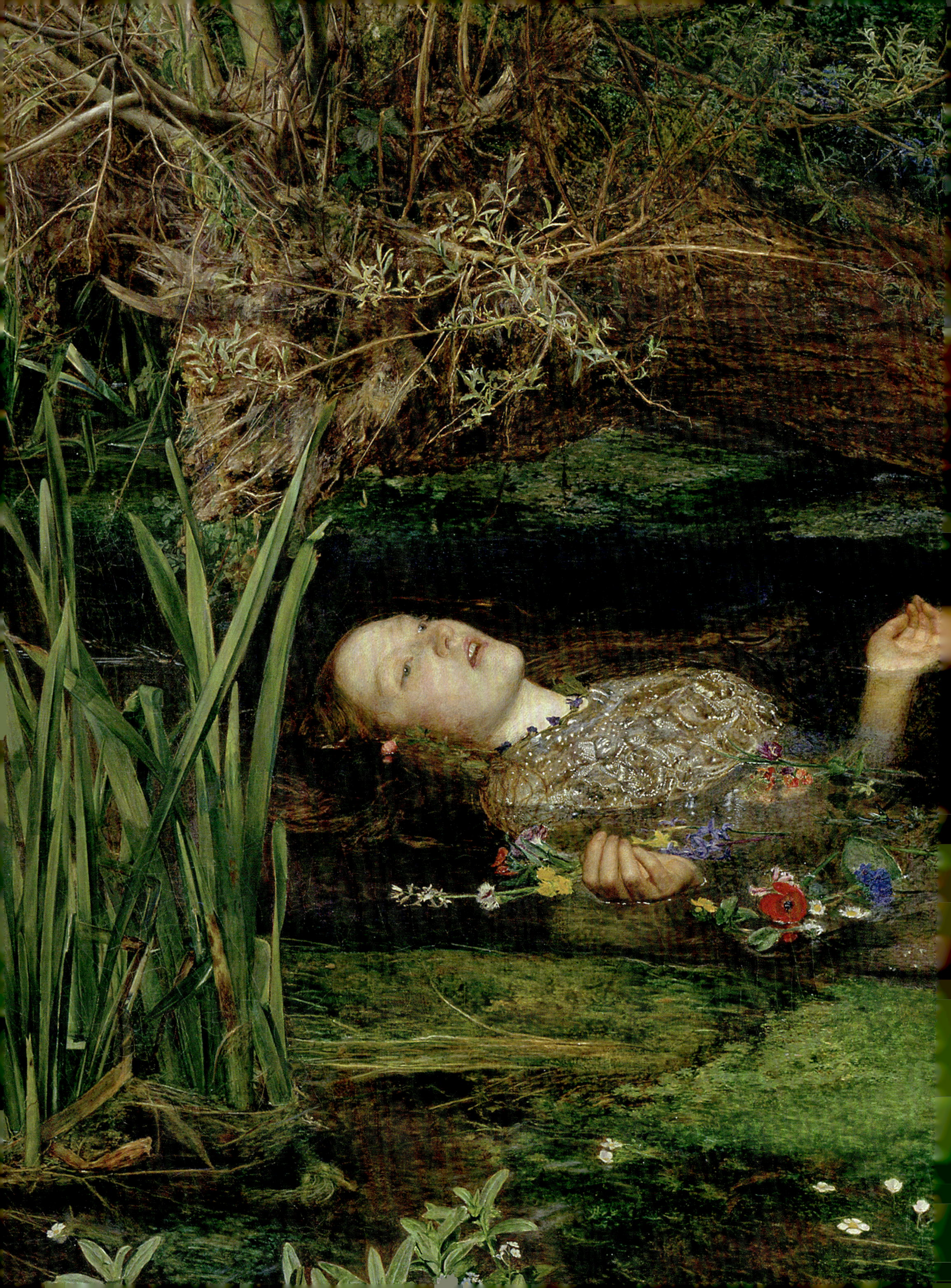

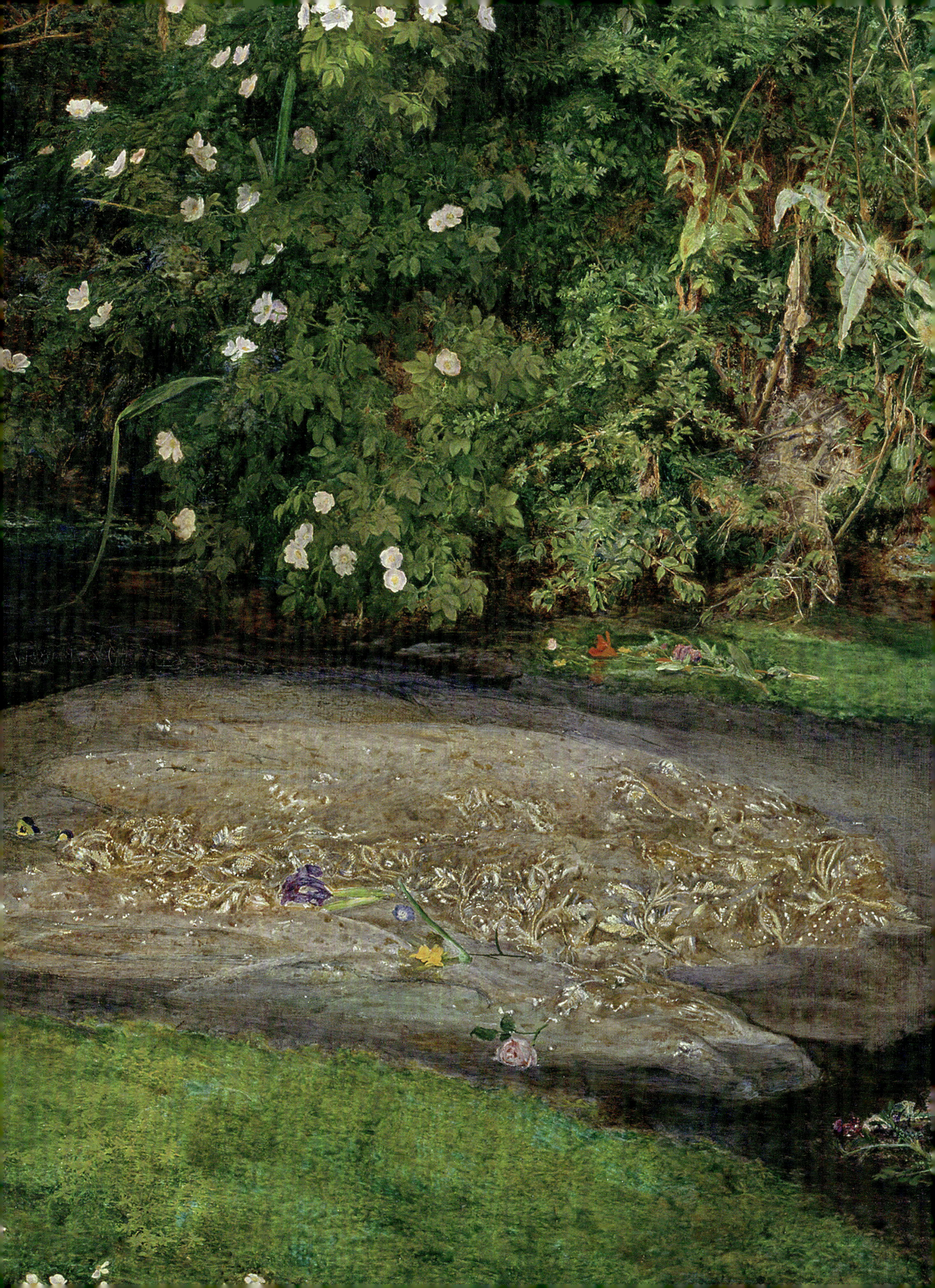

Claude Monet 1840–1926

One of the most important artists of his generation, Claude Monet was a leading figure of impressionism, a movement named after his small canvas *Impression, Sunrise* 1872 (see p.21). Such works aimed to capture fleeting moments, evoking the atmosphere and light of a scene. Working directly from nature, Monet's studies of light and its changing effect on the landscape led to large canvases in which his subject matter increasingly took second place to the formal qualities of paint, a development that paved the way for twentieth-century abstraction. In the 1890s he painted multiple versions of the same subject under different lighting conditions, capturing the passing of time. *The Seine at Port-Villez*, one of many paintings of the River Seine near his Giverny home in northern France, typifies this approach. Here, physical detail is kept to a minimum and the painting's surface is covered with small, individual brushstrokes, which together capture the morning mist and the variations of light on the water. Although the painting is dated 1885, it appears on style to be a work from the 1890s, and the records of the original owner indicate that the painting was in fact dated incorrectly by the artist.

In 1891, Monet painted *Poplars on the Epte* (p.87), one of twenty-three pictures depicting a row of tall trees lining the sinuous River Epte. Eleven show this view painted from his specially adapted flat-bottomed boat. After learning that the trees were to be felled, Monet paid for them to be left standing long enough for him to complete the series. The sketchy brushwork of this composition suggests that the painting was executed at speed and with great spontaneity. While others in the series show signs of extensive reworking, this looser version was Monet's favourite.

The Seine at Port-Villez 1894
Oil paint on canvas
65.4 × 100.3

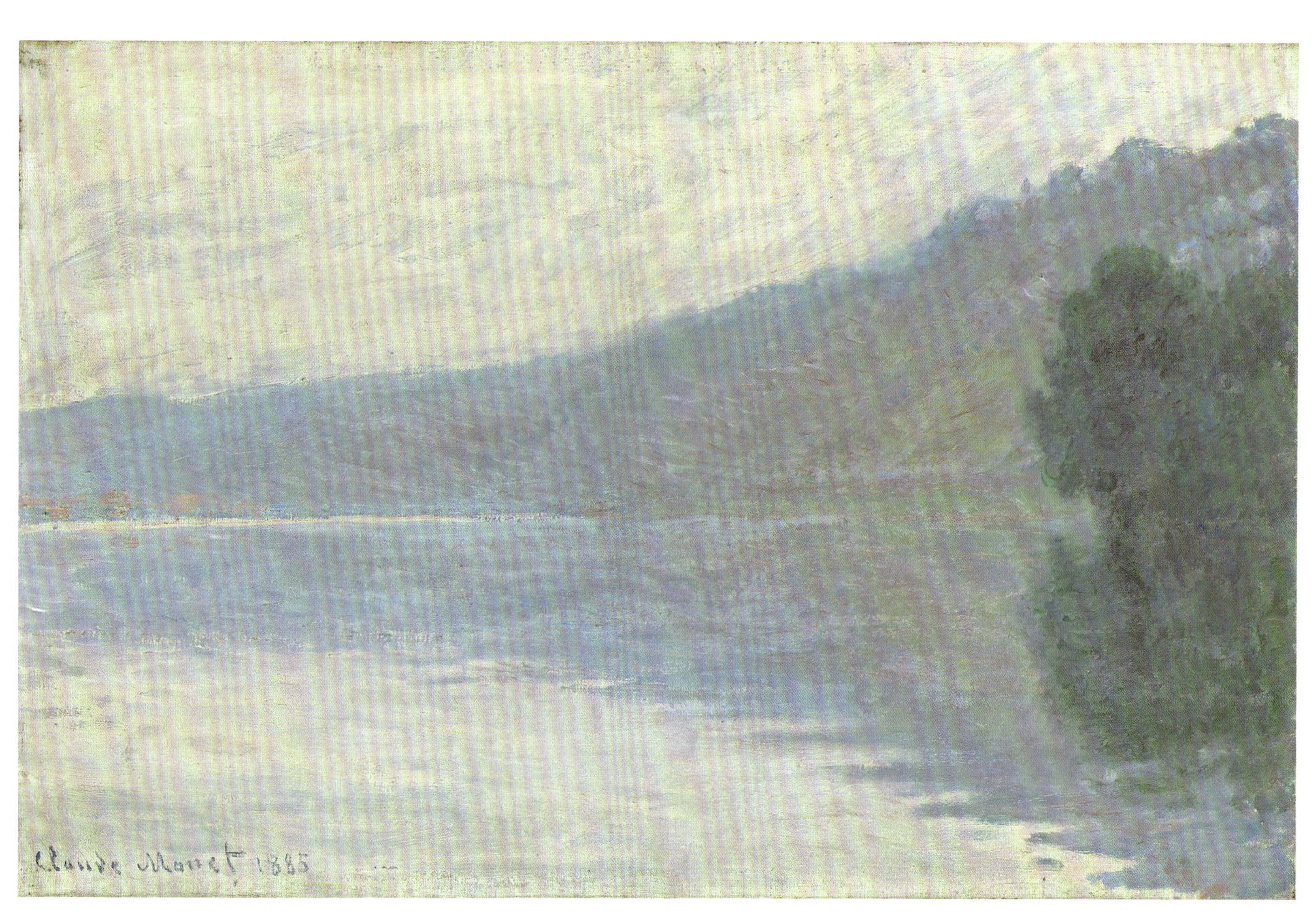
Claude Monet 1885

Poplars on the Epte 1891
Oil paint on canvas
92.4 × 73.7

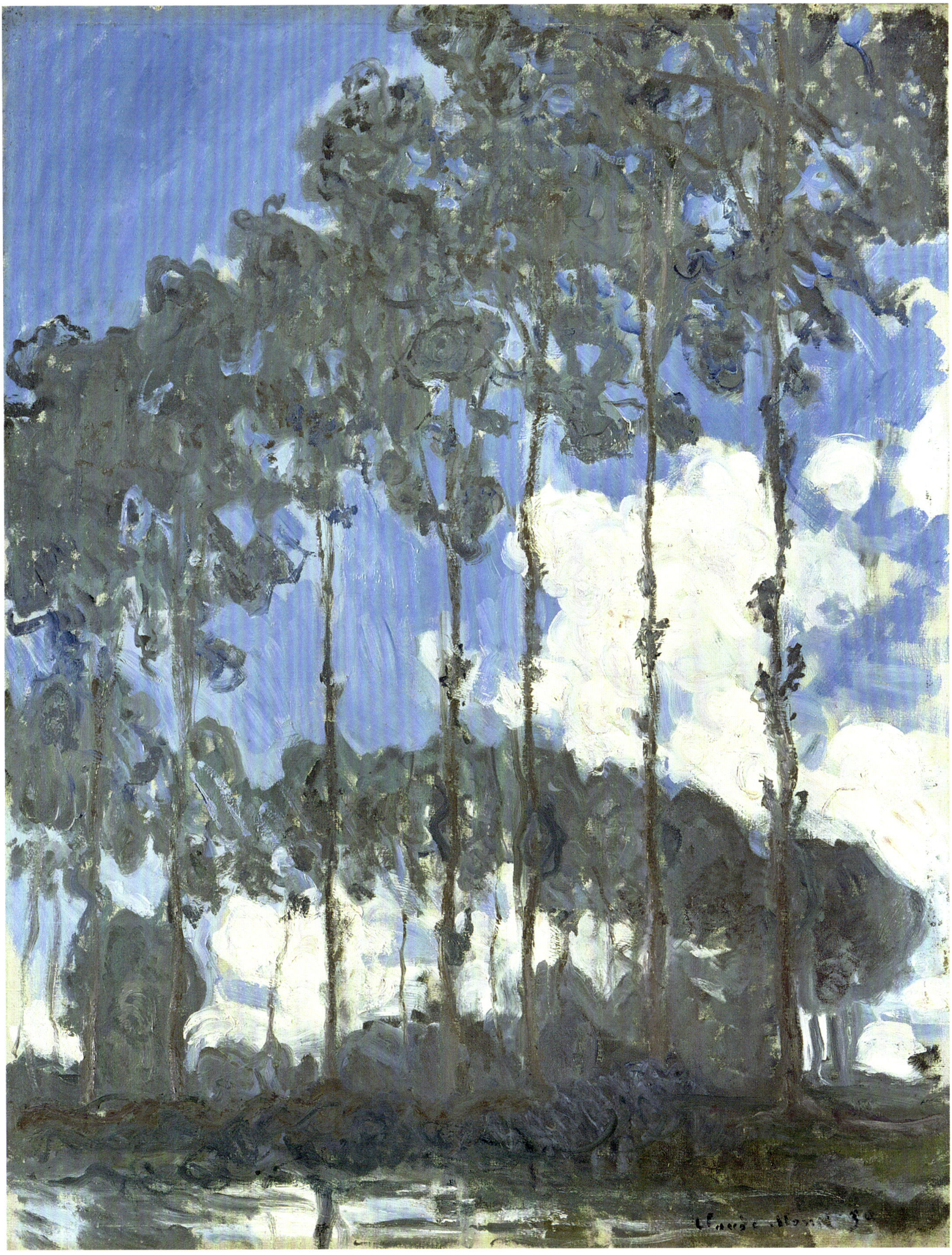

Alfred Sisley 1839–99

Born in Paris to English parents, Alfred Sisley was a founding member of the impressionists. He became friends with Claude Monet (1840–1926), Pierre-Auguste Renoir (1841–1919) and Frédéric Bazille (1841–70) in the 1860s and for a time worked regularly with them *en plein air* (in the open air), a method of painting to which he remained dedicated throughout his career. Sisley displayed a sensitive awareness of the effects of light on the landscape. As he wrote to a friend in the 1880s: 'Objects must be portrayed in their particular context, and they must, especially, be bathed in light, as is the case in nature.'[10] *The Small Meadows in Spring* illustrates this objective. A crisp light strikes the spindly trees, casting shadows across the Chemin des Petits Prés, the wooded path that once ran along the left bank of the River Seine, near the former commune of Moret-sur-Loing in north-central France. The figure in the foreground, whose bright yellow hat provides an arresting focal point, is the artist's daughter, Jeanne, who appears here as an embodiment of spring. Painted a short distance from the small meadows is *The Path to the Old Ferry at By* (pp.92–3), a scene illuminated by a warm summer light that showcases Sisley's skill at painting water. At the river's edge, three washerwomen are busy at work, while nearby a small group of figures watch the ferry across the water at Champagne. Sisley painted several pictures along this riverside path, which he discovered after moving to Veneux-Nadon, on the outskirts of Moret-sur-Loing, in 1880.

The Small Meadows in Spring 1880
Oil paint on canvas
54.3 × 73

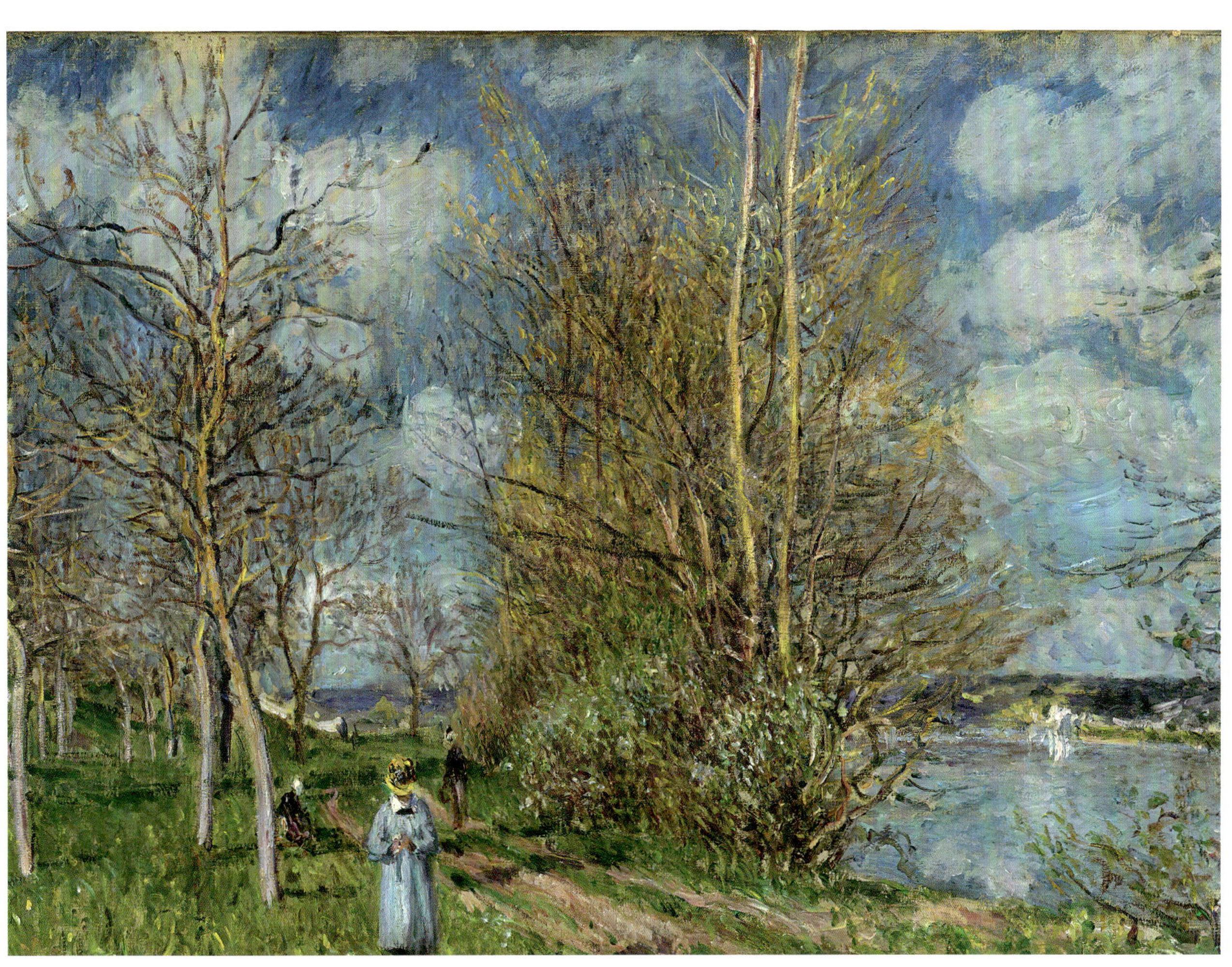

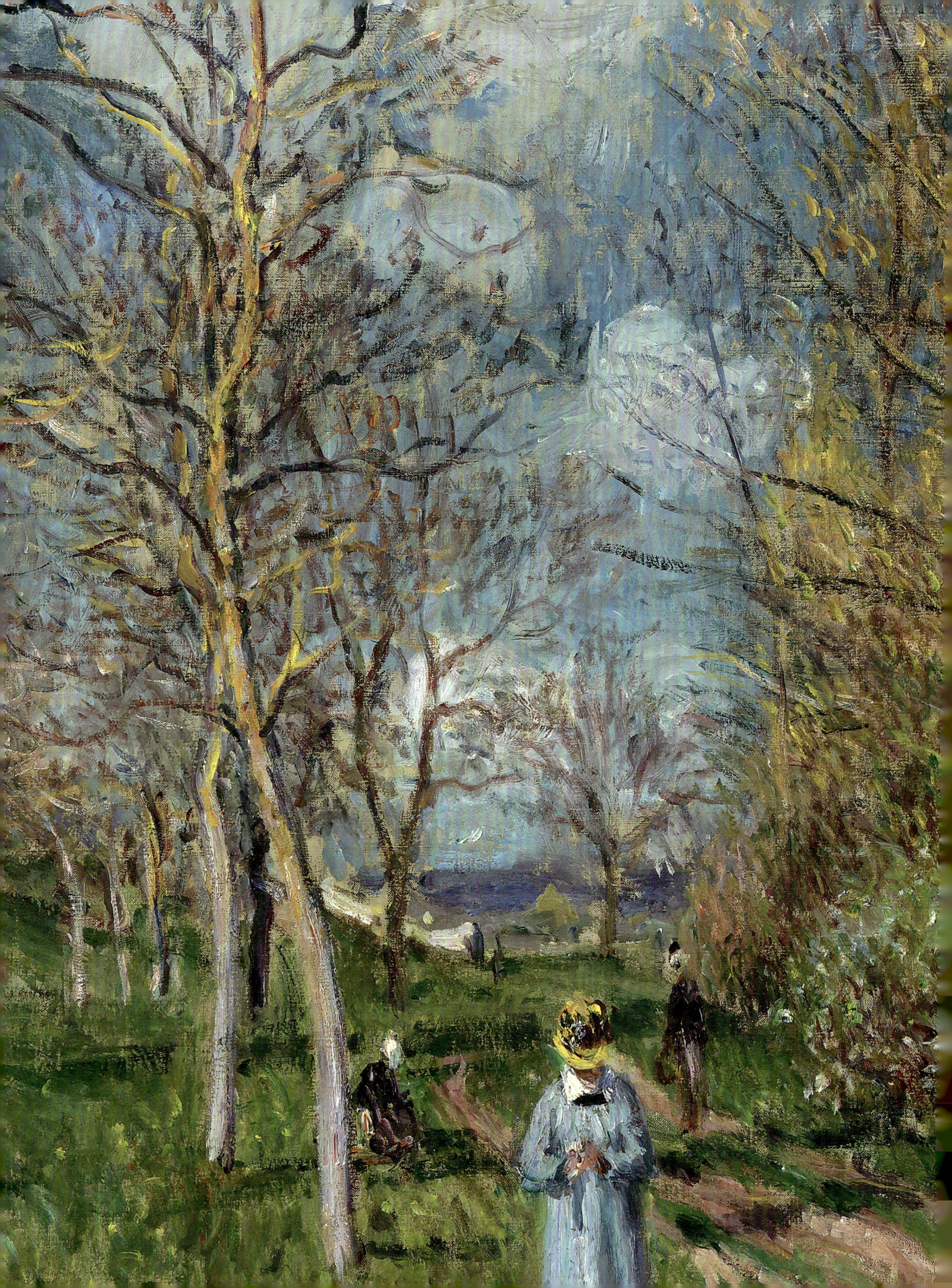

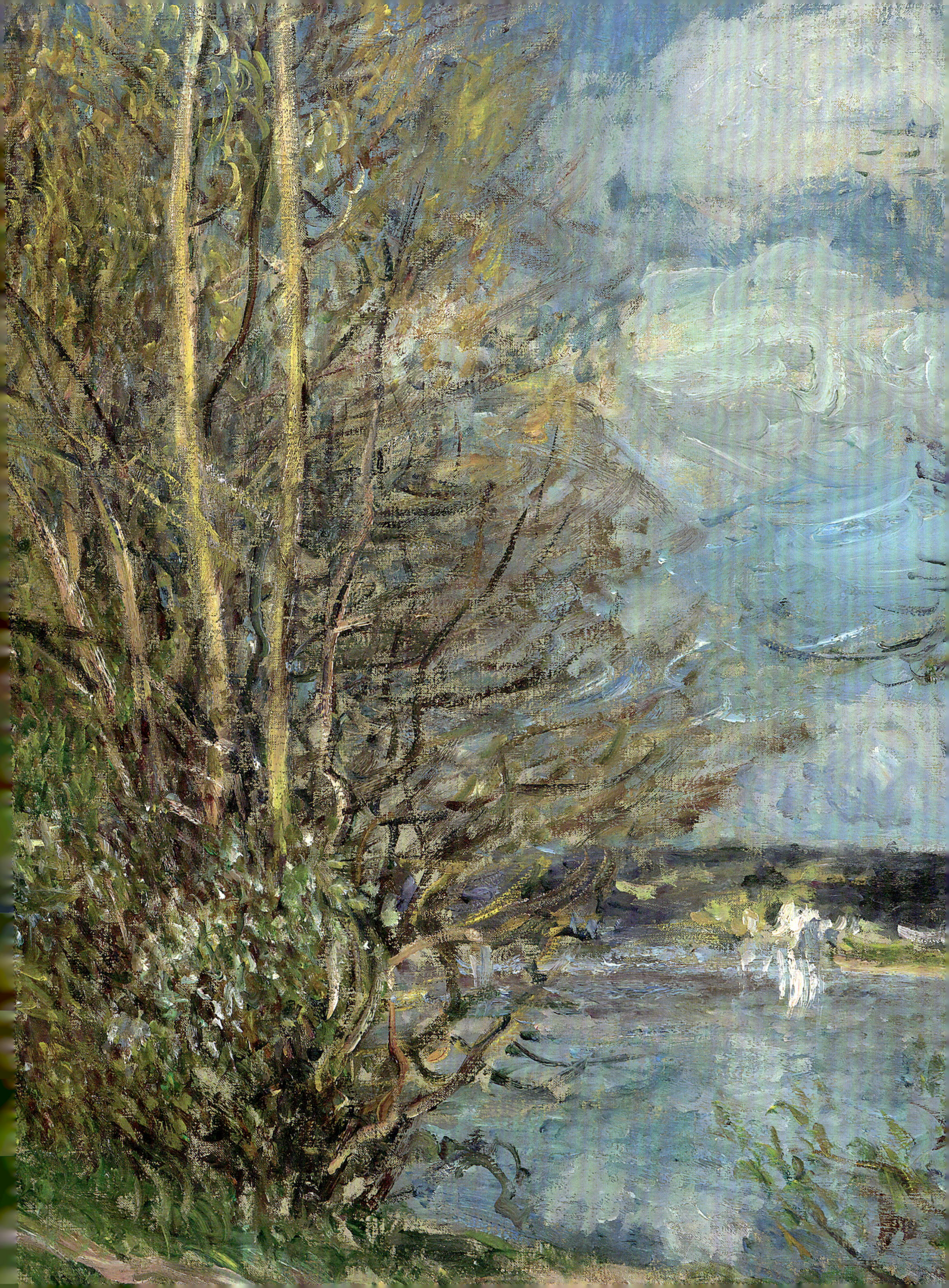

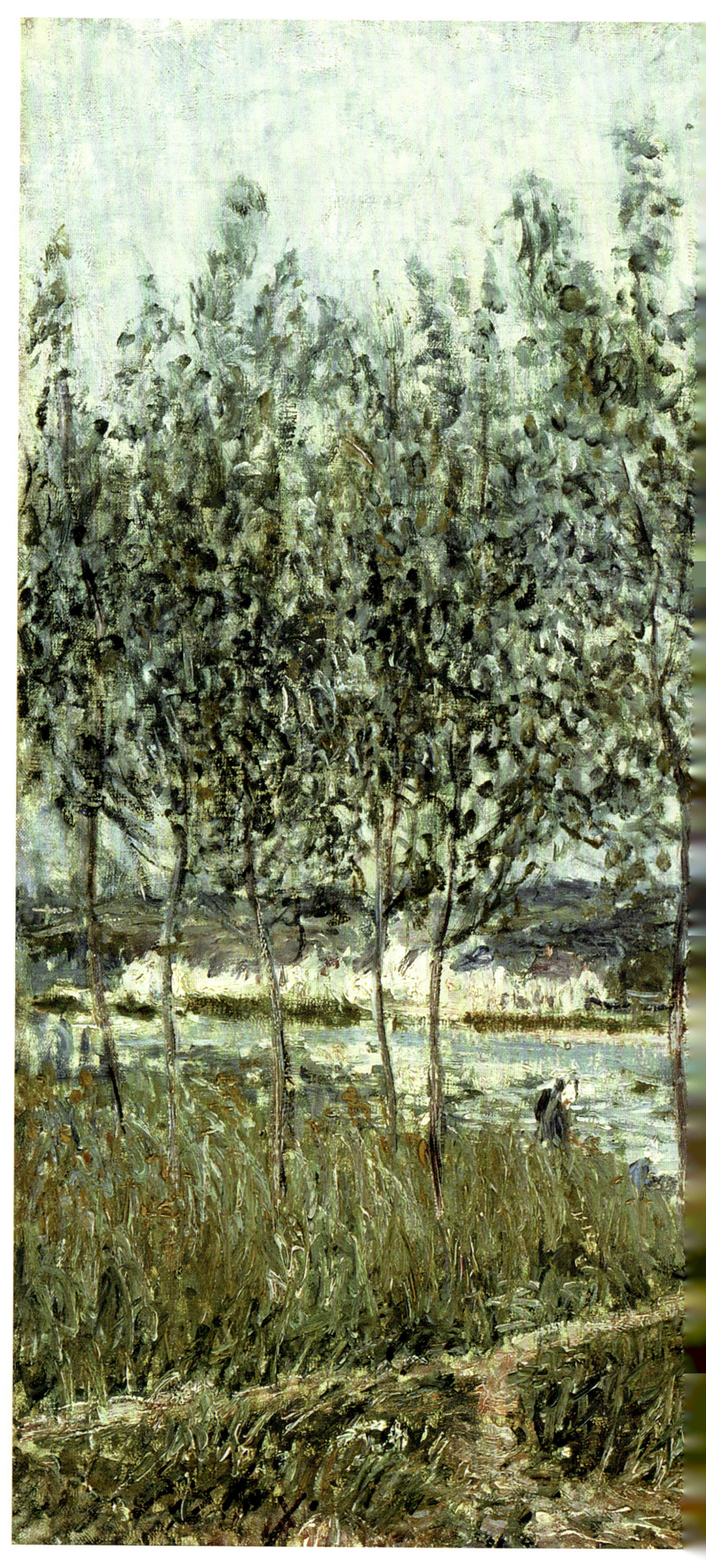

The Path to the Old Ferry at By 1880
Oil paint on canvas
49.8 × 65.1

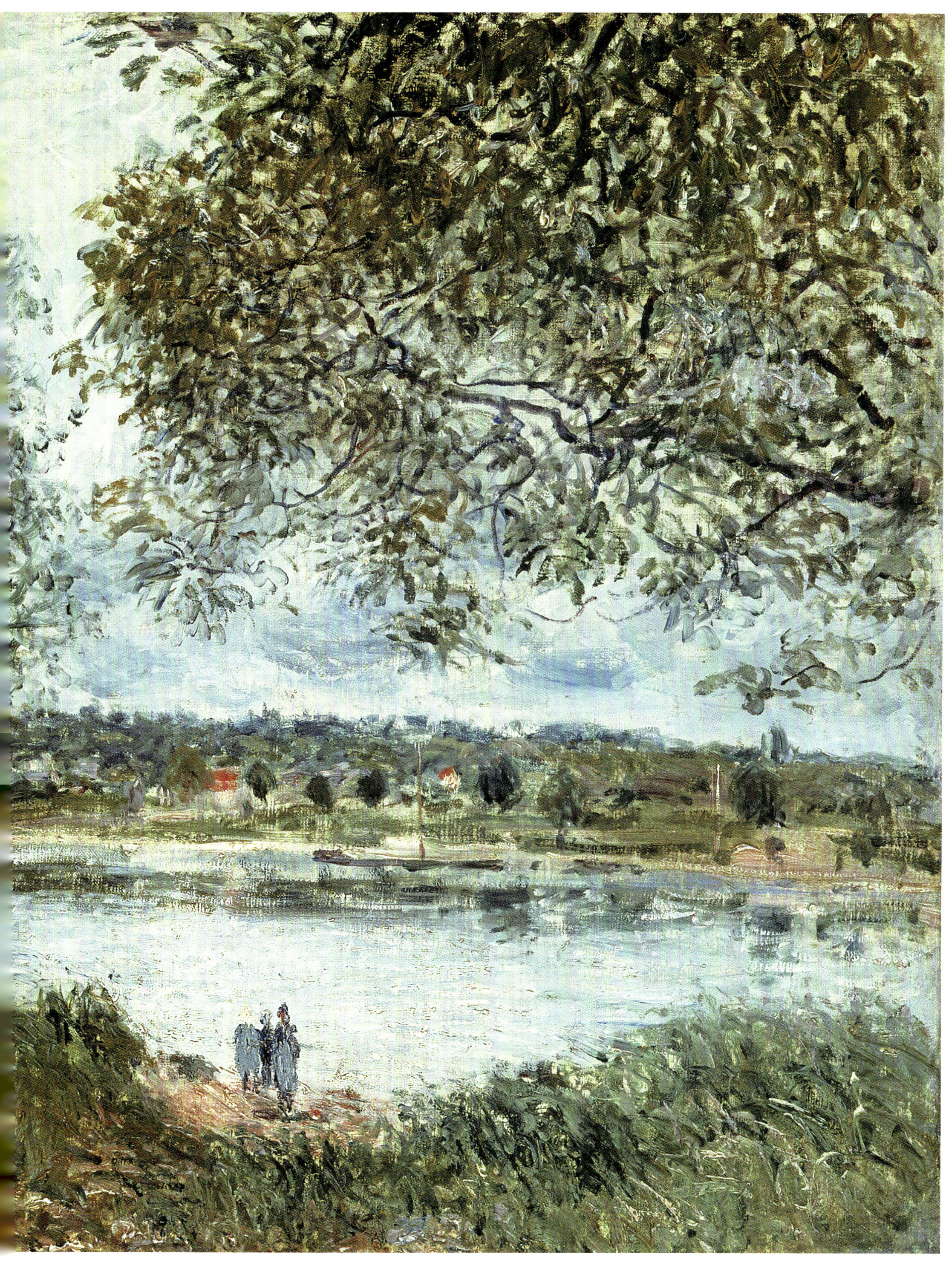

Camille Pissarro 1830–1903

Camille Pissarro was a prominent member of the impressionists, and is the only artist to have participated in all eight of the group's Paris exhibitions between 1874 and 1886. Although his style diversified over the years as he sought to find the perfect method of expressing his ideas, the play of light on the natural and built environment remained an enduring concern. Painted shortly before his death, *The Pilots' Jetty, Le Havre, Morning, Cloudy and Misty Weather* captures the overcast morning light on the harbour's choppy water. Crowds of people mill around the jetty, watching the sailing boats in the busy port. This was the location where the artist had arrived in France, at the age of twelve, from his birthplace on the island of St Thomas in the Danish West Indies (now the US Virgin Islands). The subject of Le Havre was suggested to him by local art collector Pieter van der Velde, who had admired his 1902 series of the harbour at Dieppe. Arriving in June, Pissarro took a first-floor room in the Hôtel Continental, whose balcony offered commanding views of the harbour in three main directions: towards the jetty, towards the pilot's jetty, and in the direction of the outer port. He thus worked on three different series of paintings, recording the changing light at the harbour at different times of day and in different weather conditions (as reflected by this painting's descriptive title). By the time of his departure in September, he had completed eighteen paintings and numerous drawings.

The Pilots' Jetty, Le Havre, Morning, Cloudy and Misty Weather 1903
Oil paint on canvas
65.1 × 81.3

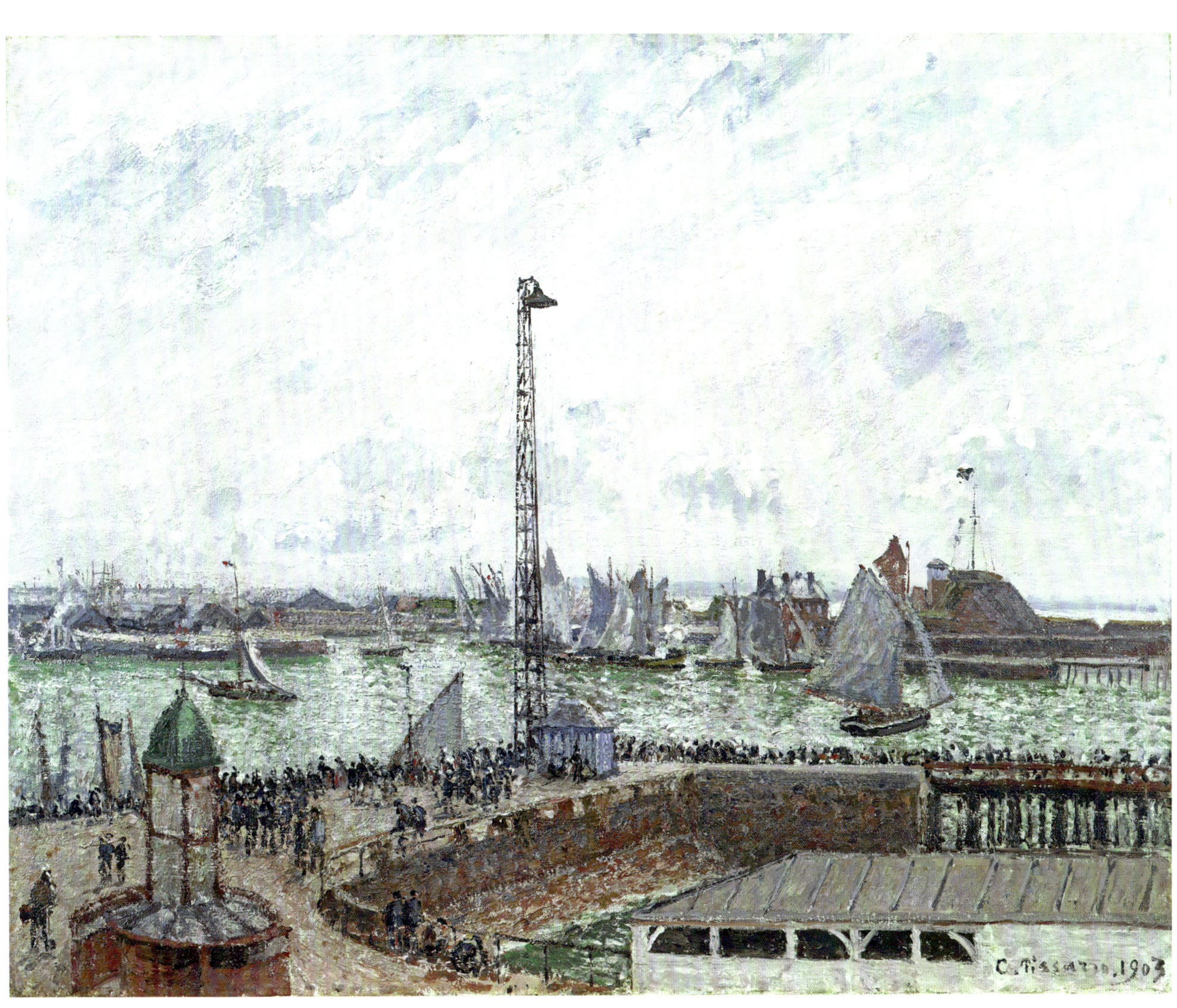
C. Pissarro. 1903

Philip Wilson Steer 1860–1942

Having studied in Paris in the 1880s, the British painter Philip Steer was strongly influenced by impressionist and neo-impressionist techniques, such as the divisionism developed by Georges Seurat (1859–91), Paul Signac (1863–1935) and their followers who, inspired by optical theory, painted with tiny dabs of colour to suggest the effects of light. The small, bright dashes seen across the surface of *A Procession of Yachts* demonstrate the way Steer incorporated such techniques into his work. Begun during a visit to Cowes on the Isle of Wight off the south coast of England in 1892, the painting shows a gathering of schooners, many with their sails raised, shining in the bright sunlight. The white sails reflect in the sparkling water, which Steer rendered with small strokes of paint, giving a suggestion of movement. Coastal landscapes featured heavily in Steer's work. In particular, he was a regular visitor to Walberswick in the east of England and completed several paintings there. Like Claude Monet (1840–1926), Steer worked in the open air, although he was just as interested in the figures as their setting. In the 1880s, he was a leading figure in the impressionist movement in England, and though he exhibited at the Paris Salon, his paintings were deemed uncompromisingly avant-garde and derided in London. Steer later dismissed his French influences, turning to a style derived from Turner and Constable.

A Procession of Yachts 1892–3
Oil paint on canvas
62.9 × 76.2

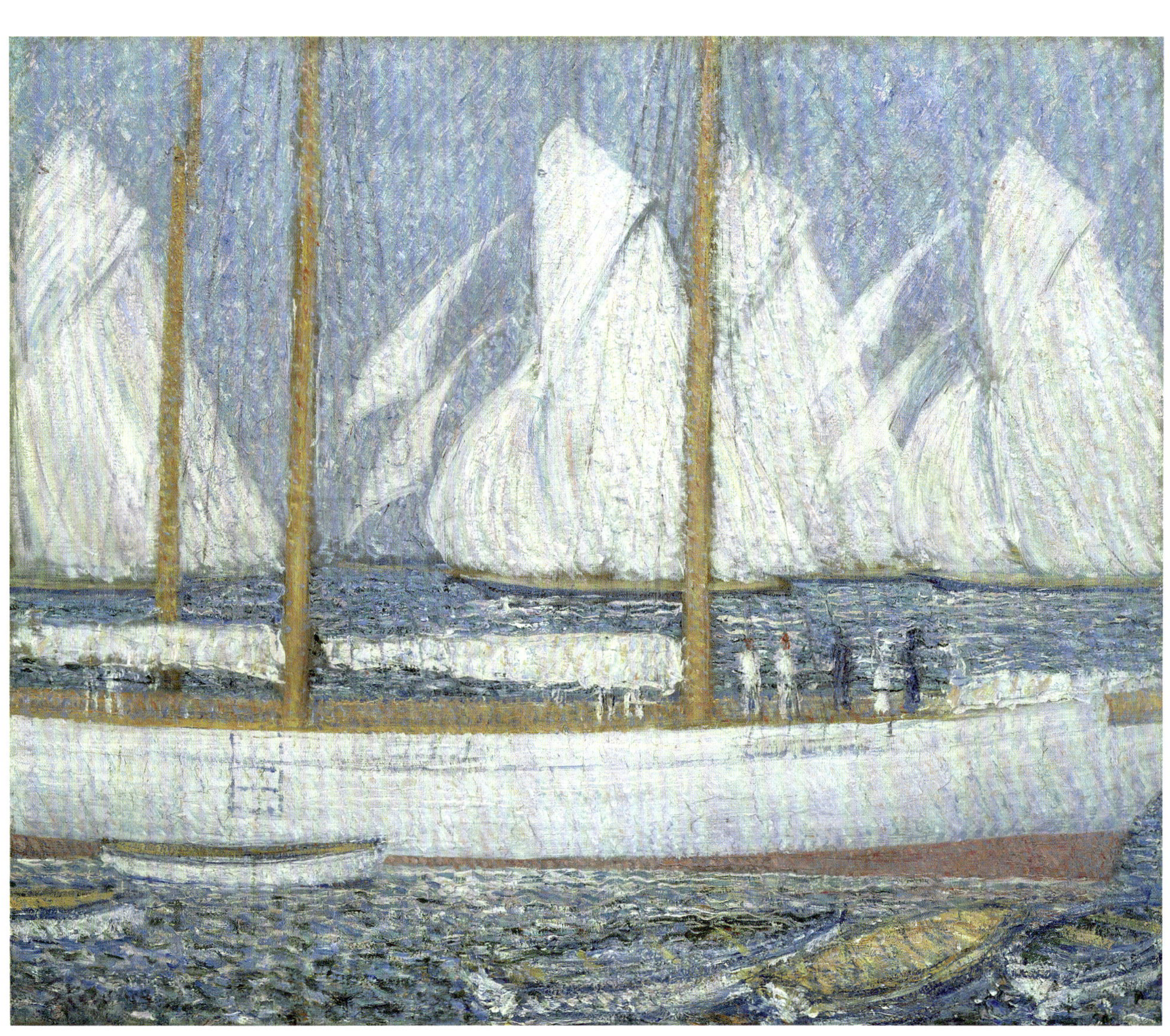

Armand Guillaumin 1841–1927

Like other impressionists drawn to the former French commune of Moret-sur-Loing – including Claude Monet (1840–1926), Pierre-Auguste Renoir (1841–1919) and Alfred Sisley (1839–99) – Armand Guillaumin was fascinated by the effect that different light and weather conditions had on this beautiful riverside location. By the time he painted *Moret-sur-Loing*, Guillaumin had established himself as a highly respected impressionist painter and engraver, having shown his work in six of the group's eight Paris exhibitions held between 1874 and 1886. Although not as revered as his friends Paul Cézanne (1839–1906) and Camille Pissarro (1830–1903), he had a considerable influence on their work (Cézanne's first etching, for instance, was based on Guillaumin's paintings of barges on the River Seine).

This radiant canvas, which shows a view looking to the south-east, up the Loing towards the bridge and church of Moret, is one of several that Guillaumin made from the same position at different times of the day. Using a bright palette and short, dabbed brushstrokes, the artist shows the afternoon light hitting the surface of the river, flooding the scene with vibrant colour (other versions capture the village in the morning and midday light). A bright red rowing boat is moored by a vivid green bank, while nearby a tree shimmers with variegated foliage. In the distance, light violet buildings and blue trees cast their reflections on the water. According to the artist's daughter Marguerite, Guillaumin painted this and similar works while visiting her in Moret as she was convalescing from a childhood illness.

Moret-sur-Loing 1902
Oil paint on canvas
60 × 73

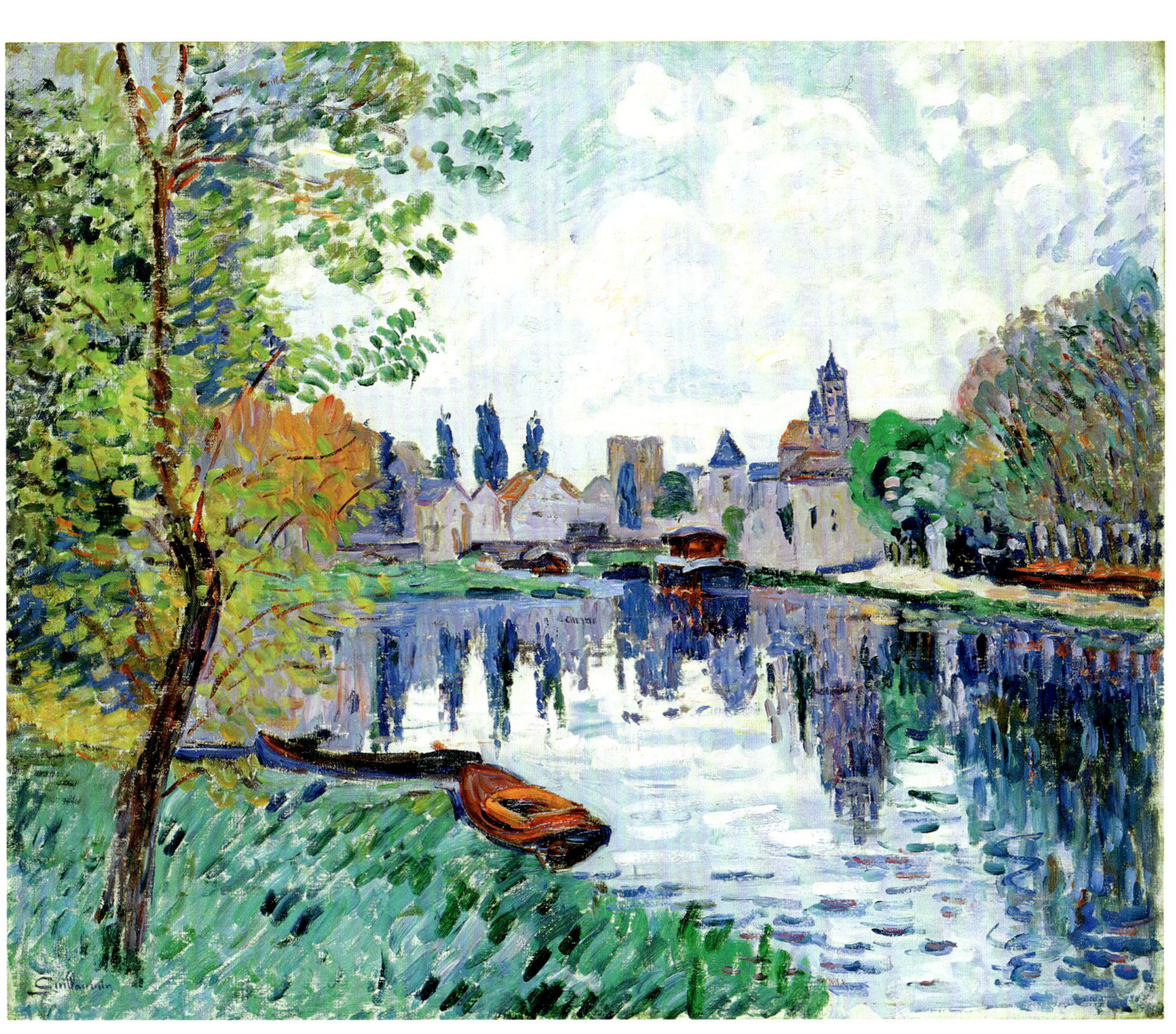

Interior Light

Dismayed at the unimaginative conventions of Victorian painting, a group of young English artists known as the Pre-Raphaelite Brotherhood responded by returning to the style of fifteenth-century Italian art. Founded by John Everett Millais (1829–96), Dante Gabriel Rossetti (1828–82) and William Holman Hunt (1827–1910), the group was encouraged by leading art critic John Ruskin, who urged these artists to 'go to nature'. Working directly from life, they paid close attention to the relationship between light and their subject matter, creating intensely coloured compositions characterised by excessive detail and symbolism. In their paintings the depiction of light is used to convey both physical and metaphorical illumination, pointing viewers to symbolic truths, while the introduction of dramatic highlights and shadows heighten the emotional impact. The Pre-Raphaelite's atmospheric paintings of interiors captured with remarkable realism the play of natural light in a room. In the early twentieth century, artists such as Vilhelm Hammershøi (1864–1916) and William Rothenstein (1872–1945) continued to record the details of their domestic environments in subdued portraits and meditative interiors – sometimes giving as much attention to a room's decor as the figures in the portraits and taking great care to accurately portray the effects of light and shadow in the home. Everyday manifestations of light in interior settings continue to be a subject for artists today. By fixing a particular moment of light, the artists featured draw attention to the connections between light and our perception of time.

John Everett Millais 1829–96

Mariana, with its abundant detail, intense colours and complex composition exemplifies the Pre-Raphaelites' approach. Inspired by literature, these artists frequently painted controversial subjects including poverty, emigration, prostitution and the double standards of sexual morality in society. Mariana is a character from William Shakespeare's (1564–1616) play *Measure for Measure* 1604. Her fiancé Angelo leaves after her family's money is lost in a shipwreck. Still in love with him, she hopes they will be reunited.

In this painting, Millais depicts Mariana stretching her back after working at some embroidery. Her longing for Angelo is suggested by her pose and the needle thrust fiercely into her embroidery. Autumn leaves scattered on the ground suggest the passage of time. When it was first exhibited at the Royal Academy in 1851 this picture was accompanied by the following lines from Alfred Tennyson's (1809–92) poem *Mariana* 1830: 'She only said, "My life is dreary; He cometh not," she said; She said, "I am aweary, aweary; I would that I were dead!"' Mariana contemplates the stained-glass windows which show the Annunciation, contrasting the Virgin's fulfilment with Mariana's frustration and longing. The motto '*In coelo quies*' means 'In Heaven there is rest', and clearly refers to the theme of yearning and Mariana's desire to be dead. The coloured windowpanes cast strong shadows, heightening the emotional charge. Millais was a master at constructing intricate psychological dramas, using the female body as a site to play out the ethical and religious debates of the Victorian era. This painting fits within a broader genre of 1800s literary and visual works that used the interiority of closed and confined spaces as a metaphor for the private thoughts of women at a time when the public were increasingly interested in the emerging field of psychology.

Mariana 1851
Oil paint on mahogany
59.7 × 49.5

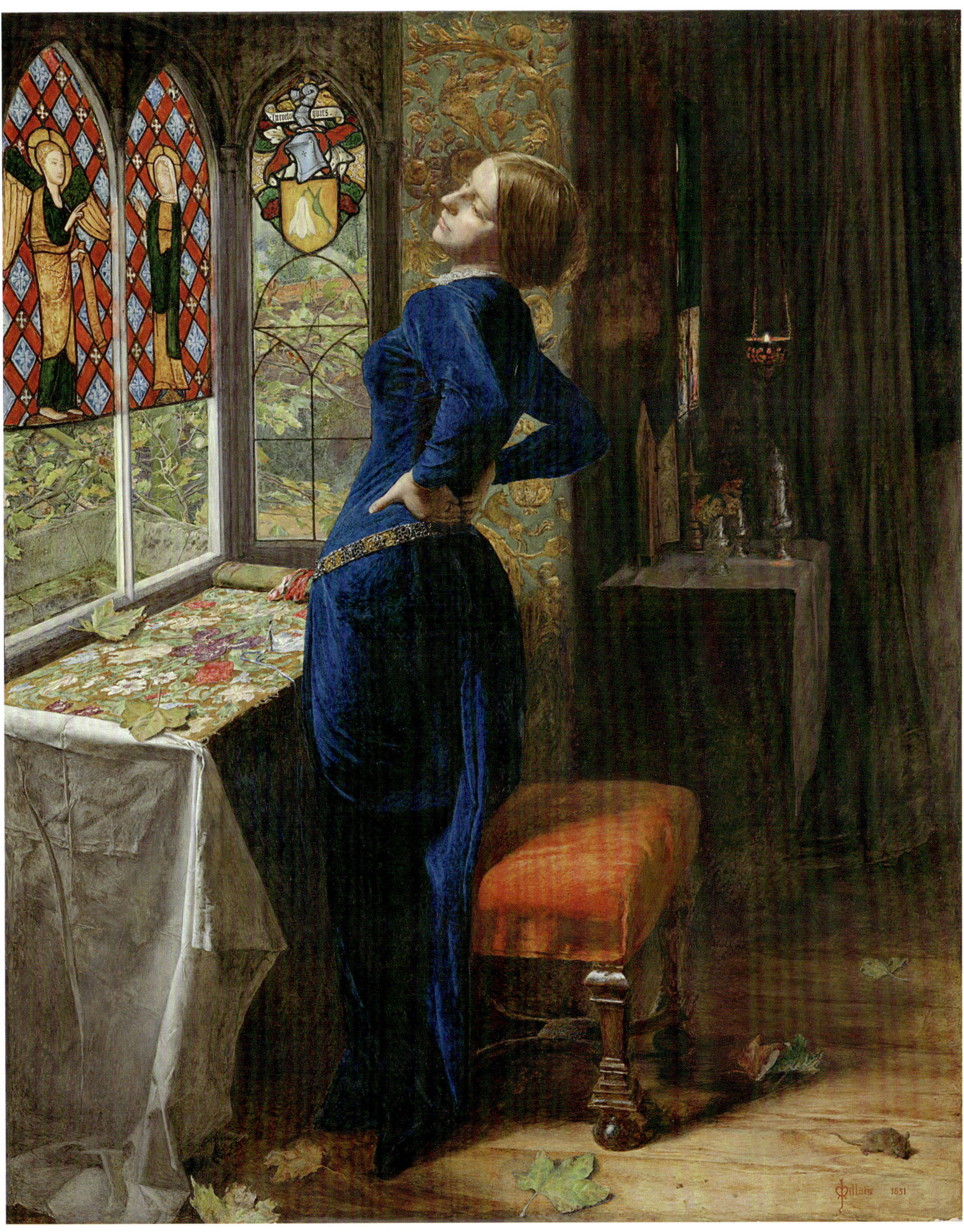
In coelo quies
Millais 1851

William Holman Hunt 1827–1910

William Holman Hunt enrolled at the Royal Academy Schools in London in 1844. There he met John Everett Millais (1829–96), and in September 1848, with Dante Gabriel Rossetti (1828–82) and Millais, he formed the Pre-Raphaelite Brotherhood. The Brotherhood enabled the confluence of several conflicting ideas of the late 1800s, uniquely combining symbolism, which proposed that art should reflect an emotion or idea, and realism, which argued for sharply focused, detail-oriented painting, in a naturalistic setting. Hunt's participation in the Royal Academy exhibition in 1853 attracted the attention of Thomas Fairbairn, a prominent English industrialist and art collector, who commissioned *The Awakening Conscience*. Hunt conceived this painting as a counterpart to *The Light of the World* 1851–3 (see p.14), with the former being painted by daylight, and the latter at night. *The Awakening Conscience* depicts a wealthy man visiting his mistress, indicated by her lack of a wedding ring. Intended to be 'read', the painting is full of symbolic elements. The man idly plays a tune on the piano, while the woman rises from his lap towards a window overlooking a sunlit garden, which is reflected in the mirror behind the couple. The claustrophobic space is filled with intricate clues which symbolise the woman's moral 'plight', such as the bird trying to escape from a cat, and the clock's female figure enclosed in a glass dome. The discarded glove at her feet represents the woman's likely fate, and the tangled yarn on the floor symbolises the web in which she is trapped. The Victorian viewer would have immediately comprehended the precariousness of her situation, the unopened writing manuals on the table indicating the hollowness of her genteel status. The model is Hunt's protégé, Annie Miller (1835–1925), an uneducated barmaid whom he met in 1850 when she was fifteen, and later sought to marry.

The Awakening Conscience 1853
Oil paint on canvas
76.2 × 55.9

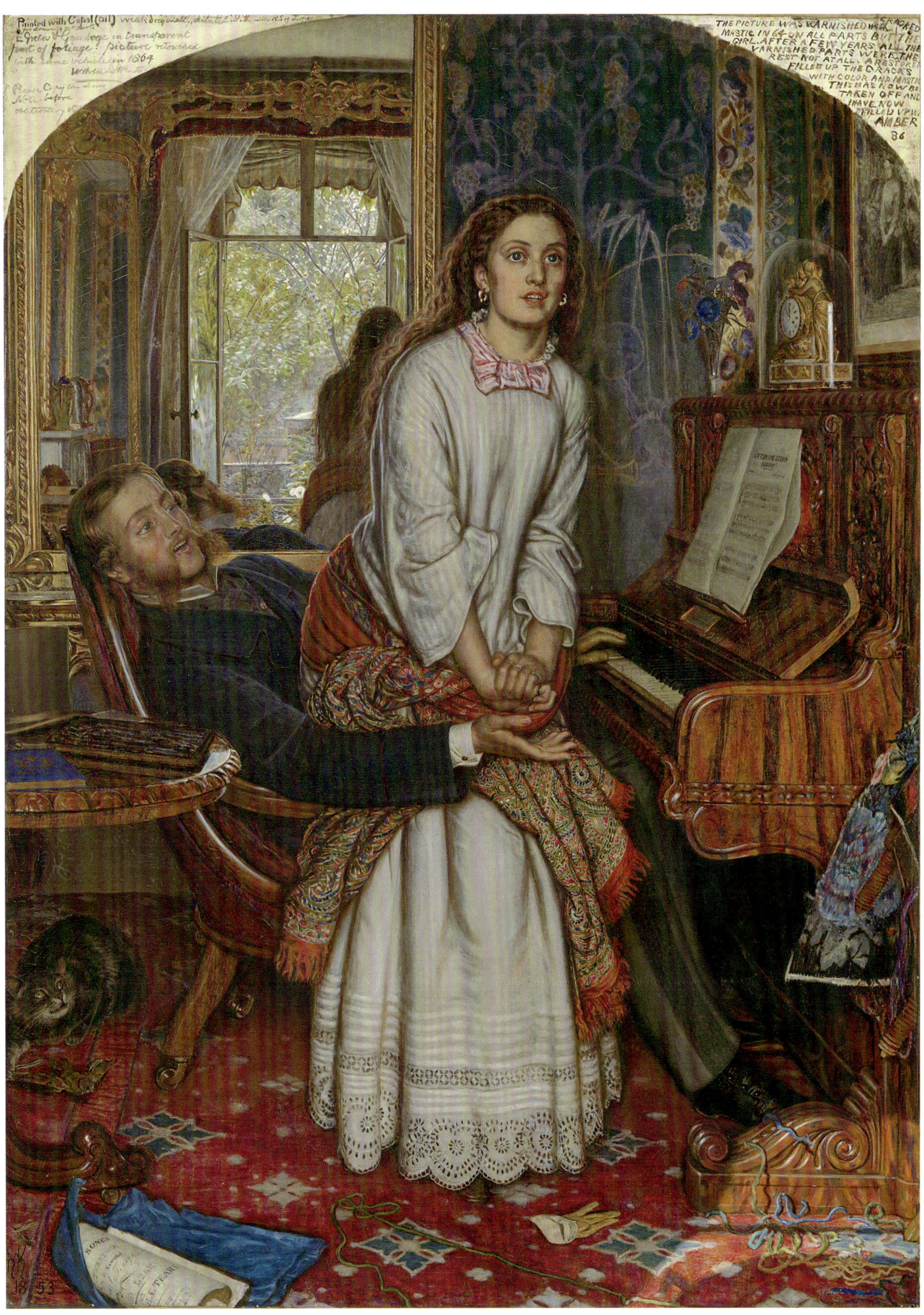
THE PICTURE WAS VARNISHED
MASTIC IN 64 ON ALL PARTS
GIRL. AFTER A FEW YEARS ALL THE
VARNISHED PARTS WERE
REST NOT AT ALL.
FILLED UP THE CRACKS
WITH COLOR AND
THIS HAS NOW
TAKEN OFF AND
I HAVE NOW
AMBER
86

Henry Wallis 1830–1916

Henry Wallis's connection to the Pre-Raphaelite Brotherhood can be seen in the vibrant colours and careful use of symbolic detail in *Chatterton*, the artist's earliest and best-known work. The picture created a sensation when it was first exhibited at the Royal Academy in 1856, accompanied by the following quotation from poet Christopher Marlowe (1564–93): 'Cut is the branch that might have grown full straight; And burned is Apollo's laurel bough.' Thomas Chatterton (1752–70) was a poet whose 'gothic' writings, melancholy life and youthful suicide fascinated artists and writers in the nineteenth century. At an early age, Chatterton wrote fake medieval histories and poems, which he copied onto old parchment and passed off as manuscripts from the Middle Ages. The fraud was later discovered, and he was widely condemned by influential figures. Penniless, Chatterton took his own life by swallowing arsenic at the age of seventeen. Later he was elevated to the status of tragic hero by the French poet Alfred de Vigny (1797–1863). Wallis may have intended this painting as a criticism of society's treatment of artists.[11] The pale light of dawn shines through the casement window, illuminating the poet's serene features, livid flesh and torn sheets of poetry scattered on the floor. The harsh lighting, dramatic shadows, vibrant colours and lifeless hand and arm increase the emotional impact of the scene. A vial of poison on the floor indicates the method of suicide. Following the Pre-Raphaelite credo of truth to nature, Wallis has attempted to recreate the same attic room in Gray's Inn where Chatterton killed himself. The model for the figure was the novelist George Meredith (1828–1909), then aged about twenty-eight. Two years later Wallis eloped with Meredith's wife, daughter of the novelist Thomas Love Peacock (1785–1866).

Chatterton 1856
Oil paint on canvas
62.2 × 93.3

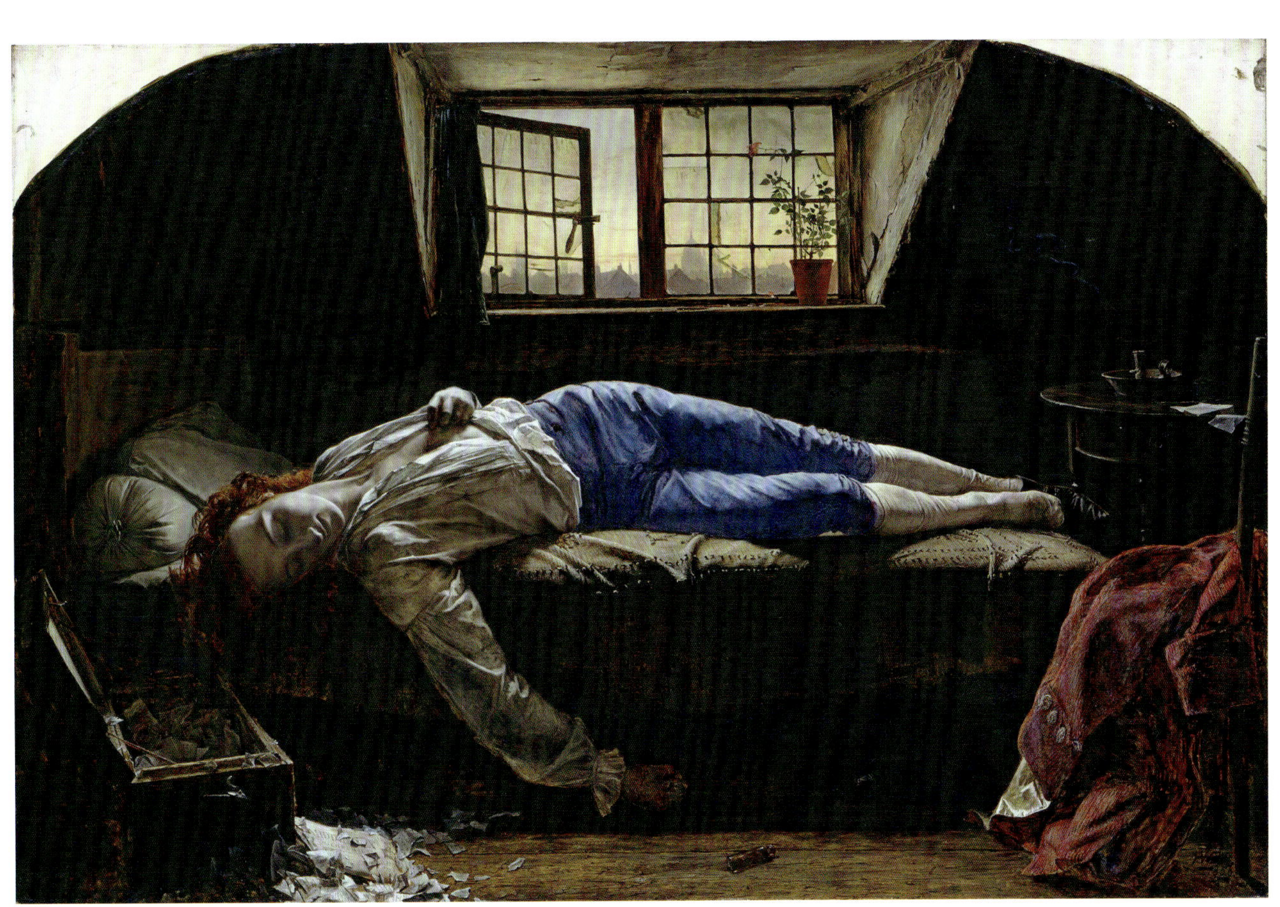

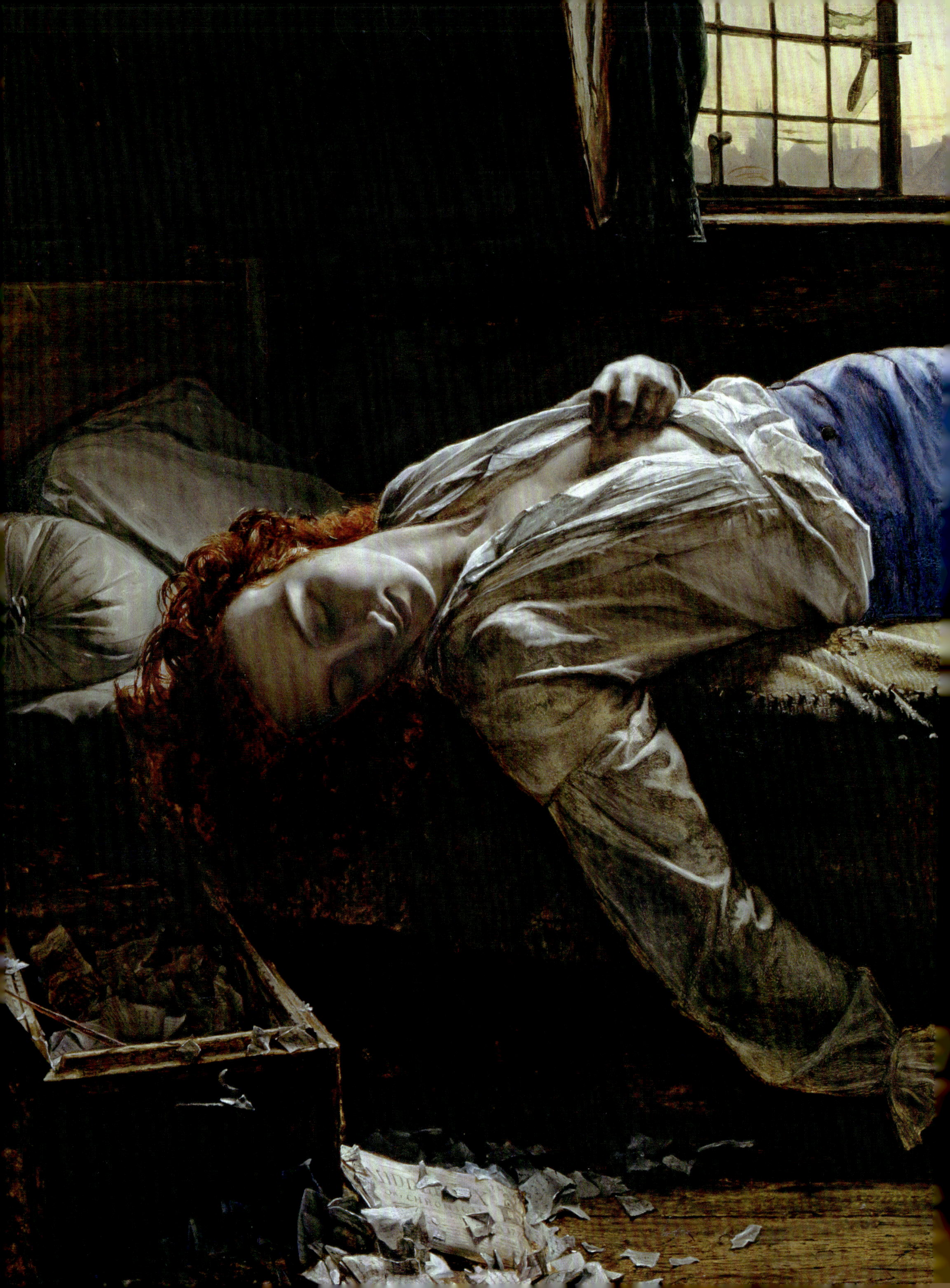

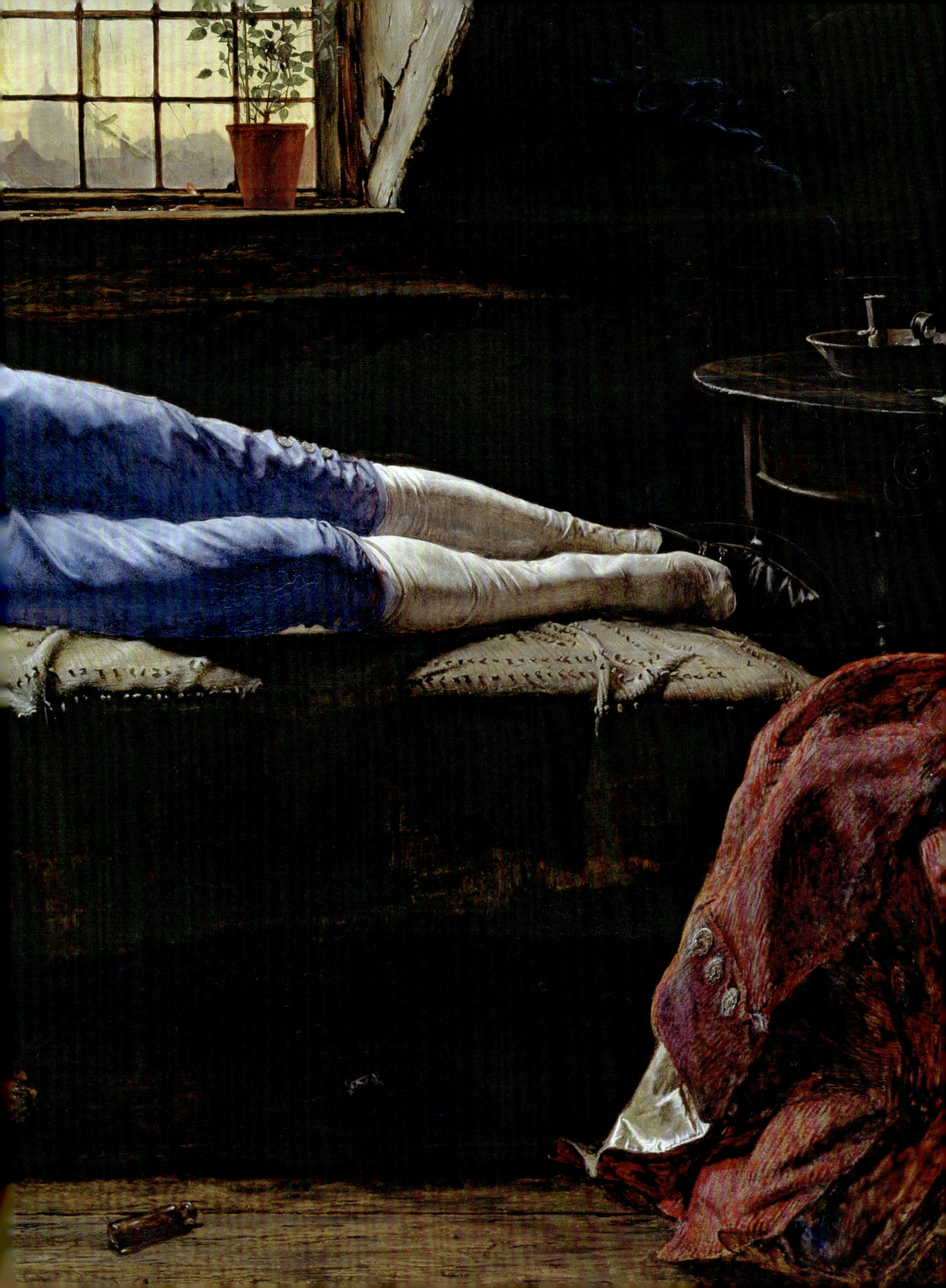

Frank Bramley 1857–1915

Frank Bramley was an English post-impressionist genre painter of the Newlyn School. After studying at the Lincoln School of Art in the East Midlands of England (1873–8) and living in Venice (1882–4), Bramley established himself in the artists' colony of Newlyn in Cornwall, south-west England, where he became one of the leading figures of the Newlyn School along with Walter Langley (1852–1922).[12] Bramley's work is particularly known for its social realism, aiming to depict the stark realities of everyday life, and commenting on the socio-political conditions of the working class. His specialisation in interiors and use of the square brush technique is, however, unusual for the Newlyn School, who preferred to paint *en plein air* (in the open air). Bramley's work exhibits a commitment to depicting natural and artificial light in combination with moving emotional and narrative subjects. When first exhibited, Bramley presented *A Hopeless Dawn* alongside a passage from *The Harbours of England* 1856 by John Ruskin (1819–1900), the leading English art critic of the Victorian era. In this excerpt Ruskin asserted that the hand of God can be found 'at the helm of every lonely boat, through starless night and hopeless dawn'.[13] The kneeling woman, comforted by her mother-in-law, realises that her husband is lost at sea, but items in the room hint at the consolations of religion. The print after Raphael's (1483–1520) drawing *Christ's Charge to Peter* 1515–16, depicted on the wall to the right, illustrates the religious undertones of Ruskin's text. An open Bible lies in front of the missing fisherman's mother, who is comforting the young wife. A candle on the windowsill is about to flicker out.

A Hopeless Dawn 1888
Oil paint on canvas
122.6 × 167.6

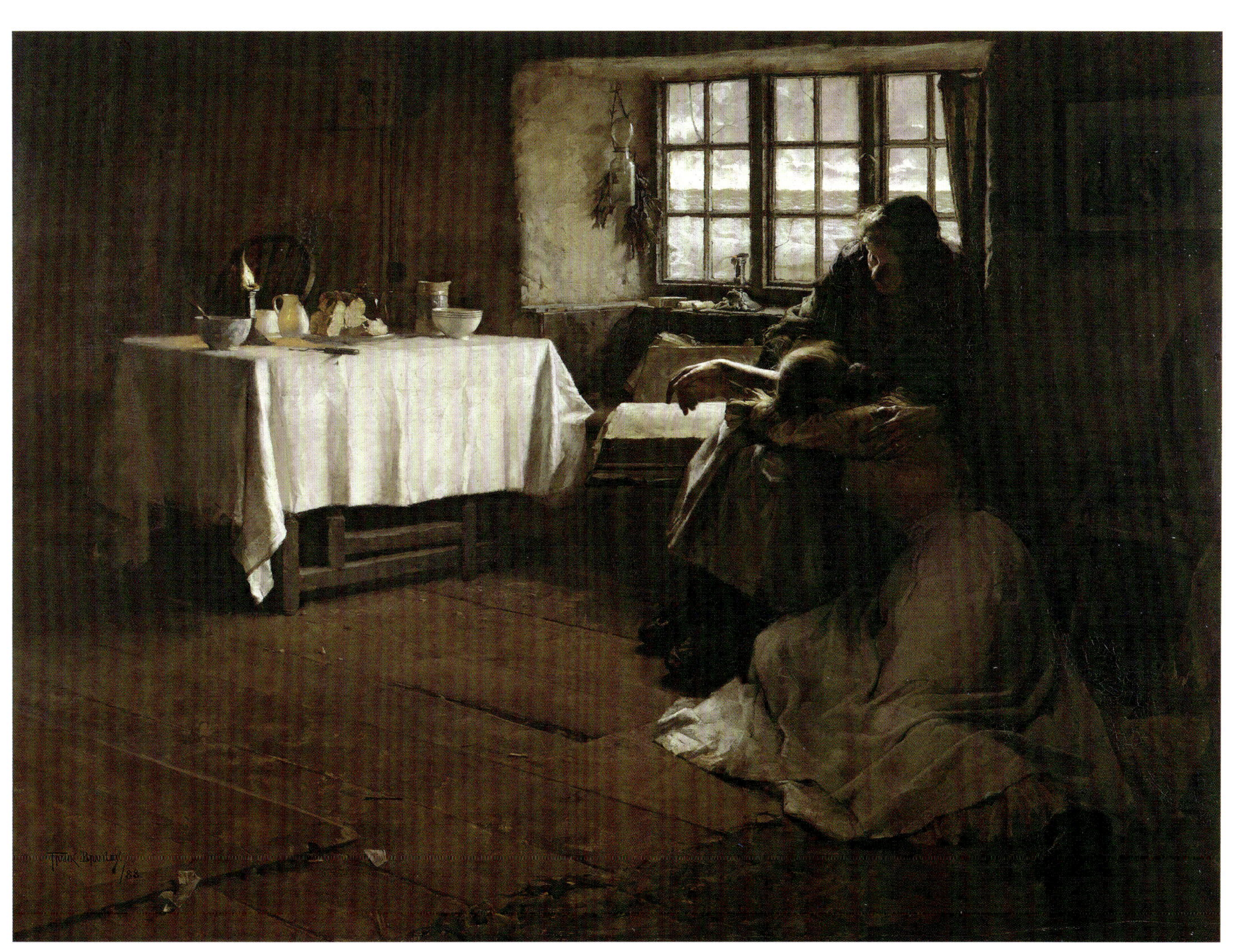

Philippe Parreno 1964–

At first glance it appears that sunlight streaming through a nearby window is casting shadows onto a carpeted floor. However, after surveying the windowless gallery space, it becomes apparent that the shadow is an illusion. Philippe Parreno created *6.00 PM* with rectangular pieces of carpet of different shades, all of which are carefully inlaid into a larger carpet that fills the room. The illusion of light is provided by cream-coloured sections, while the silhouette of the window frame is achieved using thinner, linear forms coloured the same brown as the surrounding carpet. Lighter brown sections on either side suggest partially drawn curtains through which the light is filtered. As the work's title implies, Parreno has chosen to evoke the evening light at a precise time of day. By seeming to freeze time in this way, the French artist draws attention to the temporal nature of exhibitions and in particular to the ways in which time, as well as space, impacts visibility. Similar ideas are explored in other works such as *The Marquis and the Sisters* 2016–17, Parreno's permanent public artwork at the Walker Art Center in Minneapolis. Here, a light sculpture derived from the form of a cinema marquee periodically illuminates the space with colour, while a series of automated window blinds rise and fall according to the movement of the sun and clouds outside. Through his juxtapositions of natural and artificial light, Parreno draws attention to the way that different lighting conditions affect how the world is experienced over time.

6.00 PM 2000–6
Carpet
Dimensions variable

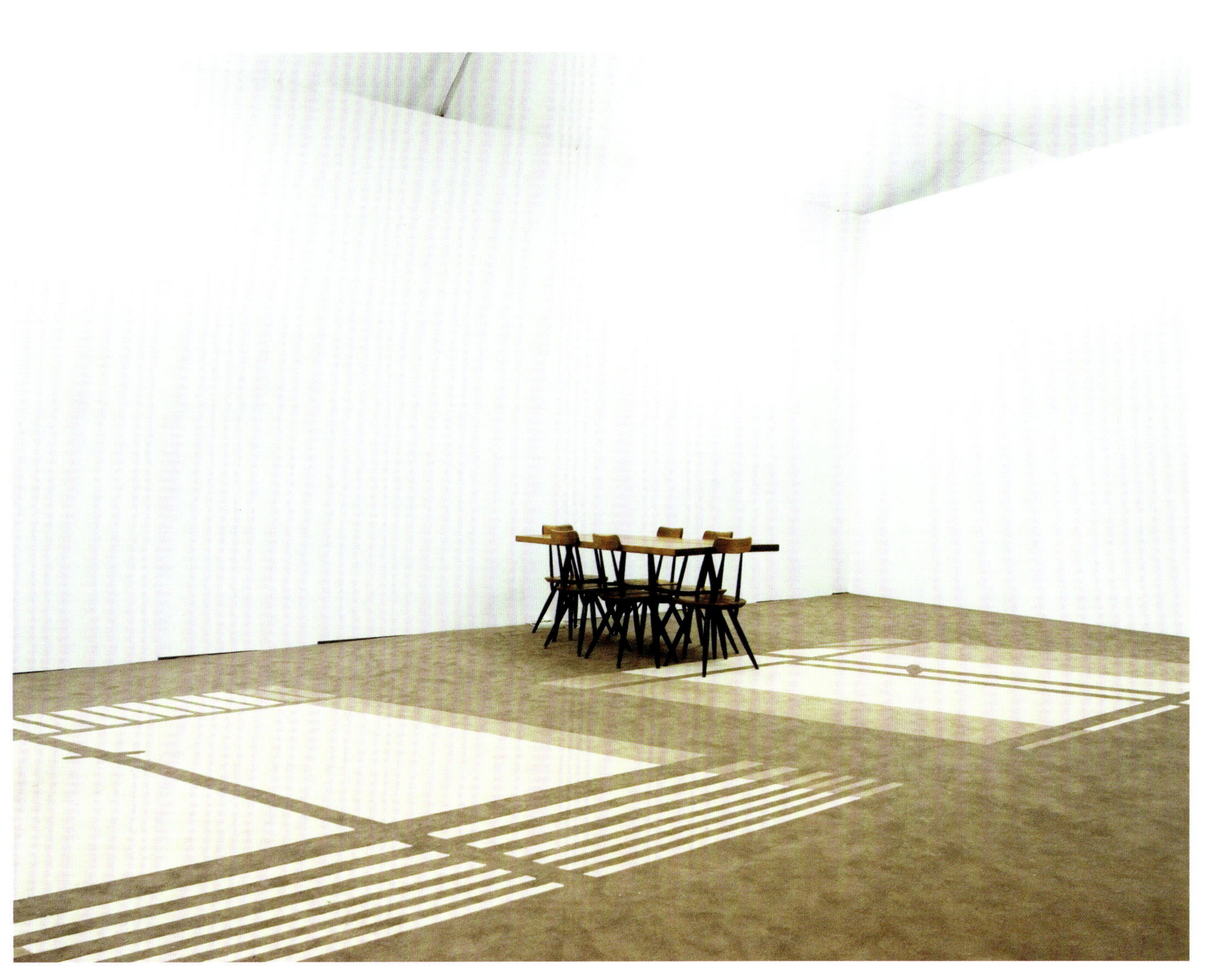

Vilhelm Hammershøi 1864–1916

Light is an essential element in Vilhelm Hammershøi's paintings, and though he produced numerous landscapes and intimate portraits, it is his meditative domestic interiors for which he is best known. The Danish artist's canvases are characterised by a restricted, predominantly grey palette coupled with a sensitivity to light that saw him compared to the Dutch Baroque master Johannes Vermeer (1632–75). Hammershøi made numerous paintings of his home in the Christianshavn district of Copenhagen, a location that became his most iconic subject. The painting *Interior, Sunlight on the Floor* depicts a room in the sparse apartment, where sunlight, pouring through a window, spills onto the floor below. It was the ageing stateliness of this building that Hammershøi loved, especially the large windows that let in the soft and atmospheric light of northern Europe. As with the French impressionists, Hammershøi painted the same rooms multiple times at different times of day, recording the subtleties of changing lighting and weather conditions. Many paintings show the rooms empty, focusing on their white-painted doors, walls and minimal furnishings. Some, such as *Interior* 1899, feature the artist's wife, Ada, who is usually seen from behind. Her presence here draws viewers into the space, to its architectural features, its furnishings and the way that the light falls on and illuminates these various elements. In fact, Ada was originally included in *Interior, Sunlight on the Floor*, positioned between the table and the back wall to the left of the window. However, a previous owner of the painting who disliked this arrangement folded the canvas over so that the figure is now unseen.

Interior, Sunlight on the Floor 1906
Oil paint on canvas
51.8 × 44

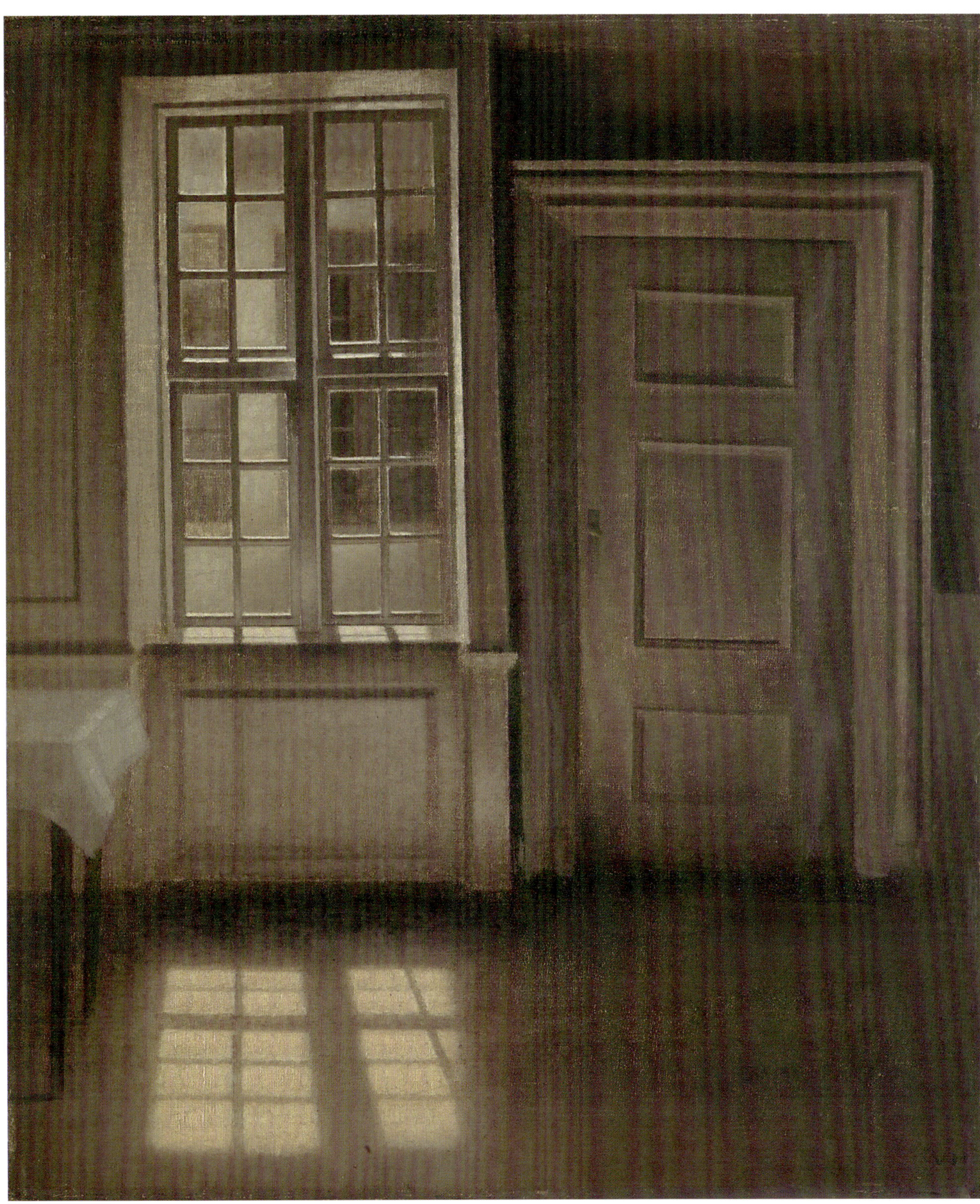

William Rothenstein 1872–1945

In 1900, William Rothenstein began painting portraits of his family and friends in which the domestic interior is considered as important as the figure. In the painting *Mother and Child*, Rothenstein's wife, Alice, is shown with their first child, John, aged about two (he would grow up to become an art historian and Director of the Tate Gallery from 1938 to 1964). Alice, seated with her back to the window, stands the child on her lap; gazing out of the window, he is illuminated by the diffused sunlight entering the first-floor room. The location is the Rothensteins' family home in Hampstead, London, a stylish house characterised by its panelled rooms, carved staircase and Queen Anne fireplaces. While the intimate scene can be interpreted as a simple celebration of motherhood, it is furthermore a masterful study of light and shadow. Rothenstein has taken great care in his naturalistic and accurate portrayal of light, from the highlights on the figures' hair, skin and clothing, to the complex play of shadows and reflections around the fireplace and panelled wall. The soft daylight entering from a single window, the exaggerated contrasts of light and dark, the shallow depth of field, and the pervading stillness all reflect the influence of the seventeenth-century Dutch master Johannes Vermeer (1632–75). At the time this painting was produced, Dutch interior painting had become very fashionable at the New English Art Club, of which Rothenstein was a member. Rothenstein greatly admired Vermeer's extraordinary ability to capture the effects of light and evidently sought to emulate this in his own painting.

Mother and Child 1903
Oil paint on canvas
96.9 × 76.5

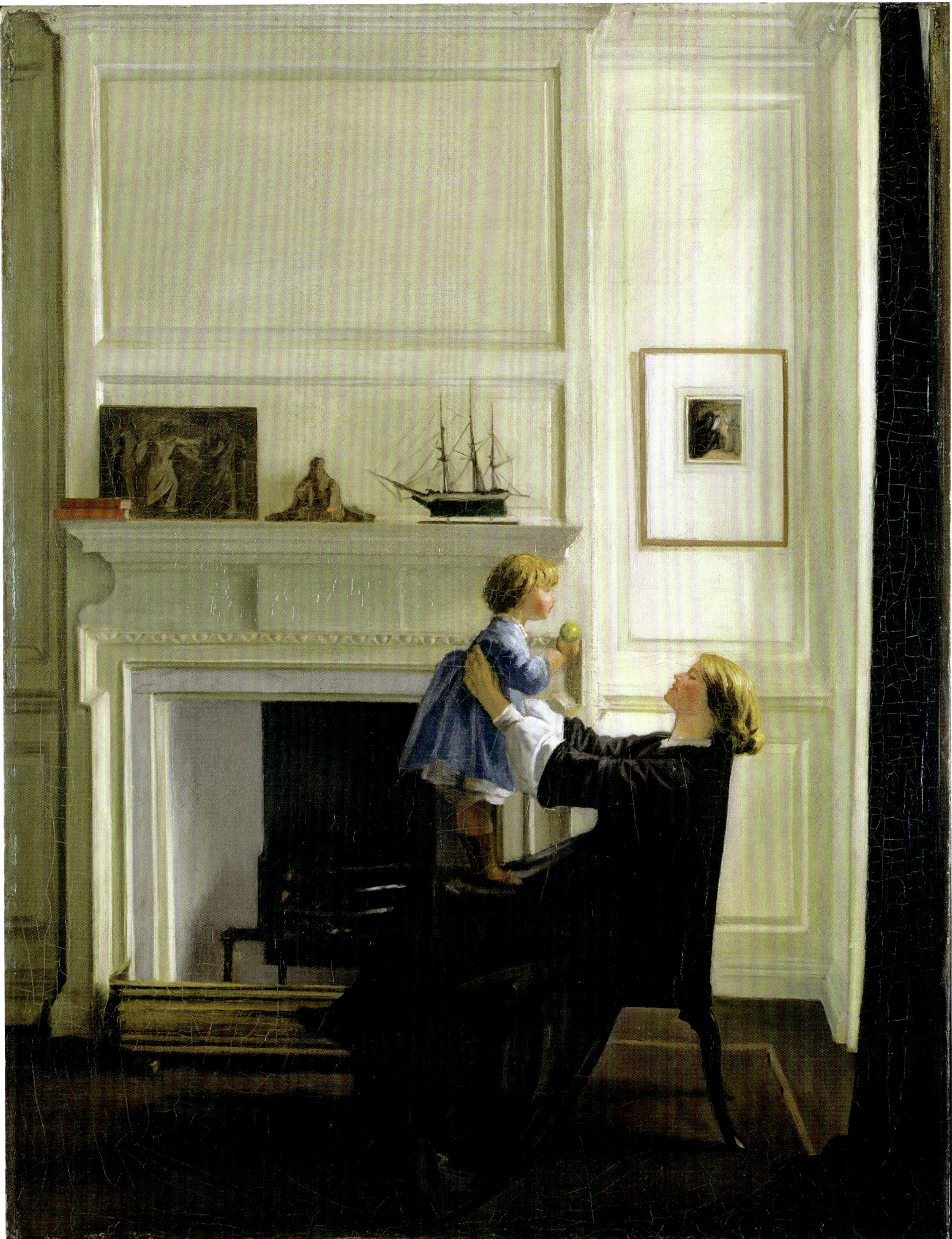

Light Effects

The intersection of art and science has been a productive area of enquiry for many artists. Nineteenth century discoveries inspired new approaches to painting and, with the invention of photography in the 1830s, innovative ways to explore the properties and effects of light. Described as the 'painter of light', J.M.W. Turner (1775–1851) drew on scientific theories and his own studies of reflection and refraction to develop new artistic techniques. In the late nineteenth century, the popularisation of electric light and developments in photographic processes paved the way for artistic experimentation in the twentieth century with light itself. Pioneering work in experimental photography considered light as a primary medium and greatly influenced a younger generation of avant-garde artists, whose photographs harnessed different lighting effects and shadows. By working directly with light, artists could explore experimental darkroom techniques that did not require a camera. Their abstract imagery revealed the way that light interacts with static objects, whereas others have used moving light to create dynamic photographic abstractions. Artists such as Yayoi Kusama (1929–) continue to be inspired by the way light behaves when it strikes different materials, using the physical effects of reflected light to disorientate and immerse.

Joseph Mallord William Turner 1775–1851

Elected an Associate of the Royal Academy in London in 1799 and Academician in 1802, J.M.W. Turner refused to be typecast and experimented with a wide range of subjects. This group of diagrams was created by Turner to support his lectures while Professor of Perspective at the Royal Academy in London, a post he held from 1807 to 1828. In these lectures, Turner discussed reflection and refraction, or what he termed 'reflexies', and their relationship to light and shade, which he illustrated with a range of technical drawings, including of globes, some made of polished metal and others, presumably of glass, half-filled with water. Turner used these diagrams to explain how to depict light from different sources. In his text, the artist observed how, indoors, light can be manipulated and shadows 'dissipated'.[14] *Lecture Diagram 65* and *Lecture Diagram 66* (p.123) show the influence of Giovanni Battista Piranesi (1720–78), an Italian printmaker whose fantastical images of the imposing architecture of ancient Rome became very popular in Britain during the second half of the eighteenth century. In the series *I Carceri* (*The Prisons*), Piranesi grimly depicted the interiors of imaginary prisons. These images of imposing spaces exerted a powerful influence on the Romantic imagination, including Turner, who was engaged to copy some examples during the mid-1790s. In these renditions, Turner used strong shading to create a sense of depth and drama, to evoke emotion in the viewer.

Top left: *Lecture Diagram 61: A Cube with Shadow* c.1810–11
Part of *I. Numbered Perspective Diagrams*
Graphite and watercolour on paper
67.5 × 101

Top right: *Lecture Diagram 62: Various Forms with Shadows* c.1810
Part of *I. Numbered Perspective Diagrams*
Graphite and watercolour on paper
67 × 99.9

Below left: *Lecture Diagram 63: Various Forms with Shadows* c.1810
Part of *I. Numbered Perspective Diagrams*
Graphite and watercolour on paper
67 × 100

Below right: *Lecture Diagram 64: Various Forms with Shadows* c.1810
Part of *I. Numbered Perspective Diagrams*
Graphite and watercolour on paper
67.1 × 100.5

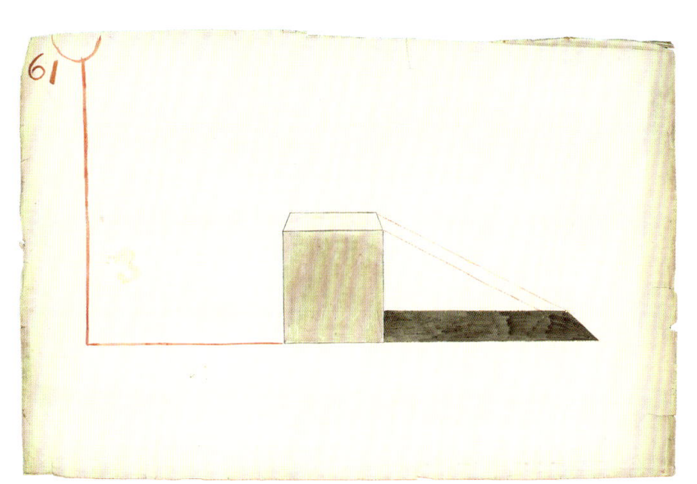
61

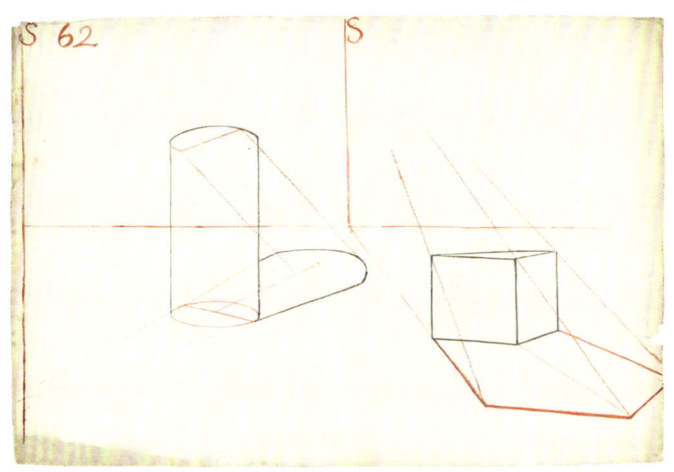
S 62
S

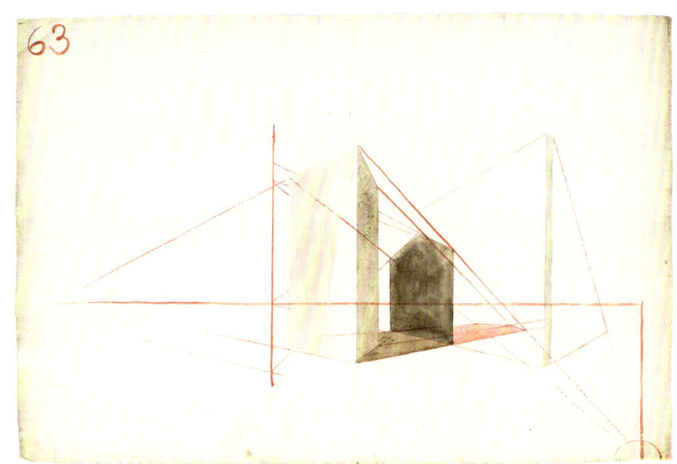
63

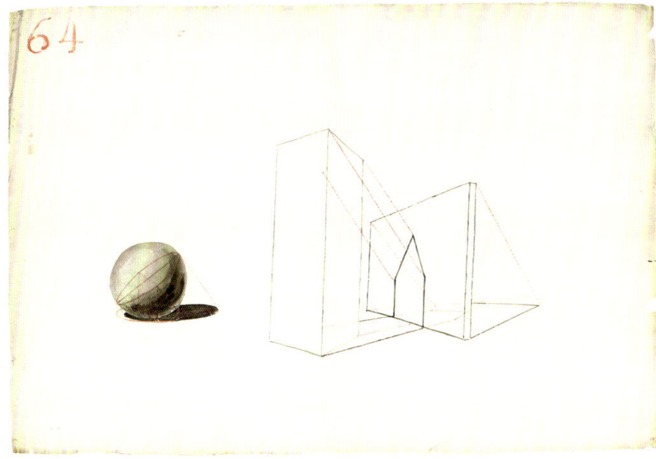
64

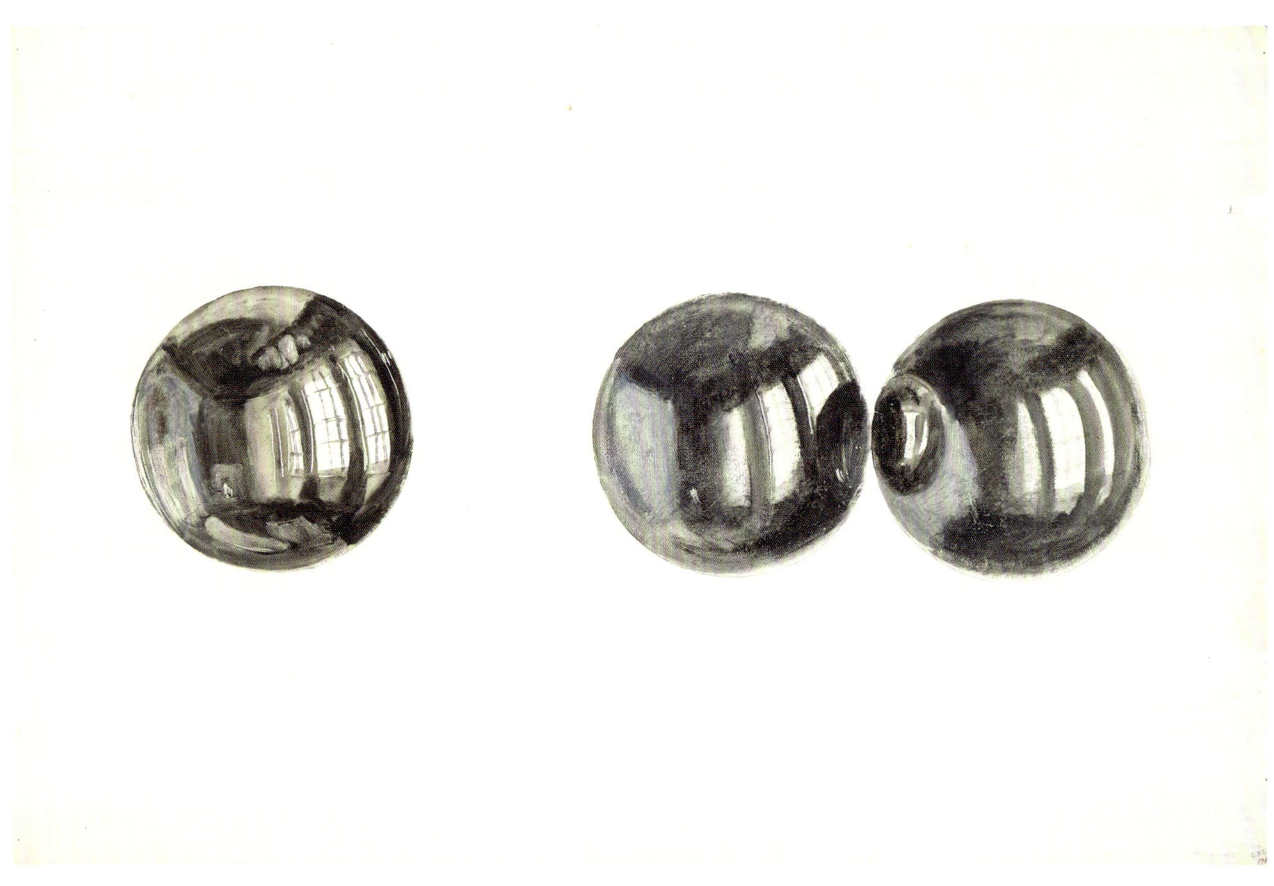

Above: *Lecture Diagram: Reflections in a Single Polished Metal Globe and in a Pair of Polished Metal Globes* c.1810
Part of *II. Various Perspective Diagrams*
Oil paint and graphite on paper
64 × 96.8

Opposite, top: *Lecture Diagram 65: Interior of a Prison* c.1810
Part of *I. Numbered Perspective Diagrams*
Gouache, graphite and watercolour on paper
48.7 × 68.7

Opposite, below: *Lecture Diagram 66: Interior of a Prison (after Giovanni Battista Piranesi)* c.1810
Part of *I. Numbered Perspective Diagrams*
Graphite and pen and ink on paper
44.3 × 59.5

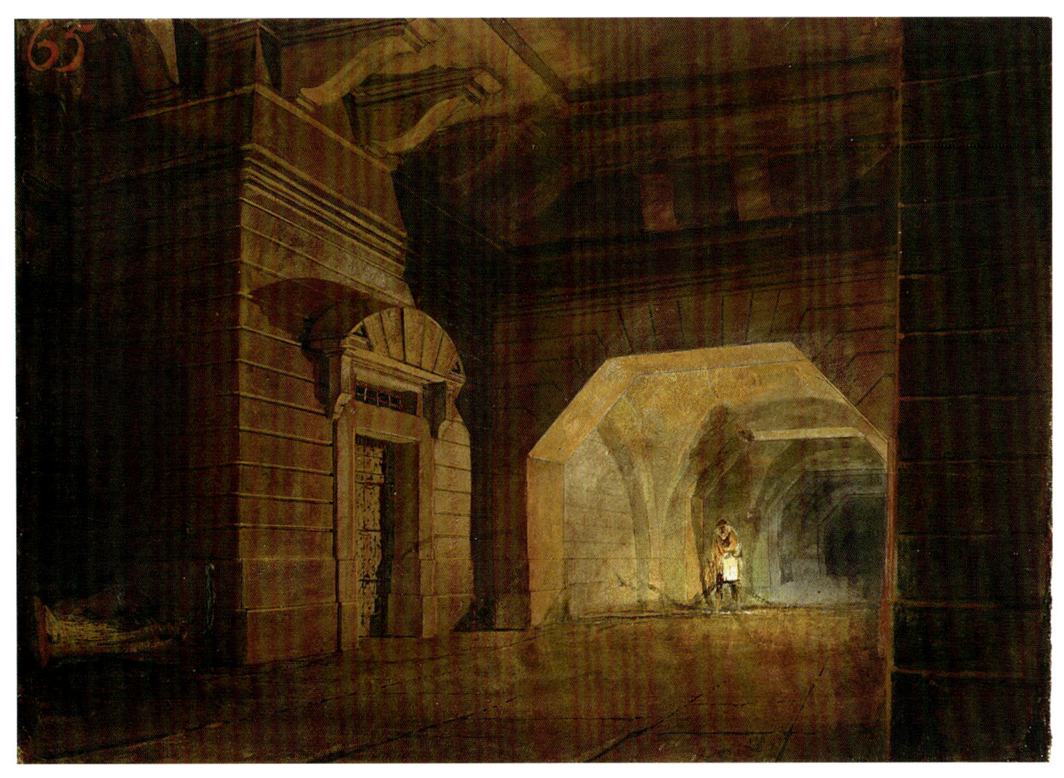
65

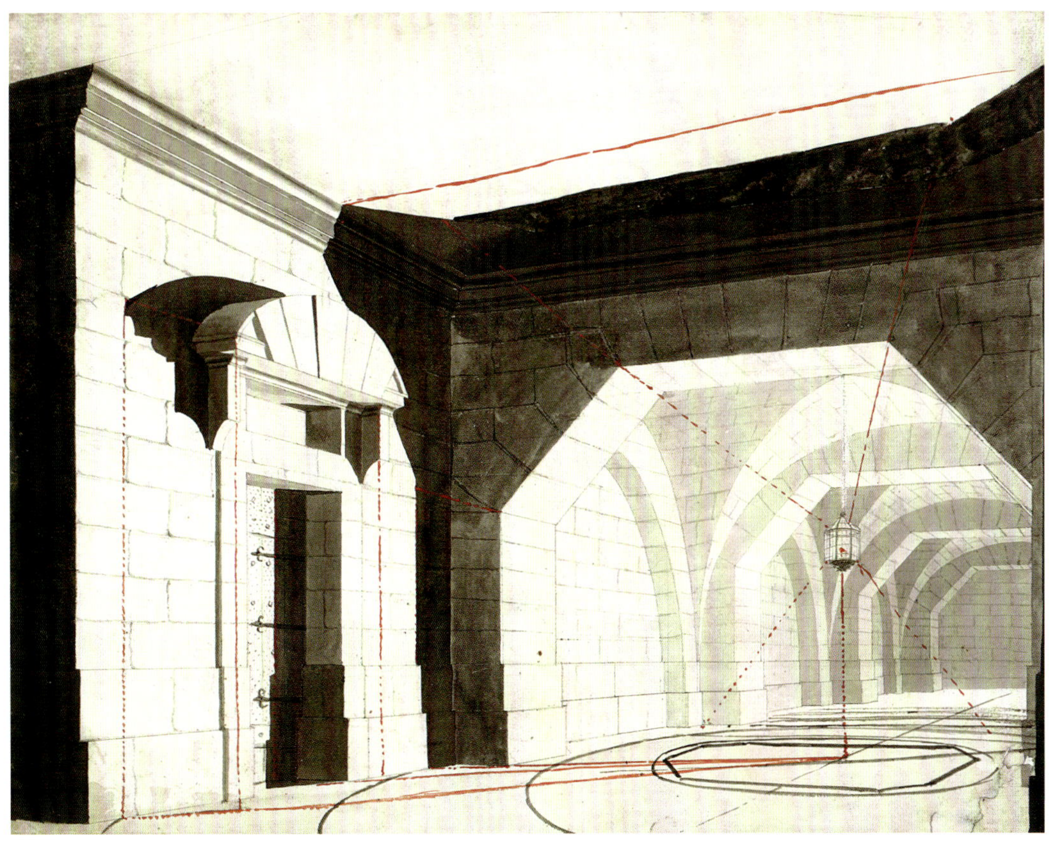

Liliane Lijn 1939–

Liliane Lijn's kinetic artworks stem from her interest in the relationship between art and science. Indeed, the American-born artist approaches all her work with the curiosity of a scientist. In the 1960s she became engrossed in the behaviour of electromagnetic waves, and began using white light as her primary medium. Inspired by her interest in astronomy and physics, she experimented with lenses, projectors, water and acrylic resins to explore different ways of reflecting and refracting light. Resulting from five years of experimentation, *Liquid Reflections* is a complex moving sculpture that combines water, Perspex and light to evoke the movement of light particles, the tiny packages of energy known as photons. It comprises a cylindrical Perspex drum containing a solution of water and liquid paraffin that forms into clusters of spherical droplets. Two Perspex balls of unequal size sit on top of the liquid, which rotates on a motorised turntable. As it revolves, the white and yellow balls move to and fro across its surface, according to the laws of momentum. A beam of light, shining on the sculpture from an adjacent lamp, is refracted by the droplets, creating myriad luminous points that Lijn has described as a 'mobile web of light'.[15] The balls also become moving lenses, animating the space in which the sculpture is shown by casting an array of reflections and shadows. Lijn has stated that with this work she intended to create a visual metaphor for the apparent paradox of light, which behaves simultaneously as a particle and a wave.

Liquid Reflections 1968
Perspex, metal, water, liquid paraffin, motor, electrical components and lamp
Diam. 106.2 cm

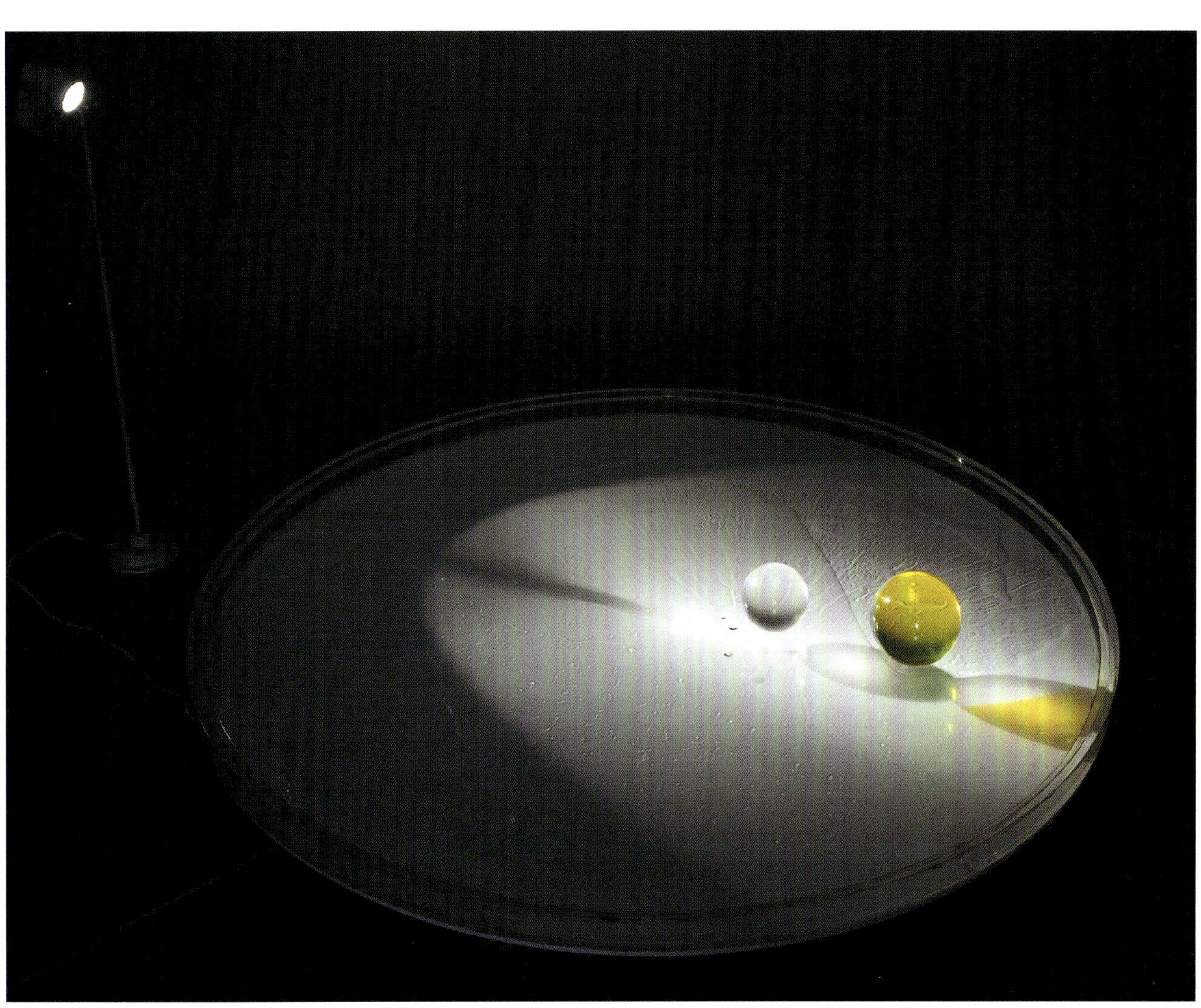

Iwao Yamawaki 1898–1987

In 1931, after training as an architect in Japan, Iwao Yamawaki travelled to Germany to study at the Bauhaus in Dessau, where he became heavily influenced by László Moholy-Nagy's (1895–1946) idea that photography could open up new ways of seeing the world beyond those available to the human eye. For these three black-and-white photographs made at the Bauhaus (opposite and overleaf), Yamawaki harnessed light in different ways to make the familiar seem strange. Showing a narrow interior space, *Untitled (Interior, Bauhaus, Dessau)* is a study in contrasts. The vertical and horizontal lines of the full-length window frames contrast with the bare twisted branches of the trees outside, while the hard surface at the right side of the image is set against the soft fabric curtain on the left. Balancing the entire scene is the contrast between the daylight entering the space through the windowpanes and the subtle shadows it casts in the lower section of the image. Stronger shadows are seen in *Untitled (Composition with Eggs and String, Bauhaus)*. Here, a bright light source hitting two eggs obliquely casts part of the composition in shadow, while further shadows are created by the tangled string. By heightening the contrast in this image, Yamawaki has transformed the objects into an abstract composition. A similar effect is achieved in *Set of Bowls*, where a collection of nested bowls becomes a study of light, shadow and form. As well as capturing everyday life at the Bauhaus, Yamawaki travelled widely in Europe and the Soviet Union, documenting modernist architecture and design.

Untitled (Interior, Bauhaus, Dessau) 1930–2
Photograph; gelatin silver print on paper
23.3 × 15.2

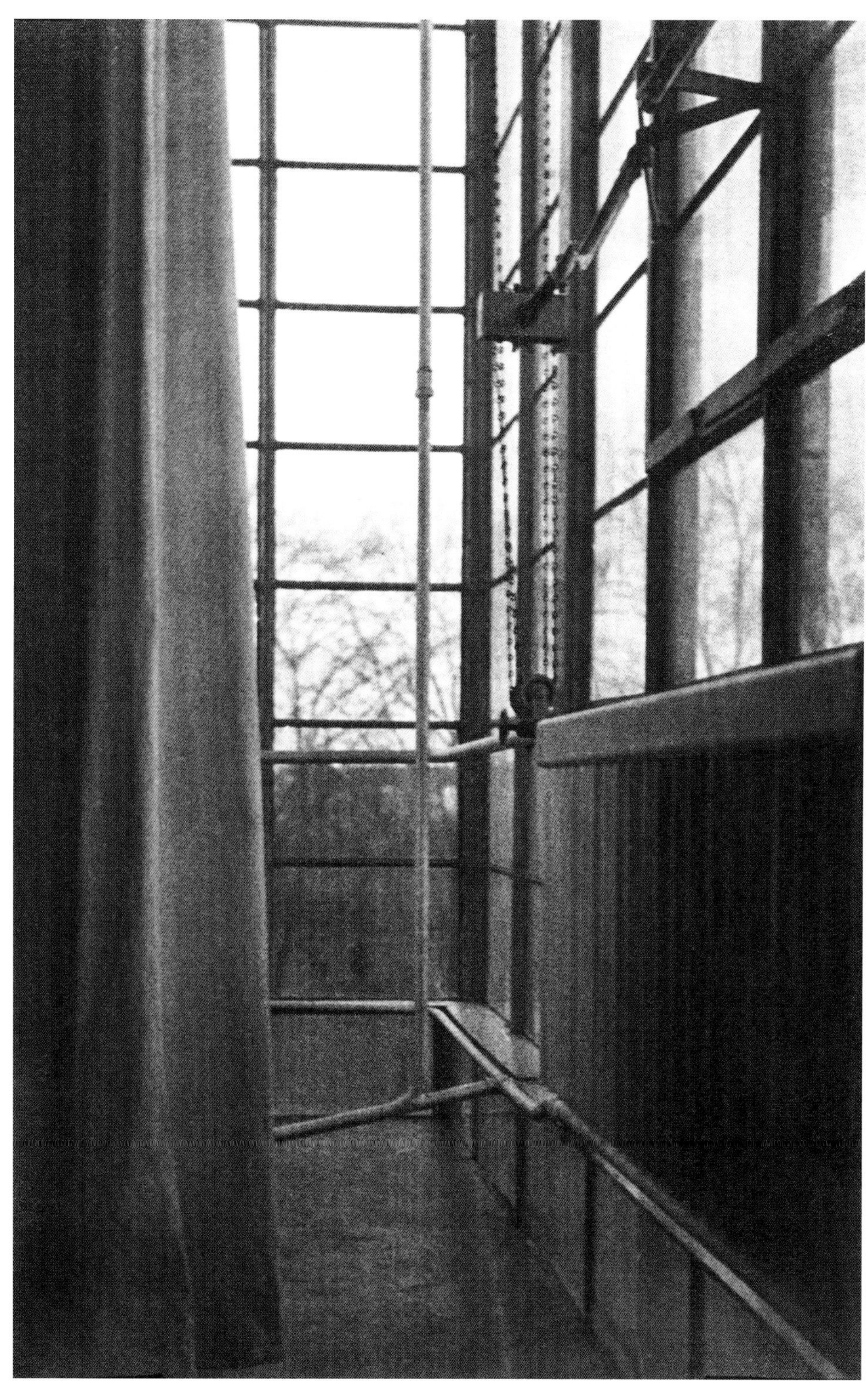

Opposite, left: *Untitled (Composition with Eggs and String, Bauhaus)* 1930–2
Photograph; gelatin silver print on paper
11.3 × 8

Opposite, right: *Set of Bowls* 1930–2
Photograph; gelatin silver print on paper
12.7 × 10

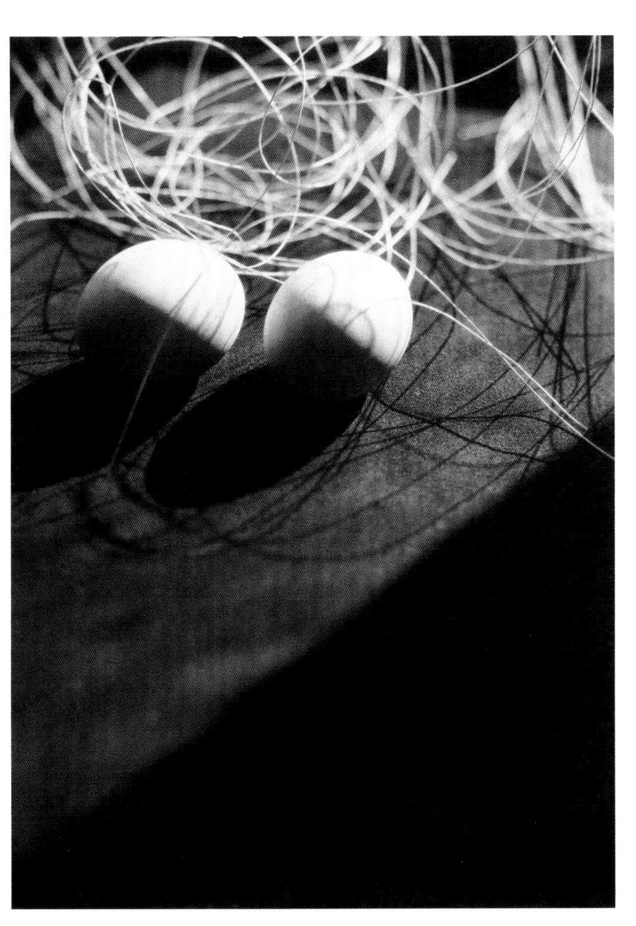

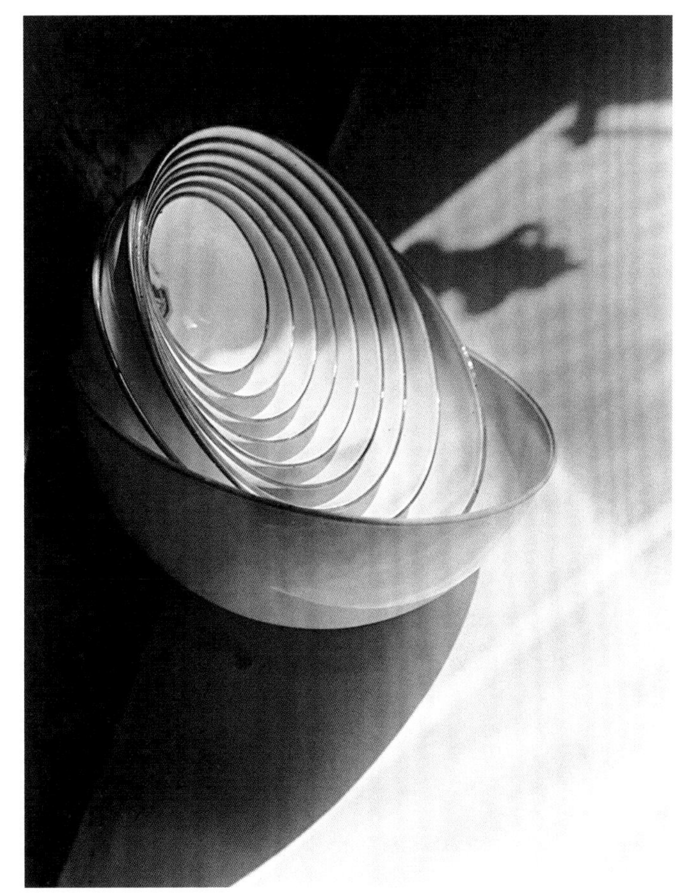

Edmund Collein 1906–92

Originally trained as an architect, Edmund Collein studied at the Bauhaus in Dessau from 1927 to 1930. It was while on the preliminary course that he came under the influence of László Moholy-Nagy (1895–1946) and Josef Albers (1888–1976). Although he never studied photography formally, all that survives from his time at the revolutionary school of art, architecture and design is a series of black-and-white photographs, several of which document works produced during Albers's material studies classes, during which Bauhaus students were instructed to use simple materials such as metal, wood, plastic and paper to design spatial structures. In these photographs Collein employs strong directional light to create striking shadows with a structural presence. The emphasis of light and shadow reflects Moholy-Nagy's recommendation to transform the appearance of reality – whether structure, texture or facture – into pure light phenomena by way of 'rare views, oblique, upward, downward, distortions, shadow effects, tonal contrasts.'[16] In *Untitled (Material Study by Otti Berger, Josef Albers' Preliminary Course, Bauhaus Dessau)*, Collein captures a work by fellow student and textile artist Otti Berger (1898–1944). Berger's grid-like structure, made from plastic and gauze, is transformed into a study of tonal variation as an unseen light source illuminates its various textures and translucent surfaces. After earning the Bauhaus diploma, Collein returned to architecture and, following the Second World War, worked for the municipal authorities in Berlin, becoming an important figure in urban planning in the German Democratic Republic.

Untitled (Material Study by Otti Berger, Josef Albers' Preliminary Course, Bauhaus Dessau) c.1927
Photograph; gelatin silver print on paper
8.6 × 6.5

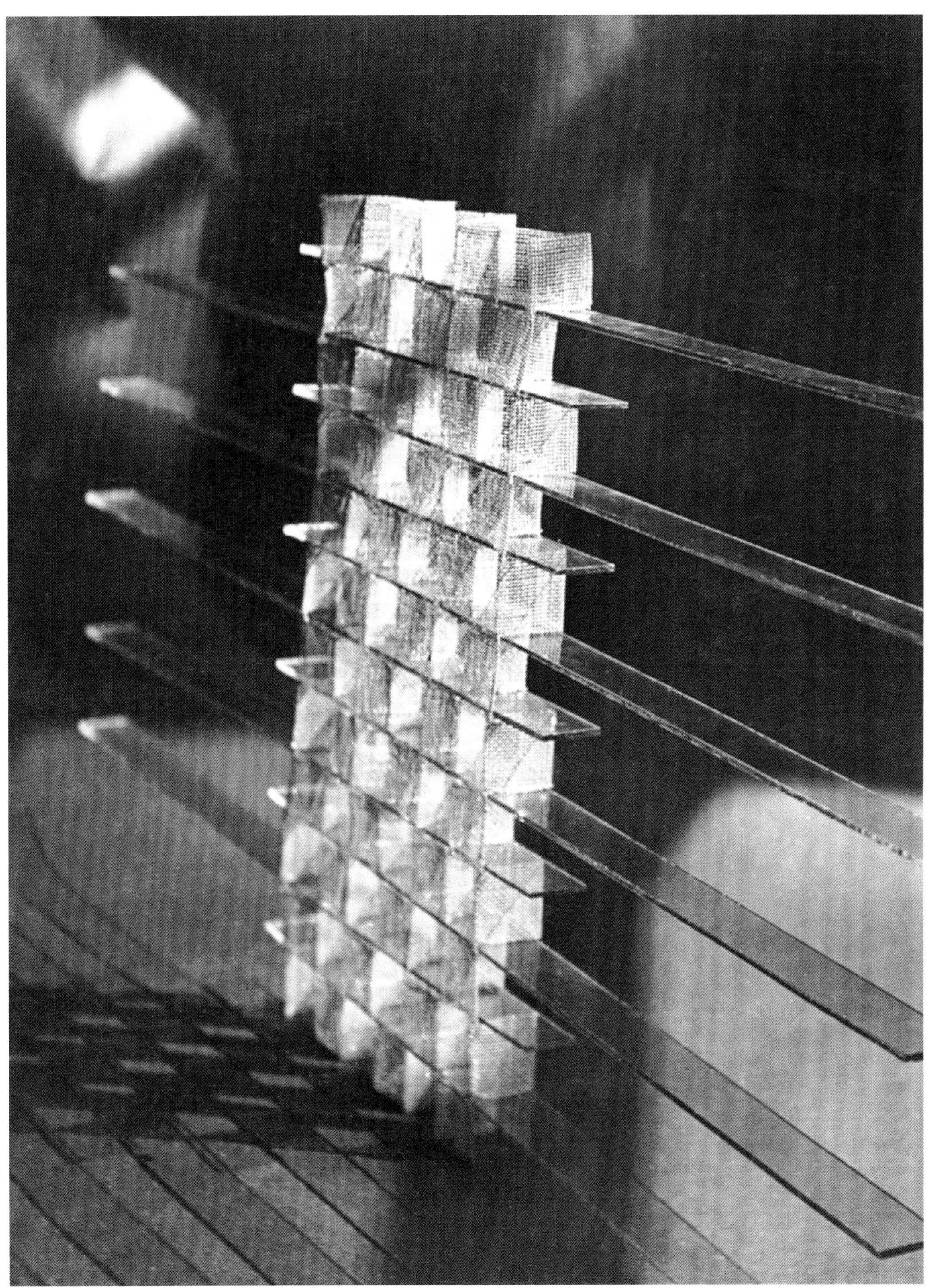

Stefan Themerson 1910–88

In 1928, after spending a year studying physics and then architecture in Warsaw, Stefan Themerson discovered that his true passion lay with experimental photography and filmmaking. The Polish artist employed a number of darkroom techniques in the creation of his abstract images, most notably the photogram, in which objects are placed directly onto photosensitive paper that is then exposed to light. Made without a camera, the resulting images invert the tonal values of lens-based photography – the greater the opacity of an object, the lighter its trace appears in the print. For example, in *Untitled* 1928 Themerson combined plant branches with smoke to create an ethereal image; the leaves that touched the paper left stark white silhouettes, while the wispy vapour that drifted in front of the light produced hazy grey tones. In 1929, Stefan met Franciszka Weinles (1907–88), an art student he began collaborating with and later married. Advancing the concept of the photogram, the couple began experimenting with what Stefan referred to as his 'trick table', a construction that held a flat horizontal piece of glass covered with tracing paper. Stefan would lie underneath, pointing his camera upwards, while Franciszka arranged objects on the shelf above and moved lights. The abstract photographs they produced were concerned with the interplay of light and shadow on various objects and liquids. This technique was also used for the five experimental films they made in Poland, of which only one has survived, *The Adventure of a Good Citizen* 1937. Stefan called these pioneering films 'photograms in motion'.

Untitled 1930, printed later
Photograph; gelatin silver print on paper
19.2 × 24.5

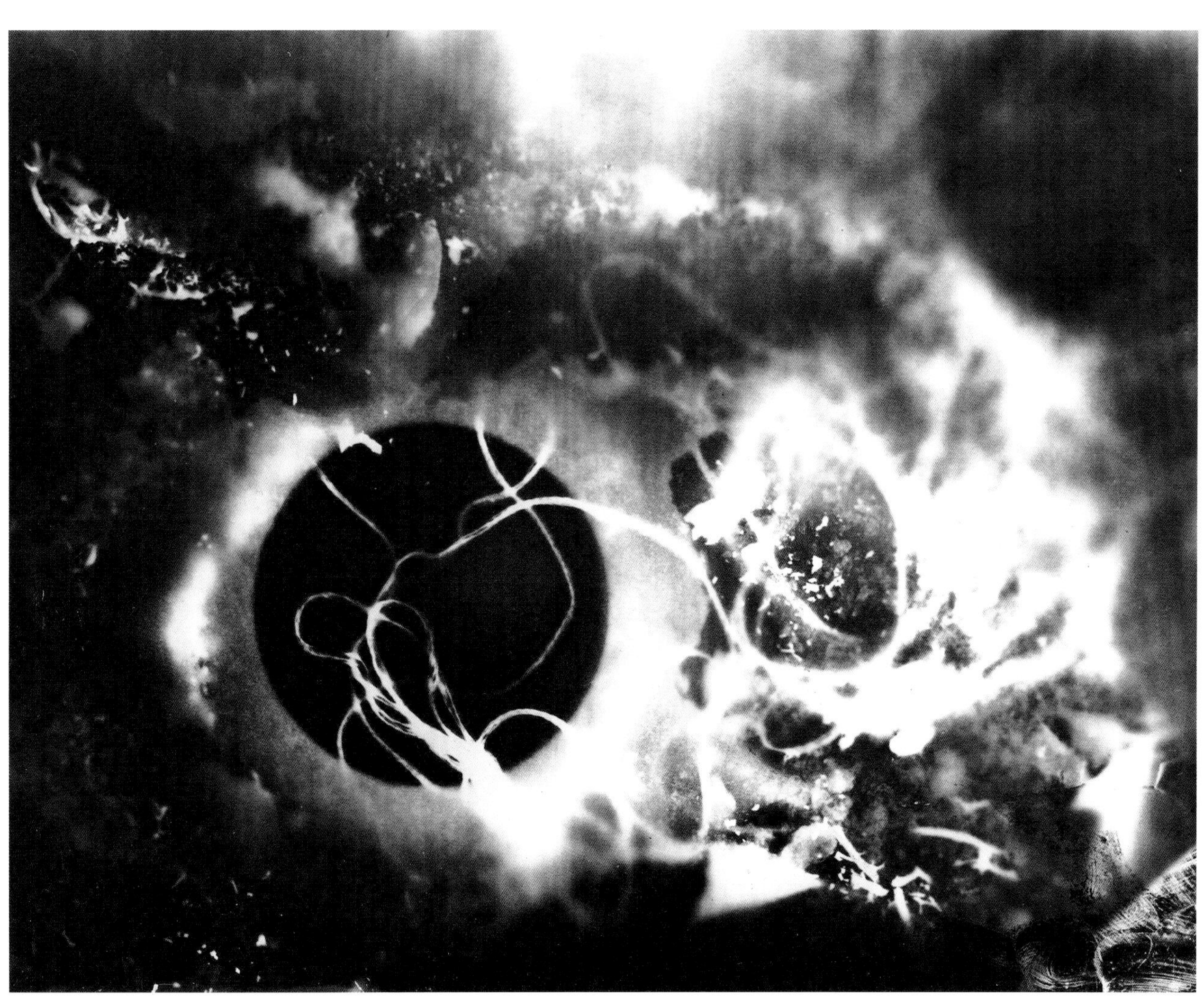

György Kepes 1906–2001

György Kepes was a Hungarian-born photographer, painter, designer, teacher and writer. In the late 1920s, he joined the Berlin design studio of former Bauhaus master László Moholy-Nagy (1895–1946), who introduced him to the 'new vision' provided by the possibilities of modern photographic techniques. In 1937, at the invitation of Moholy-Nagy, Kepes emigrated to the United States to run the Color and Light Department at the recently founded New Bauhaus in Chicago (later known as the Illinois Institute of Design). Light was central to Kepes's practice, and in Chicago he produced a large body of photographic work focusing primarily on darkroom experiments and abstract imagery. He investigated how light reflects, refracts and scatters in response to different objects, and he experimented with mirrors, prisms and filters.

The artist's interest in the formal qualities of light can be seen in the photograms and photographs he produced during this period. In *Structure Photogram* (p.137), Kepes placed a selection of leaves directly onto photographic paper before exposing it to light to create an abstract image inspired by nature. He also produced prints he called 'photo-drawings', such as *Branches* (opposite), in which he applied paint to a glass plate that he then used as though it were a photographic negative to produce abstract prints. In later works, such as *Circles and Dots*, *Blobs 3* and *Light Reflection* (p.137), he left the darkroom to photograph the effects of light reflecting on water in various outdoor contexts. While photography was not a major preoccupation for Kepes, it formed a link between his painting, films and other art projects.

Branches c.1939–40
Photograph; gelatin silver print on paper
35.5 × 28.3

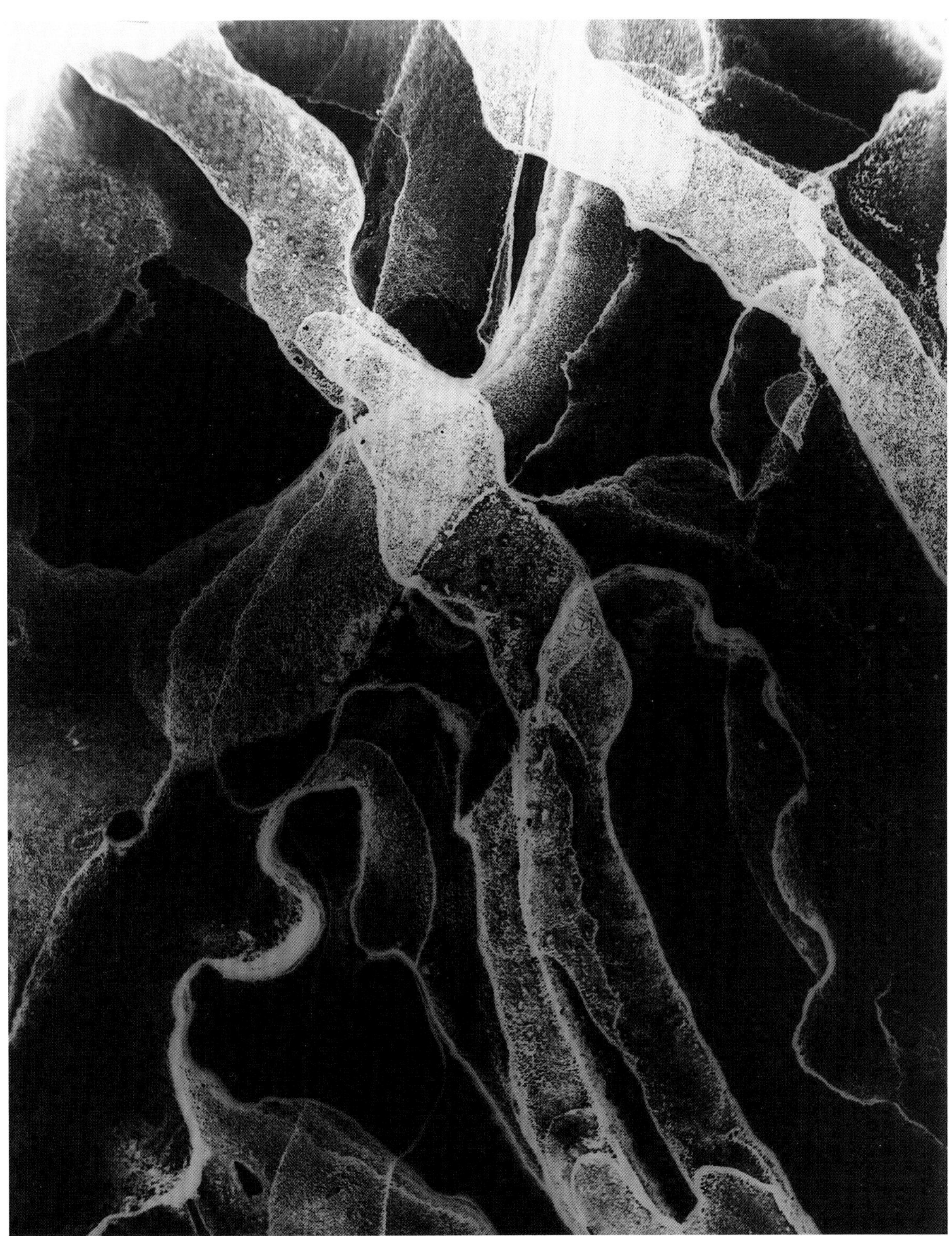

Opposite, top left: *Circles and Dots* c.1939–40
Photograph; gelatin silver print on paper
35.3 × 28.3

Opposite, top right: *Blobs 3* c.1939–40
Photograph; gelatin silver print on paper
35.5 × 28.4

Opposite, below left: *Light Reflection* 1941
Photograph; gelatin silver print on paper
35.5 × 28.4

Opposite, below right: *Structure Photogram* c.1939–40
Photograph; gelatin silver print on paper
25.4 × 20.3

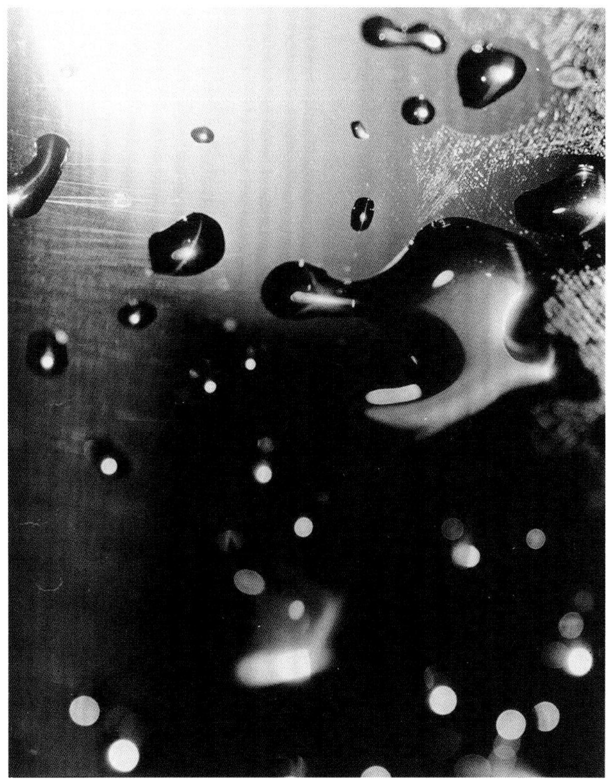
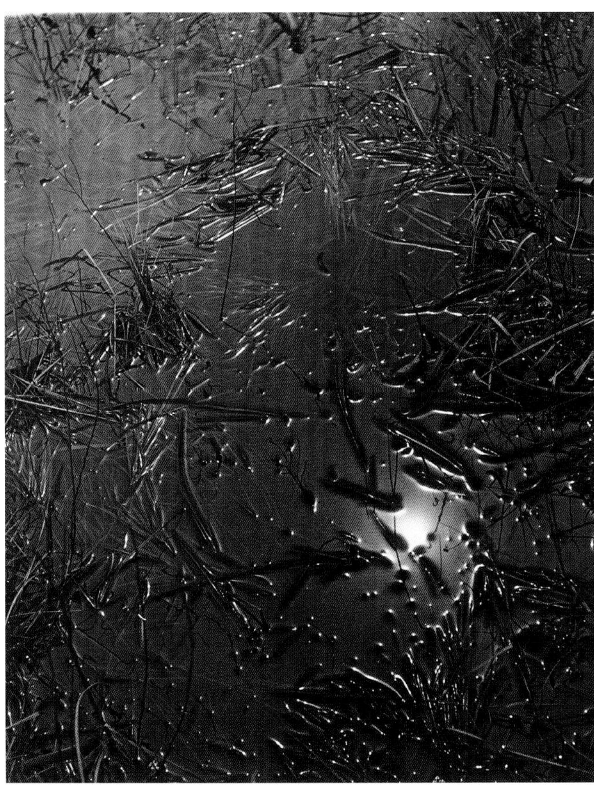
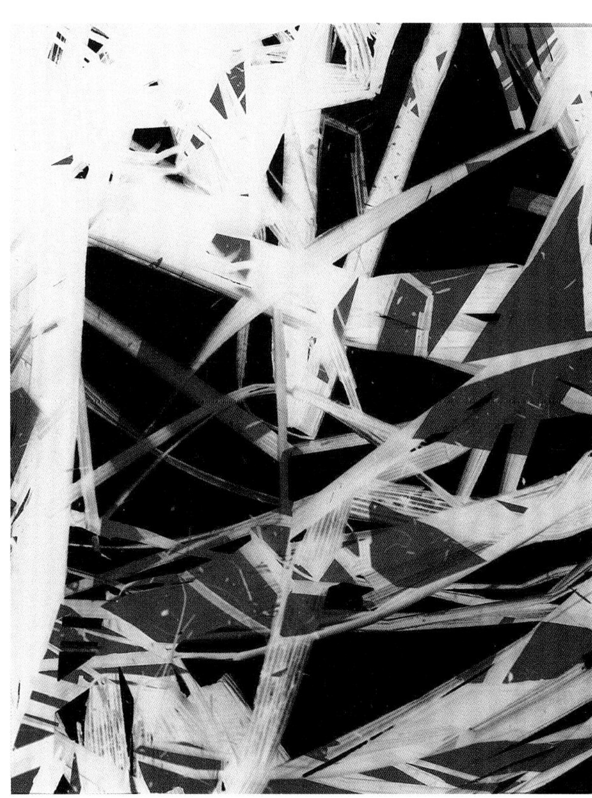

Hanaya Kanbee 1903–91

To create this ethereal image, one of a series, the Japanese photographer Hanaya Kanbee used an experimental technique known as long exposure, in which a camera's shutter is left open for a much longer duration than normal so that the paths of moving objects are recorded as blurs and smears. Using an unidentified light source in a darkened space, Kanbee experimented with different movements and gestures to create abstractions of light and shadow. In *Light B* traces of light appear as parallel diagonal lines moving across the image and are joined by several small, triangular flecks of light. The expressive and experimental style seen in Kanbee's *Light* series is typical of his practice. It was made in the same year that he co-founded the Ashiva Camera Club, which became the leading avant-garde photography group in Japan until it disbanded in 1942. Kanbee encouraged the group's members to experiment with various darkroom techniques and approaches to composition that connected them with the modernist sensibilities of their contemporaries in Western Europe, particularly those associated with the New Vision movement championed by artists such as László Moholy-Nagy (1895–1946) at the Bauhaus, as well as with the practices of dada and surrealism. Indeed, Kanbee's light paintings predate Man Ray's better-known *Space Writing* series by five years.

Light B 1930, printed 1970s
Photograph; gelatin silver print on paper
25.7 × 20.3

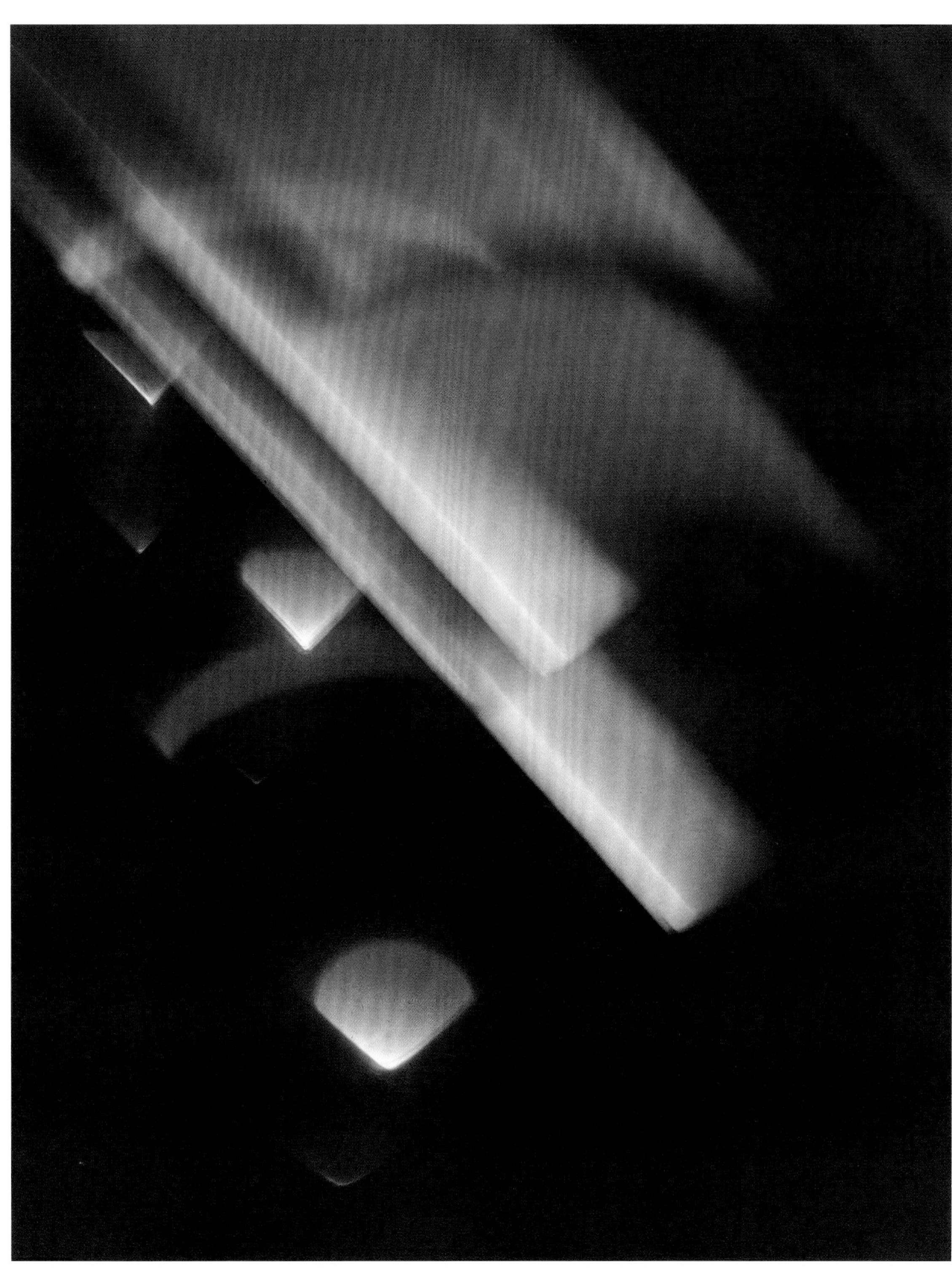

Luigi Veronesi 1908–98

The Italian photographer Luigi Veronesi was central to the development of avant-garde photography in Italy during the 1930s and 1940s. He sought to distance photography from traditional associations with documentary and reportage, promoting its status as an autonomous art form. His engagement with the medium came after he moved to Paris in 1932. While there, he encountered the work of international modern artists such as László Moholy-Nagy (1895–1946), which had been inaccessible to him under the Fascist regime in Italy. Inspired by Moholy-Nagy's photographic experiments, Veronesi began exploring the possibilities of the photogram, a technique in which a sheet of photosensitive paper is covered with objects and then exposed to light. The artworks *Construction* and *Untitled (Spiral)* (pp.142–3) are representative of the approach he adopted in the late 1930s, which saw him applying to photography the lessons in abstraction and geometry that he had learned from painting and graphic design. Fascinated by the aesthetic possibilities of this camera-less process, he experimented with many different objects in the creation of these photograms, though their configurations of lines, dots and spirals make it difficult to decipher the original sources. In later works, such as *Photo n.145* (opposite), *Photo n.152* 1940 and *Kinetic Study* 1941, Veronesi incorporated movement, experimenting with longer exposures and moving either the objects or the light source in order to 'draw' his compositions with light. With these photographic drawings he achieved a range of different effects, creating a sense of motion and depth.

Photo n.145 1940, printed 1970s
Photograph; gelatin silver print on paper
31.8 × 28.7

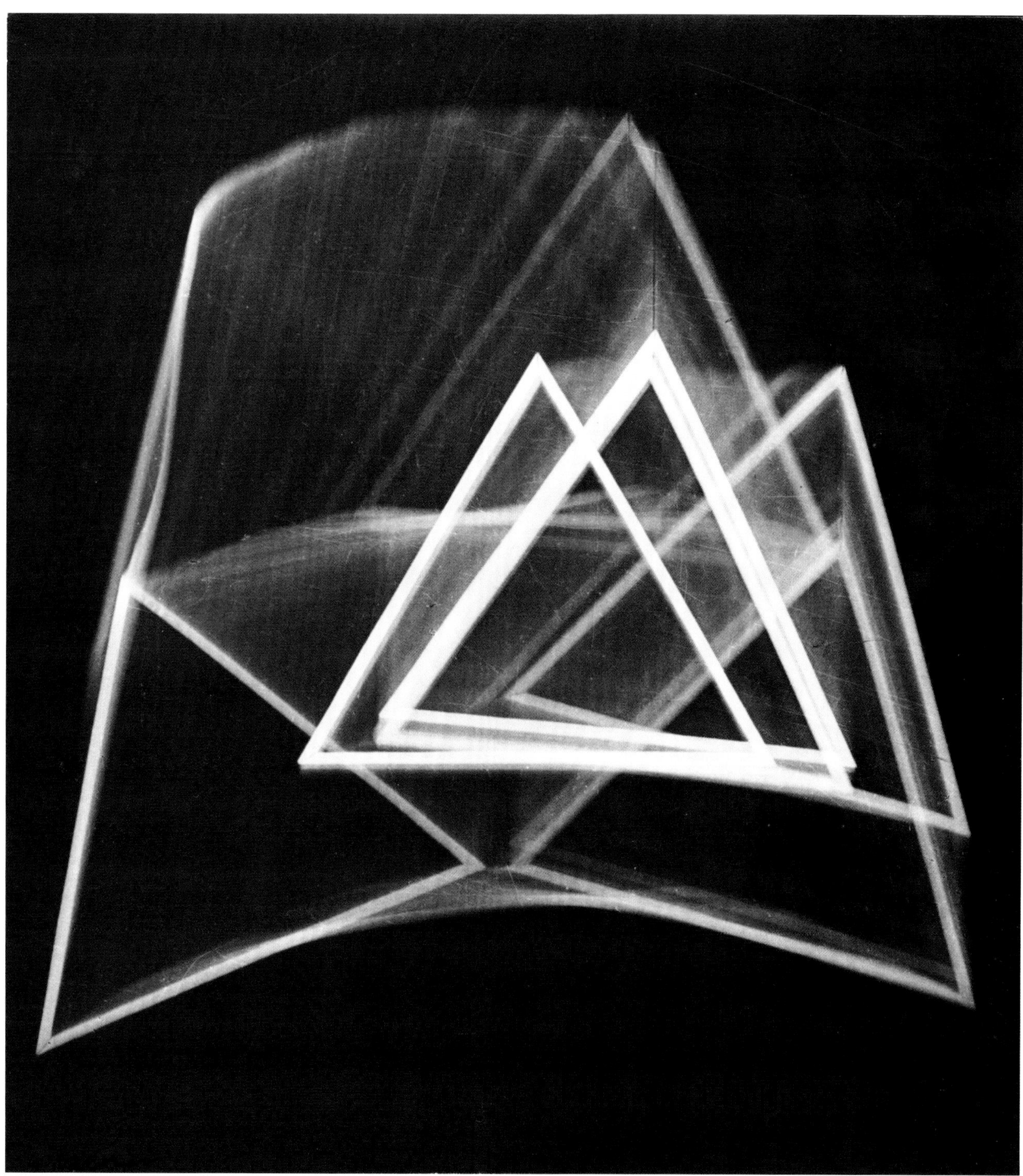

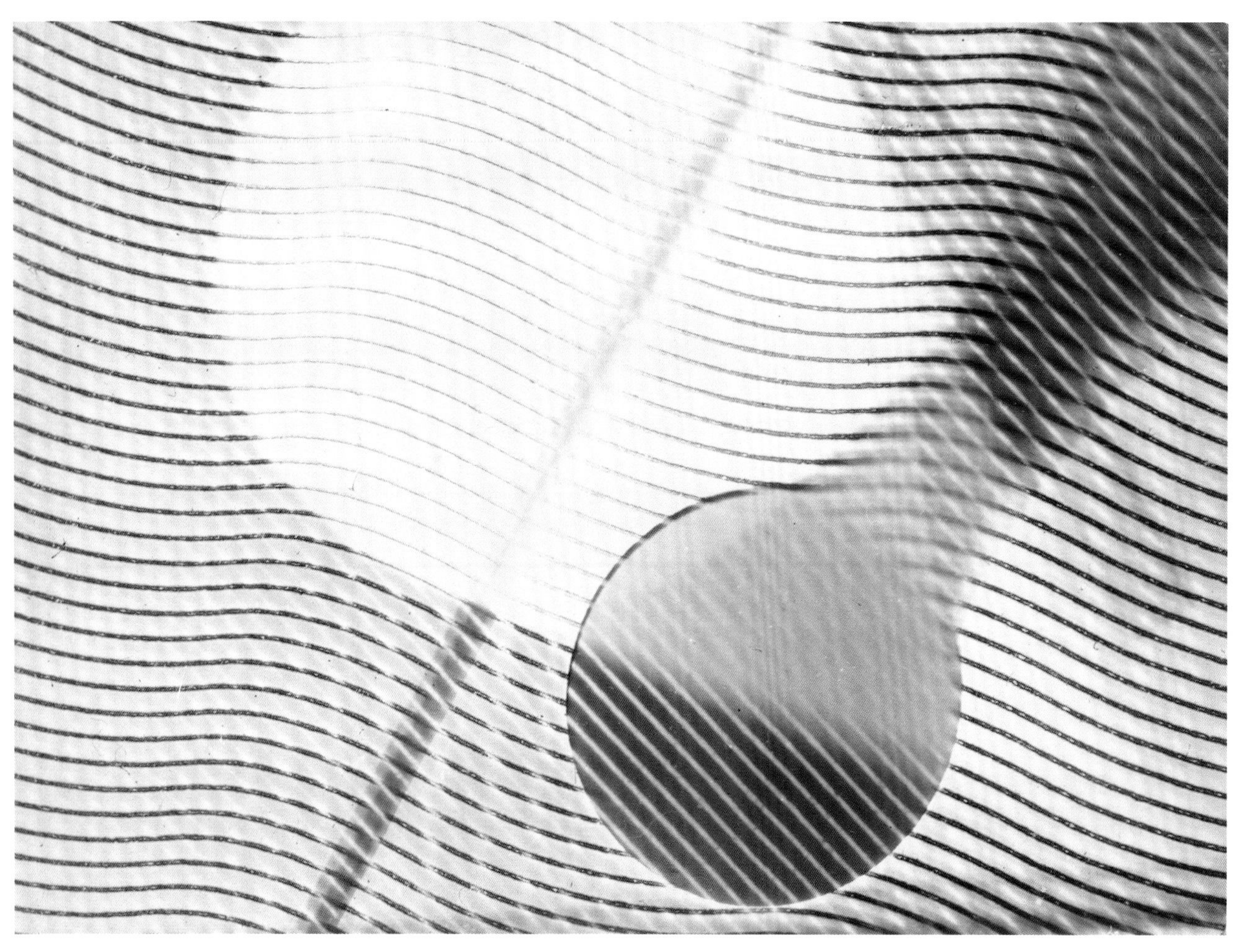

Above: *Construction* 1938
Photograph; gelatin silver print on paper
28.6 × 38.8

Opposite: *Untitled (Spiral)* 1938
Photograph; gelatin silver print on paper
29.8 × 23.5

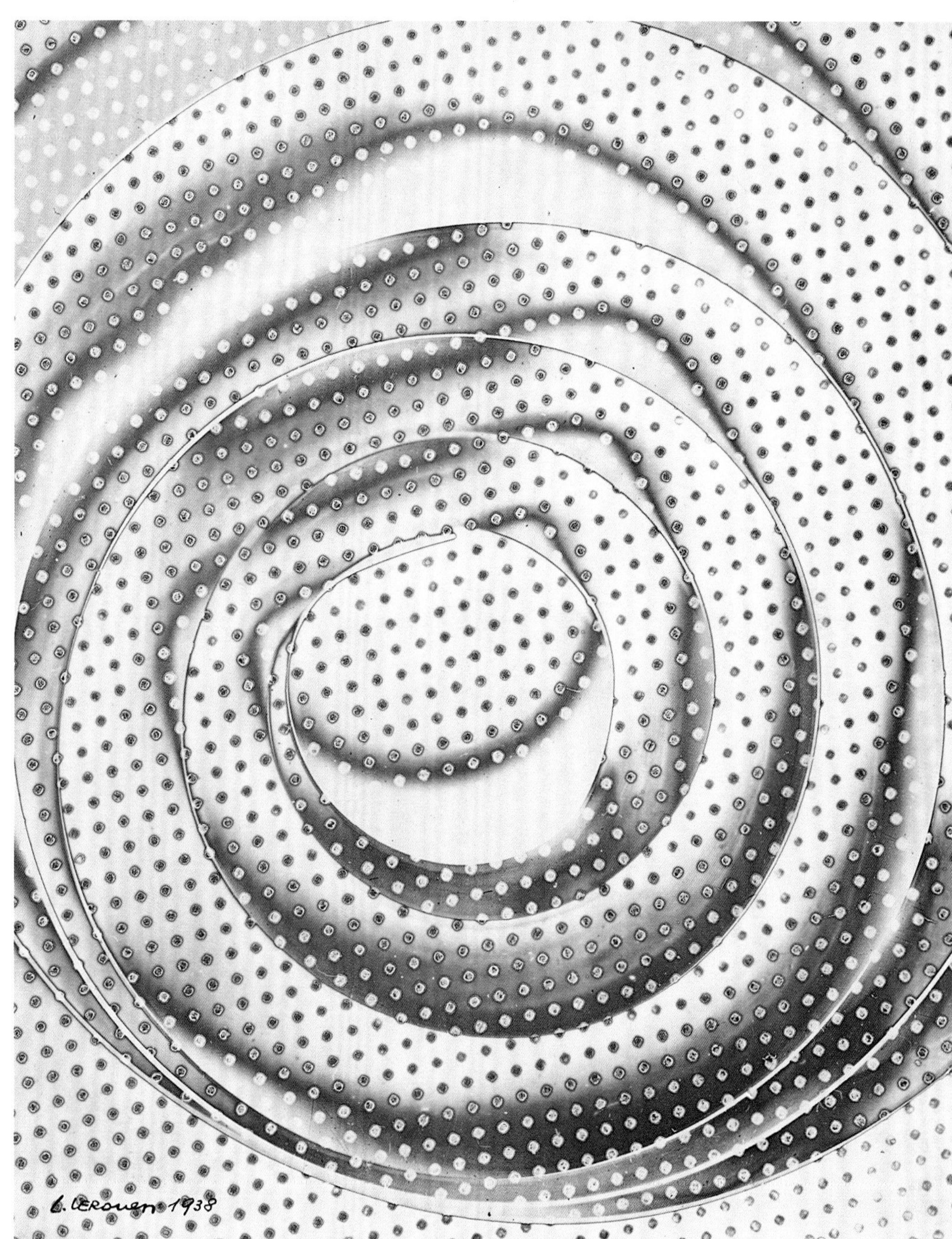

Yayoi Kusama 1929–

Reflections occur when light bounces off an object. Smooth and shiny materials, such as mirror and glass, are highly reflective – when light hits these surfaces, it is reflected back at the same angle in a phenomenon known as specular reflection. This behaviour of light lies at the heart of Yayoi Kusama's interactive sculpture *The Passing Winter*. A mirrored cube positioned at eye level invites viewers to peer through circular holes on each of its sides. Each aperture reveals a mirrored interior, which reflects light entering the cube. As light bounces around the cube, multiple reflections are created, giving the illusion of infinite space (see pp.146–7). The appearance of the interior varies in relation to external conditions, such as the light levels in the room and the surrounding objects and colours, including other viewers engaging with the work. *The Passing Winter* is part of the Japanese artist's ongoing series of mirrored interiors, including her immersive *Infinity Mirror Rooms*, which involve large mirror-lined rooms filled with coloured lights. Kusama's artworks are infused with autobiographical and psychological content, often referencing her own mental fragility. As a child she suffered from hallucinations in which nets or spots dominated her field of vision, and she has written about a serious psychological condition that causes her to feel as if she has 'returned to infinity, to eternal time and absolute space'.[17] The disorienting appearance of *The Passing Winter* may therefore be a visual approximation of Kusama's mental experiences, while its title can perhaps be understood as a reference to the hope of better days.

The Passing Winter 2005
Mirror and glass
180 × 80.5 × 80.5

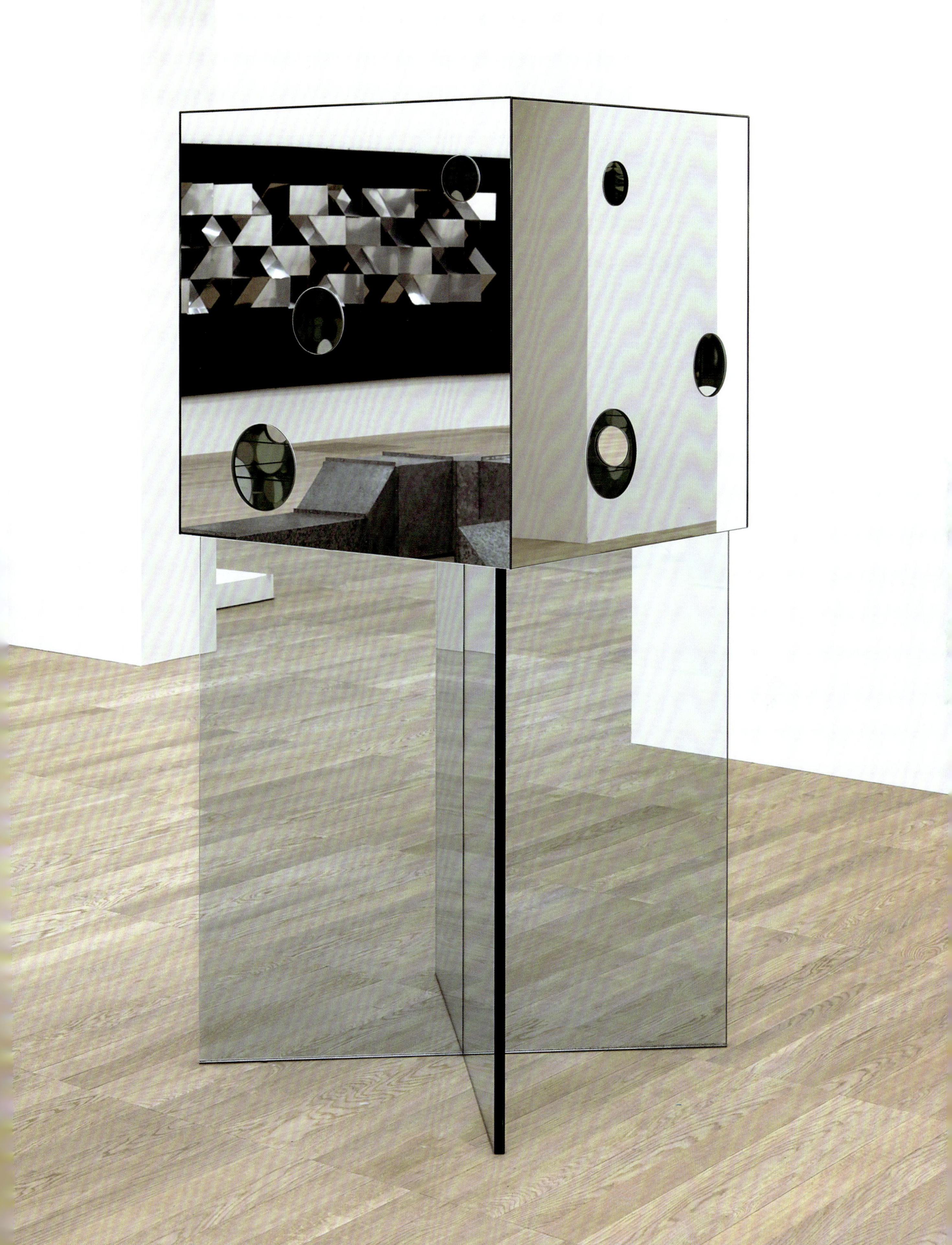

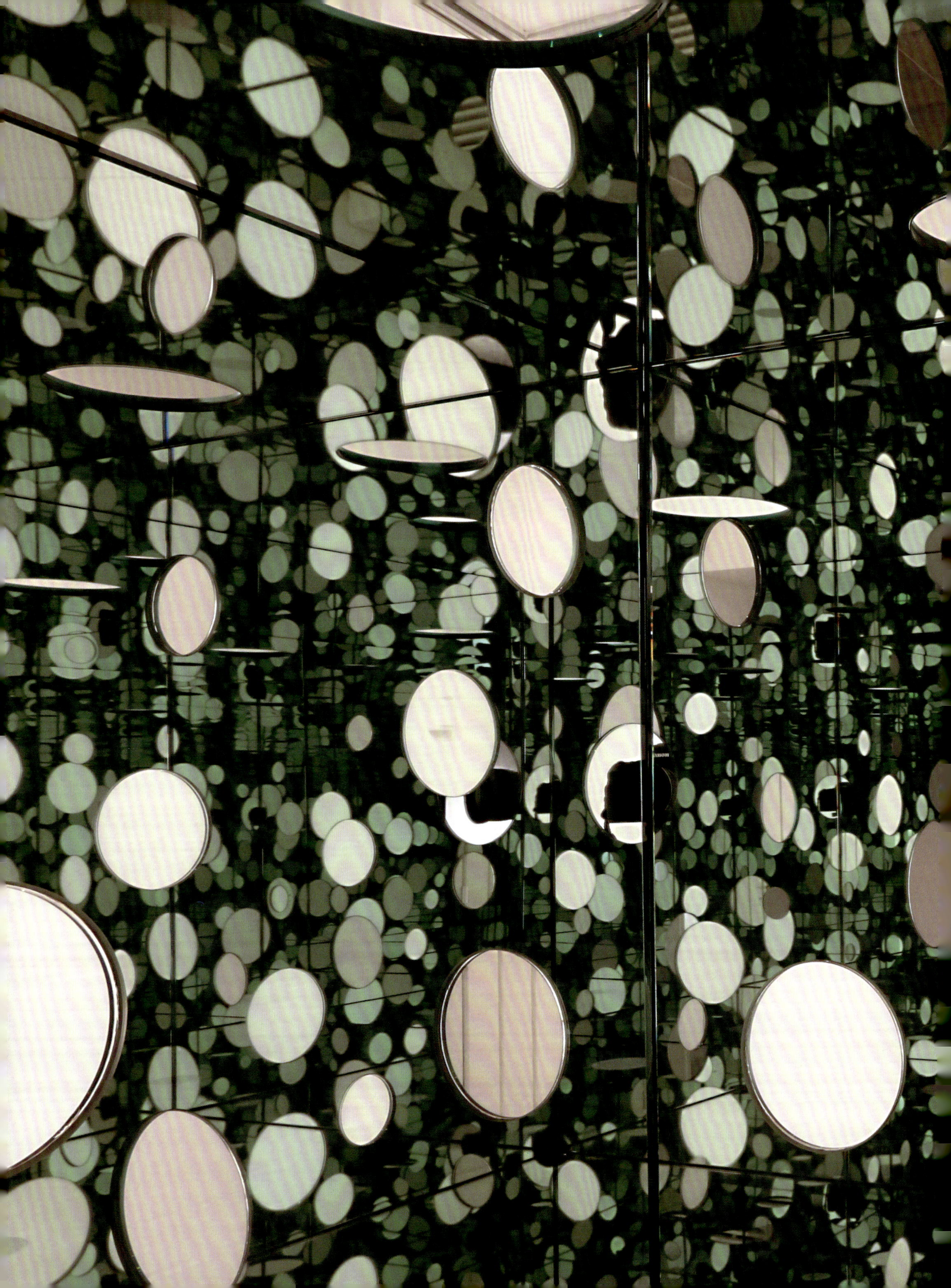

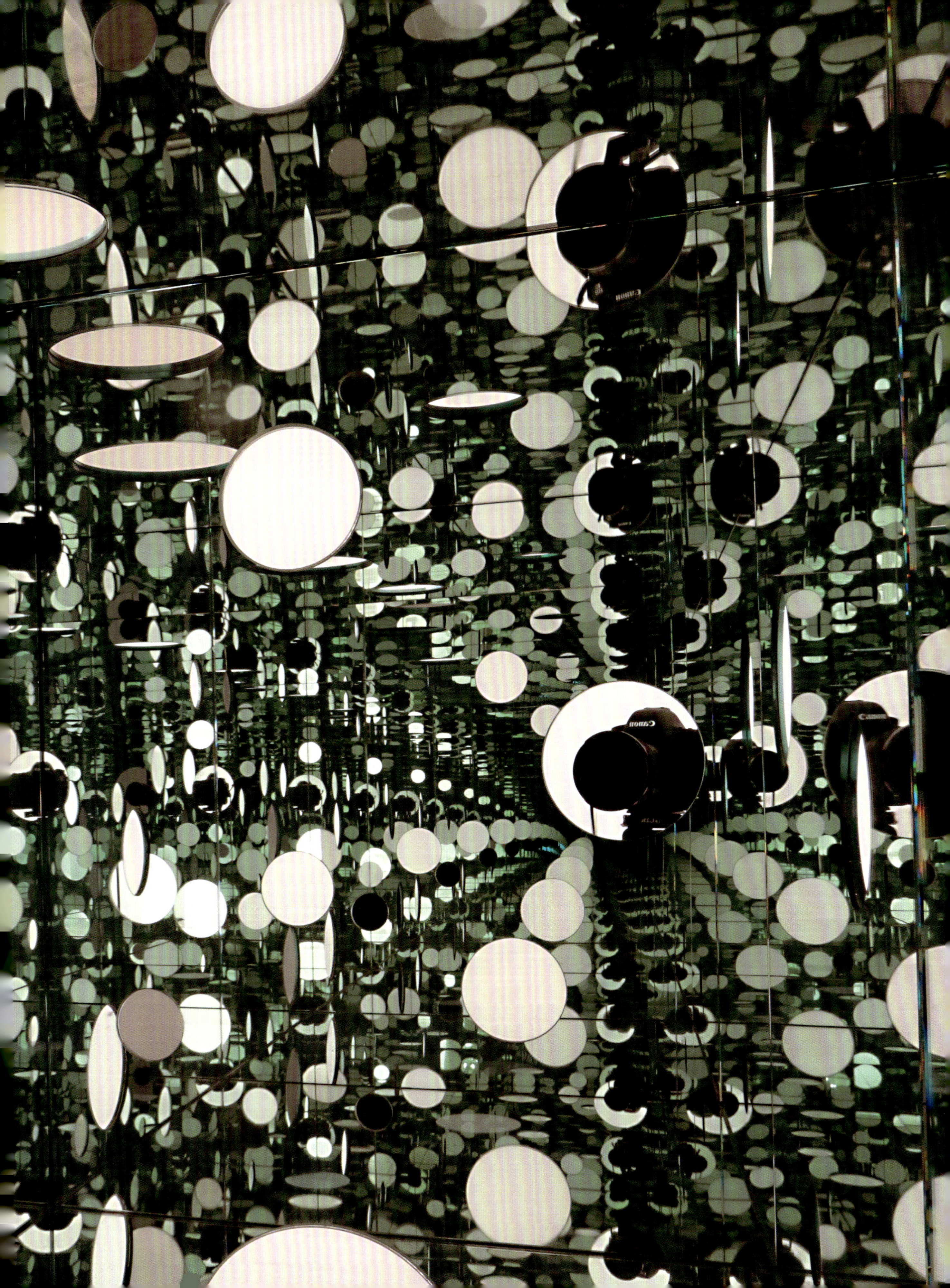

Colour and Light

Light is fundamental to our perception of colour; different hues are made visible in accordance with the particular wavelength of light reflected by an object. This fact preoccupied Josef Albers (1888–1976) who taught at the Bauhaus, an avant-garde art school in Germany. He believed that colour is relative and that the experience of colour is dictated by the interaction of one hue with another. He explored this idea in his signature series, *Homage to the Square*, which he worked on for twenty-six years from 1950. In the 1960s, many artists moved away from traditional painting and sculpture and began incorporating artificial light directly into their works, but they were still fascinated by the central concept of colour perception. All of the works featured here explore colour, and how, through the creation of various optical effects, it can be used to give the impression of light and movement.

László Moholy-Nagy 1895–1946

In 1923, after emigrating from his native Hungary to Berlin, the pioneering artist László Moholy-Nagy was appointed to run the metal workshop at the Bauhaus, the revolutionary school of art, architecture and design founded by Walter Gropius (1883–1969) at Weimar in Germany in 1919. His arrival coincided with the school's shift away from its initial focus on handicrafts towards the machine aesthetics of industrial production and an emphasis on the fusing of art and technology with everyday life. Like other Bauhaus masters, Moholy-Nagy firmly believed in art's potential as a force for positive social reform. His utopian vision, inspired by Russian constructivism's rigorously abstract language, was characterised by an emphasis on transparency and light. Paintings such as *K VII* exemplify his approach. The abstract composition is constructed from a series of overlapping lines and rectangles that appear to float on top of one another. Transparent elements seem to filter an unseen light source, achieving a subtle effect of illumination and a sense of layered space. The painting reflects Moholy-Nagy's preoccupation with light – which he came to consider his primary medium – and anticipates subsequent experiments, such as his *Light Prop for an Electric Stage* 1930, an electrically powered kinetic sculpture made from glass and metal (see p.29). When in motion, its many reflective and translucent surfaces interact with coloured lights to create moving light displays. With its fluctuating play of light, shadow and reflection, the rotating device is the subject of many of Moholy-Nagy's photographs and is recorded in the film *Lichtspiel Schwarz-Weiss-Grau (Lightplay Black-White-Grey)* 1930.

K VII 1922
Oil paint and graphite on canvas
115.3 × 135.9

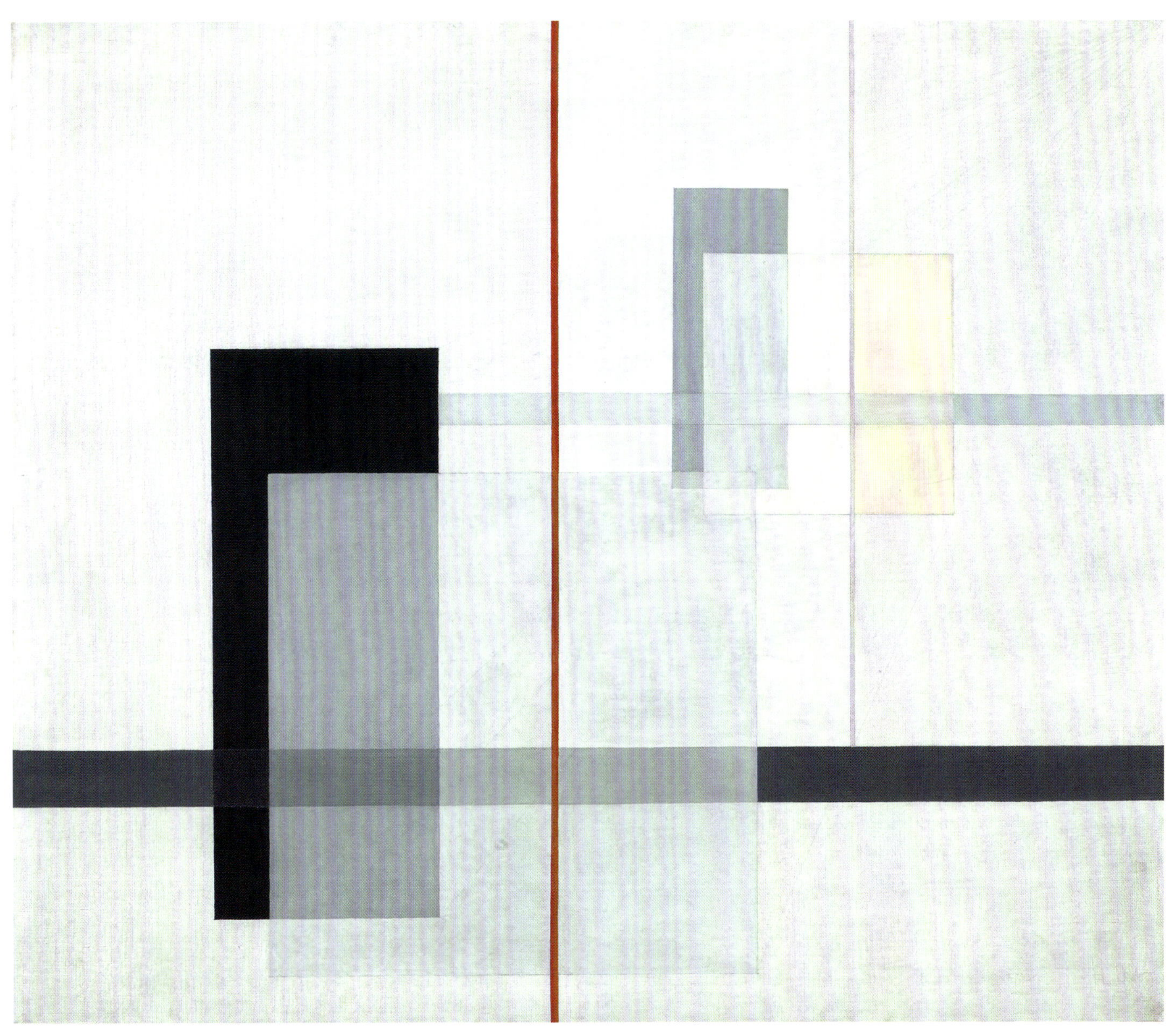

Josef Albers 1888–1976

As Isaac Newton (1642–1727) observed in 1666, colour is not inherent in objects, rather it is a property intrinsic to light. When light hits an object, some is absorbed while the rest is reflected. It is the human brain that translates the reflected light into colour, as determined by its wavelength. The perception of colour was a preoccupation of the influential German-born artist Josef Albers, who taught at the Bauhaus in Dessau, Germany, in the 1920s and later at Black Mountain College in North Carolina, USA. In 1950 he began his famous *Homage to the Square* series, exploring the optical and psychological effects of colour. Each painting is a variation on a simple compositional scheme: three or four differently coloured squares nesting inside one another, with the squares slightly gravitating towards the bottom edge. This approach enabled Albers to investigate the complex interaction of colours, adjusting their hue, tone and intensity so that the squares connect and separate in different ways, sometimes giving the illusion of receding, at other times appearing to be advancing. In works such as *Study for Homage to the Square: Beaming*, they almost seem to glow. Here, the largest square, painted in bright blue paint, stretches to the edges of the fibreboard support. Within this is a smaller, darker blue square, which in turn contains a much smaller blue-green painted square. For works such as *Study for Homage to the Square: Departing in Yellow* and *Study for Homage to the Square* (overleaf), Albers used closely related hues to explore the interaction of similar colours. In 1963 he elucidated his ideas in the book *Interaction of Color*, in which he emphasised practical exploration over theoretical concerns.

Opposite: *Study for Homage to the Square: Beaming* 1963
Oil paint on fibreboard
76.2 × 76.2

Overleaf, left: *Study for Homage to the Square: Departing in Yellow* 1964
Oil paint on fibreboard
76.2 × 76.2

Overleaf, right: *Study for Homage to the Square* 1964
Oil paint on fibreboard
76.2 × 76.2

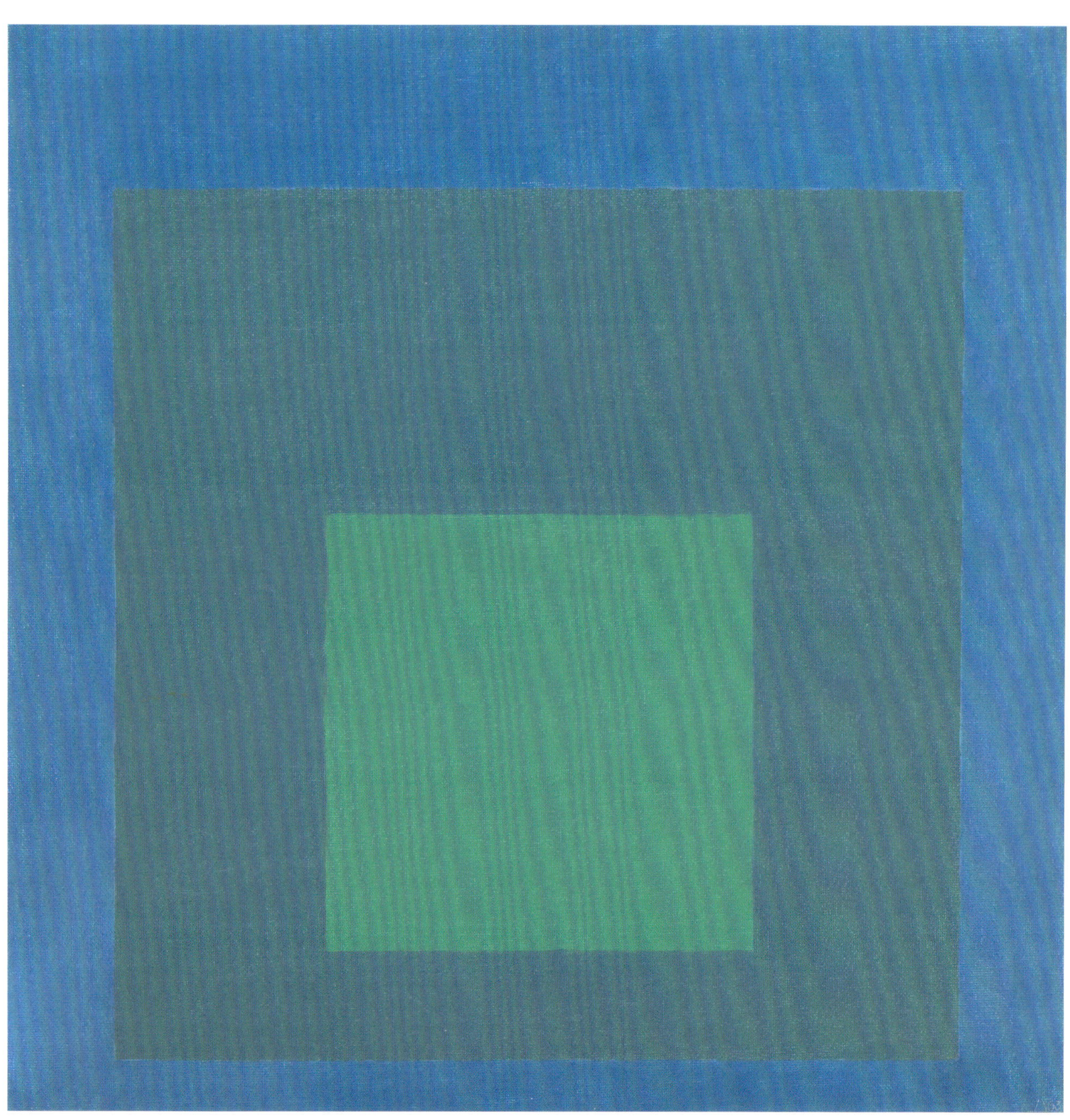

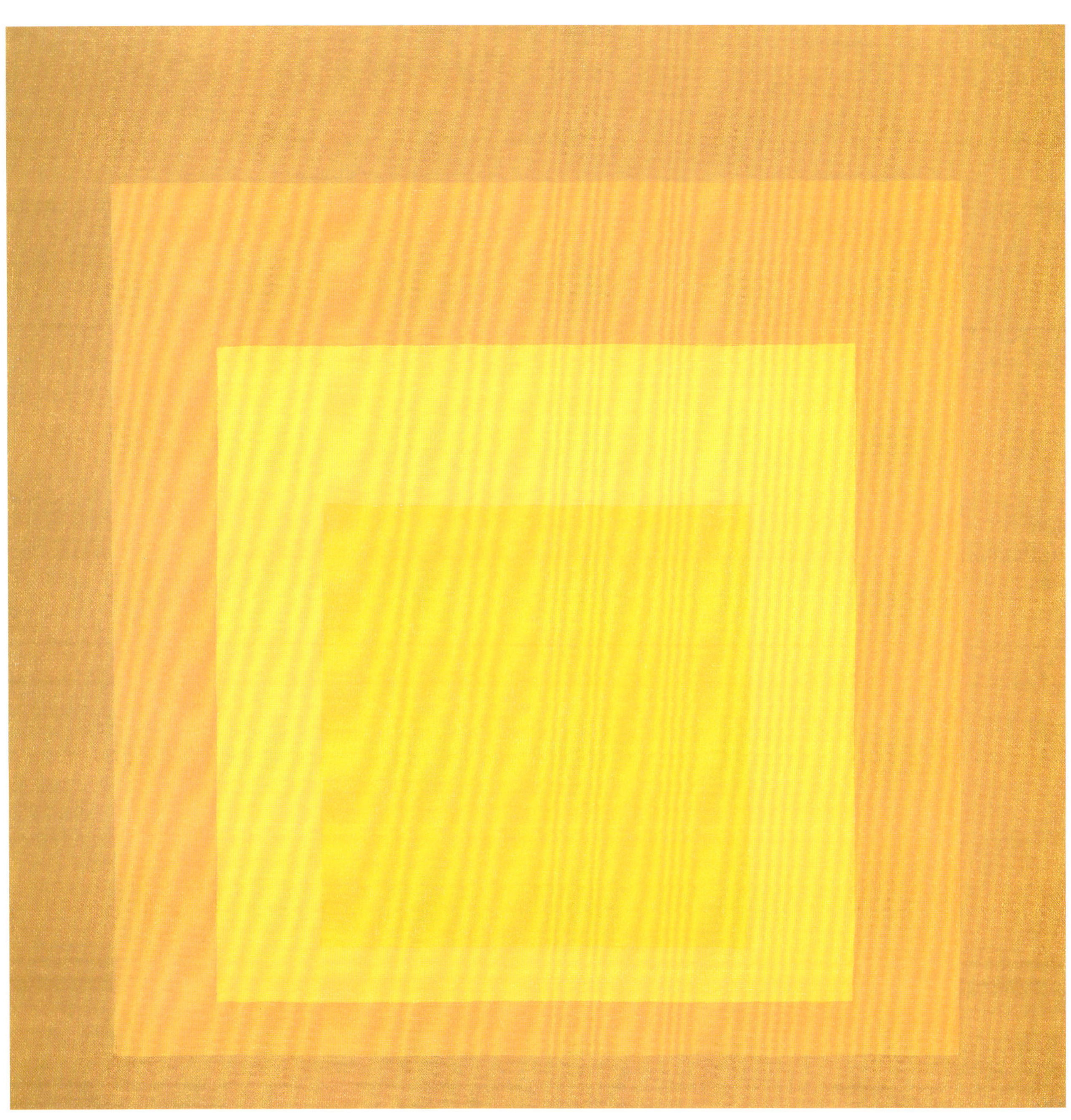

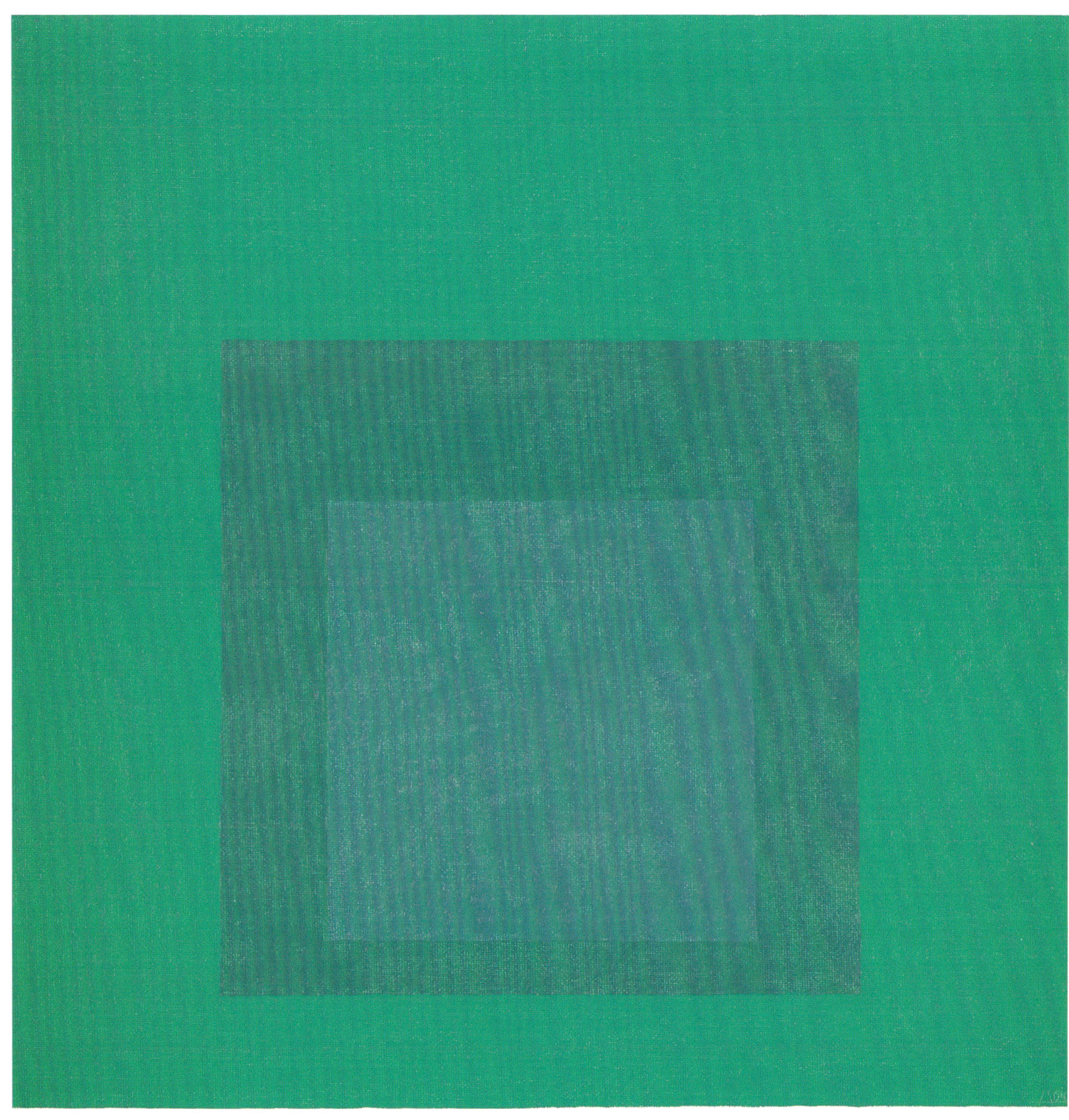

Stephen Willats 1943–

Stephen Willats was a pioneer in the emerging field of conceptual art in the 1960s, which sought to prioritise the ideas behind an artwork over the finished art object. Willats developed an interest in phenomenological and behavioural theories while studying at the Ealing School of Art in London from 1962 to 1963. This experimental course encouraged a multidisciplinary approach to art practice through the understanding of mechanical, physical, biological, cognitive and social systems. *Visual Field Automatic No.1* was first displayed in 1966 in the exhibition *Kunst-Licht-Kunst* at the Van Abbemuseum, the Netherlands, alongside works by other artists working with light, including Dan Flavin (1933–96) and László Moholy-Nagy (1895–1946).[18] Willats conceived *Visual Field Automatic No.1* as a behavioural artwork that invites a response from the spectator, exploring the intersection between art and social behaviour. A single, circular white light is positioned at the centre of the structure with four square protruding areas of coloured light linked to a circuit board that is hidden from view. These lights flash one at a time in a series of random computer-generated sequences. In this sculpture and others in the series, the random flashing lights often provoke the viewer to attempt to impose some order on what they are seeing, yet the desire to systemise is left unfulfilled by the unpredictable pattern of the lights.

Visual Field Automatic No.1 1964
Plywood, wood, plastic, metal, light bulbs and circuit board
191 × 122 × 22

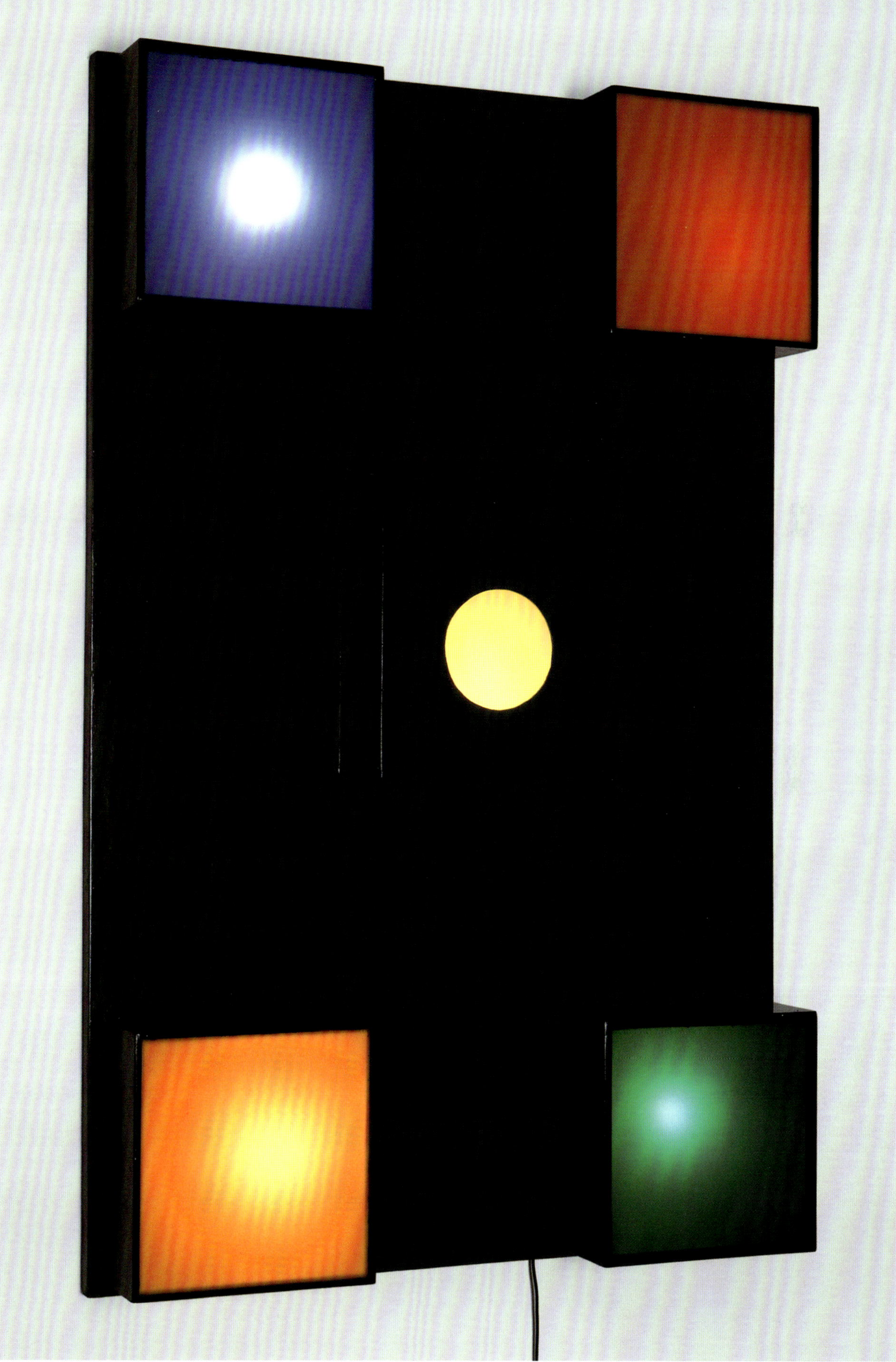

Wassily Kandinsky 1866–1944

Inspired by folklore scenes and icons of his native Russia, Wassily Kandinsky was also influenced by the landscape outside Munich, where he lived with his first wife, artist Gabriele Münter (1877–1962), in the early 1900s. By 1913, Kandinsky had already been instrumental in the founding of two influential groups of artists, the Phalanx and Der Blaue Reiter, exhibited several times in the Salon d'Automne in Paris, and produced the most radically abstract work presented in the famed Armory Show in New York. When the First World War broke out, Kandinsky returned to Russia and contributed to the artistic activities of the fledgling Bolshevik State. There his paintings evolved towards a more centred and linear expression in response to the work of artists such as Kazimir Malevich (1879–1935) and El Lissitzky (1890–1941). However, disenchanted with the increasing political control over artistic expression, Kandinsky returned to Germany in 1921 where he taught at the Bauhaus, an interdisciplinary school of art, architecture and design, until the school was forced to close in 1933. This painting was made while Kandinsky was at Weimar before the Bauhaus moved to Dessau in 1925. Kandinsky believed painting should aim to be as abstract as music, and he worked to create art that was free from all references to the material world. For him, colour was essential in liberating art from representation. By stripping away the details of recognisable motifs, he left calligraphic lines as structuring devices within his compositions. *Swinging* epitomises this approach, while the title makes these allusions to music and movement explicit. Kandinsky conceived of his art as an alternative pathway to a spiritual realm, made more powerful by not being tied to the observed world.

Swinging 1925
Oil paint on board
70.5 × 50.2

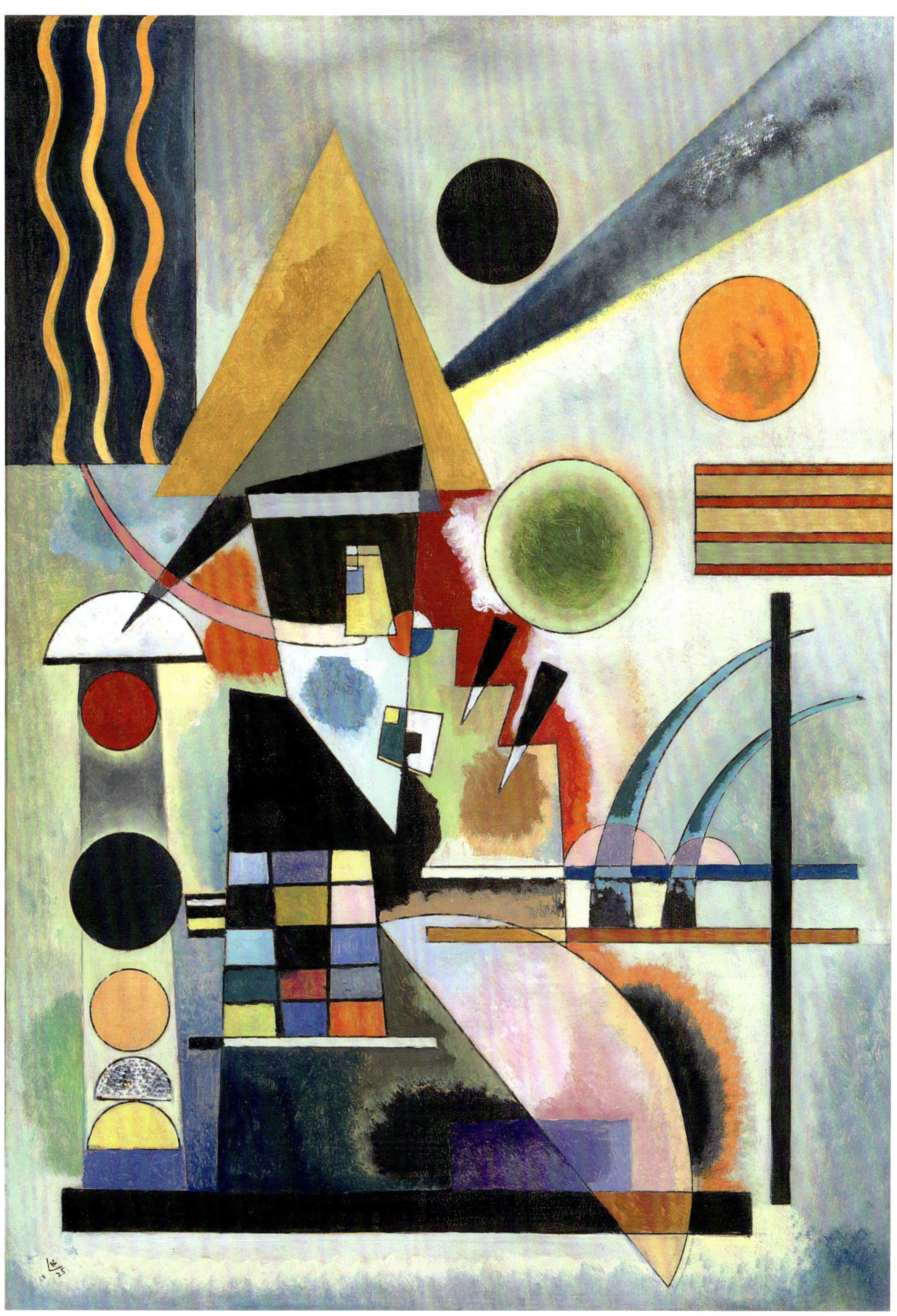

Pae White 1963–

Pae White is known for her large-scale, mixed-media installations that, although they frequently change in size and form, share a common concern for the ephemeral and forgotten aspects of everyday life.[19] *Morceau Accrochant* is a hanging mobile installation consisting of 482 strands of thread and screenprinted paper suspended from the ceiling to create a three-dimensional volume of dense colour; an experience the artist has called 'an exploration of movement contained'.[20] Each strand has a long yellow and a shorter red length onto which five or six discs of colour-saturated paper are threaded. White envisions this shape as a stylised leaf, hoping to capture 'the incoherence of a swirl of leaves or the frenzy of birds into a freeze frame'.[21] Through an interplay of movement, colour and light, she challenges the architectural aspects of installation art by suggesting the concreteness of a sculptural object without creating it: the work asserts 'so much volume but could also fit in a shoebox'.[22] As is characteristic of installation art, *Morceau Accrochant* encourages engagement on different axes. *Morceau Accrochant* is French for 'hanging piece', in deference to the idea of these multiple axes.[23]

Morceau Accrochant 2004
Paper and thread
Display dimensions variable

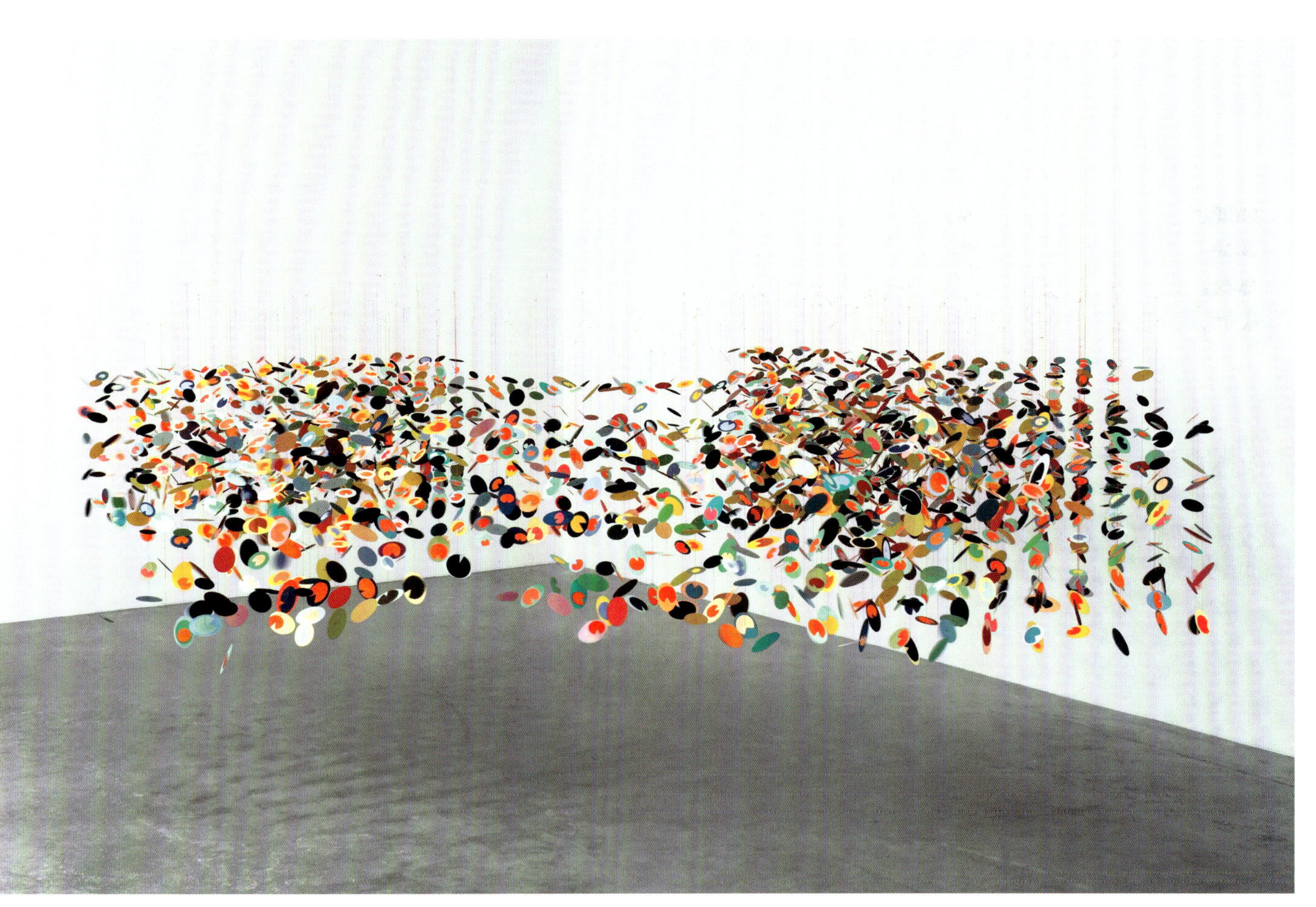

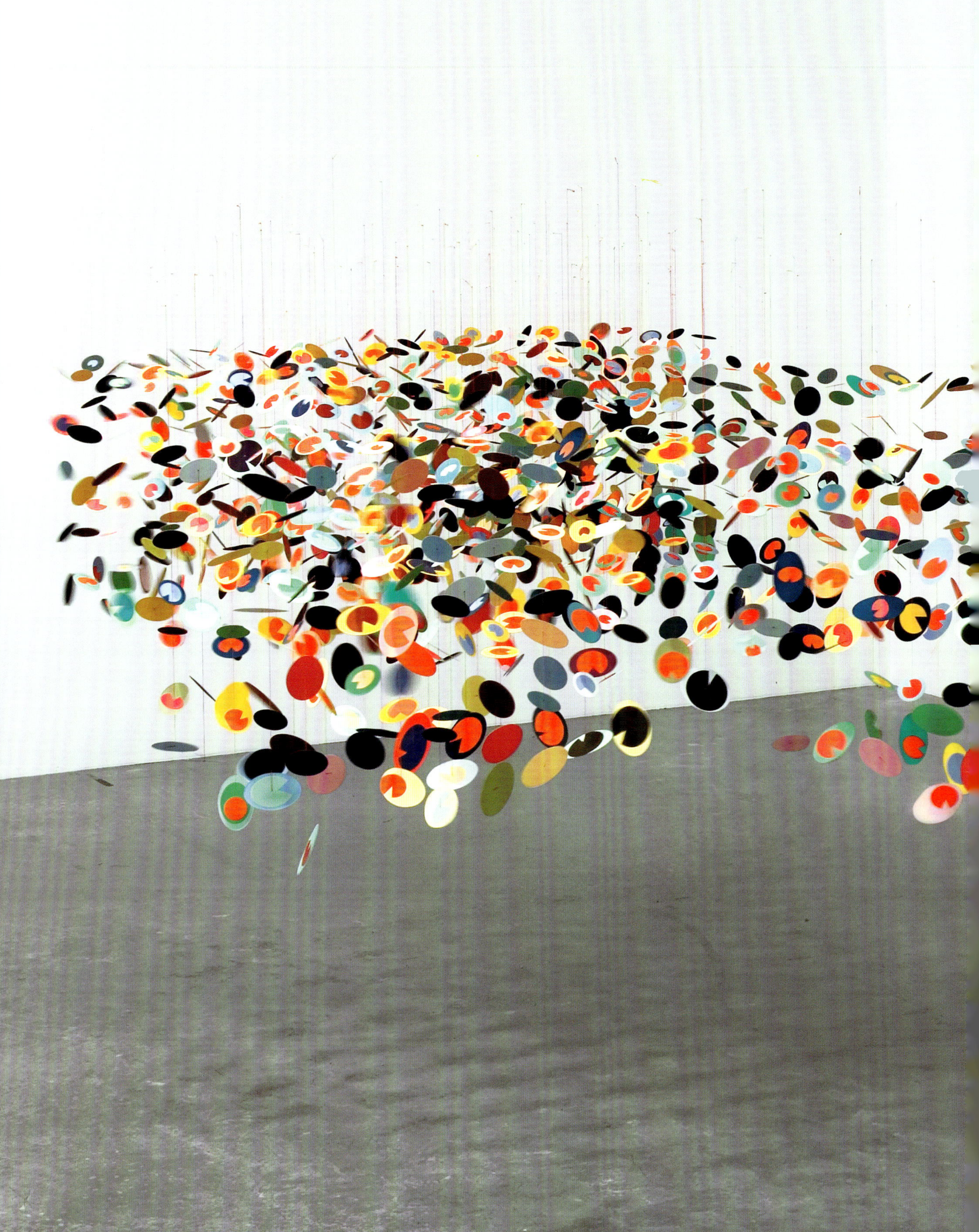

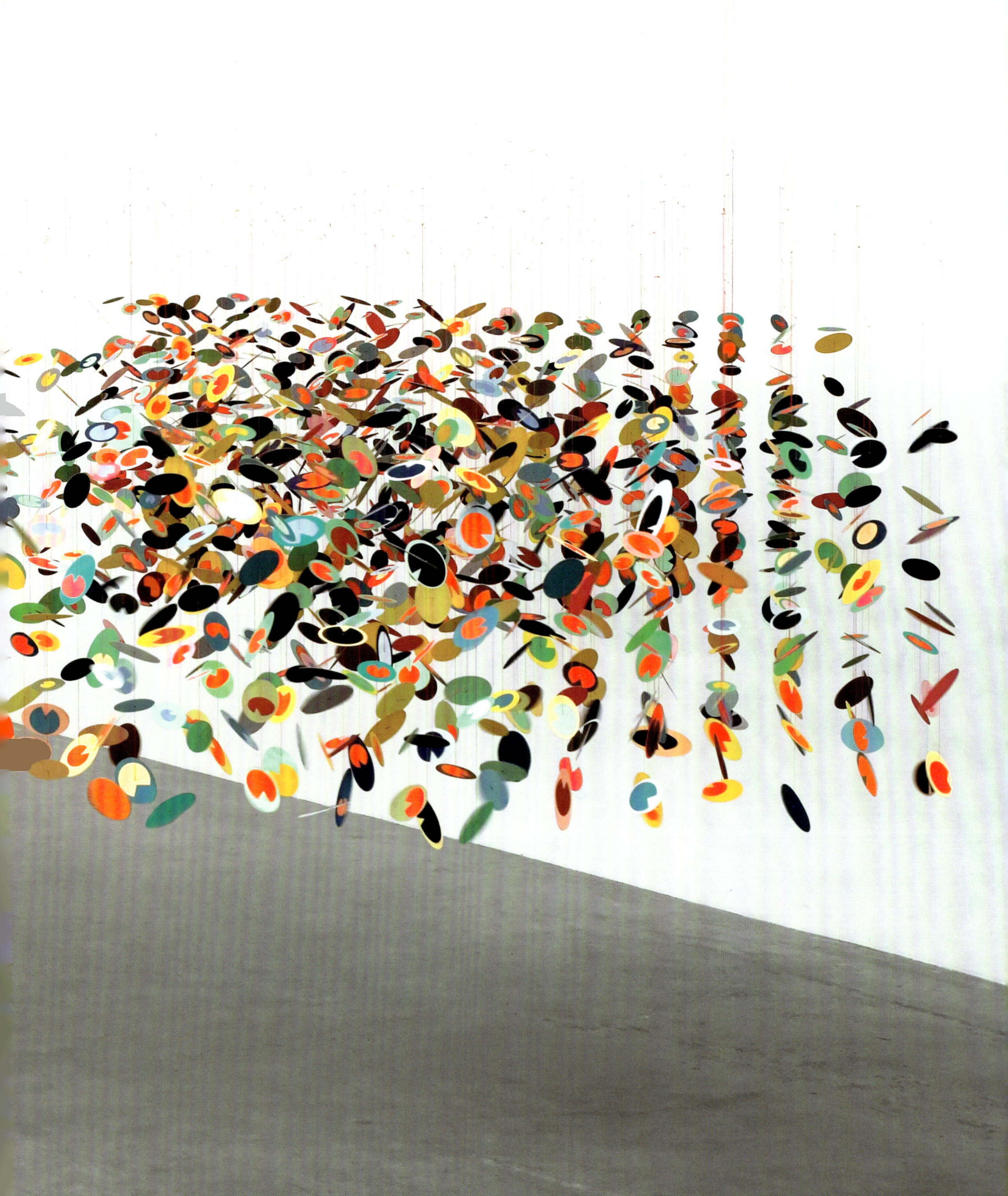

Bridget Riley 1931–

In 1959 Bridget Riley painted a copy of French post-impressionist artist Georges Seurat's (1859–91) *Bridge at Courbevoie* 1886–7 (see p.23). This experience represented a significant breakthrough for Riley, offering her a new understanding of colour and perception and emboldening her to work differently. By the mid-1960s she had risen to international prominence with abstract paintings based on repeated geometric patterns that utilised optical illusions to create a sense of movement. Riley began working with colour in the early 1970s and, after a visit to Egypt in 1986, her work attained a new chromatic intensity. In *Nataraja*, the surface is divided vertically and diagonally, creating a multiplicity of discrete areas of colour. The complexity of the colour relationships is formidable. A principal difficulty of this kind of composition is that of creating a unified and balanced field of visual sensation which, at the same time, is organised dynamically in terms of individual colours. Riley often alludes to her impressions of foreign cultures in her paintings. In 1981 she travelled to India. *Nataraja* is a term from Hindu mythology meaning 'Lord of the Dance' and refers to the Hindu god Shiva, who is usually depicted with many arms in his form as the cosmic dancer. *Nataraja* thus refers to the emphasis on rhythm and counter-rhythm, which are central elements in this painting. Here we see vertical bands of colour cut across by diagonals, creating a sense of dynamic movement. The position of each of these elements has been carefully judged in terms of correspondence, contrast and proportion. In this painting Riley has related similar and contrasting colours in a way that sustains a saturated intensity of colour, creating an overall impression of light and movement.

Nataraja 1993
Oil paint on canvas
165.1 × 227.7

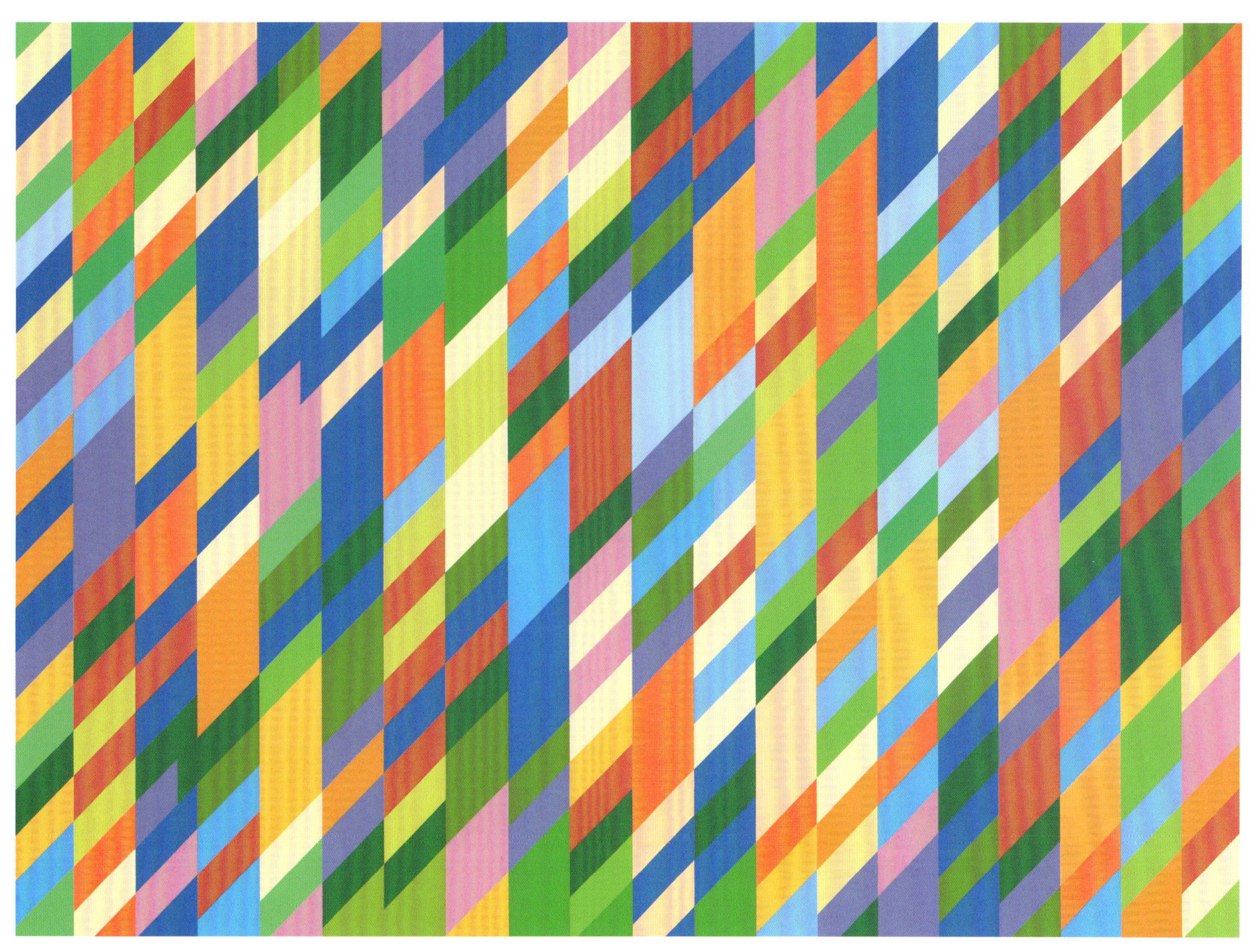

Reconfiguring Light

The invention and popularisation of electric light was an essential characteristic of modernity that revolutionised life in the twentieth century. Today, modern illumination in the form of interior and exterior lighting, colourful street signage and advertising billboards illuminate our towns and cities twenty-four hours a day. In 1963, American artist Dan Flavin (1933–96) began working with fluorescent lighting tubes to create sculptures and installations exploring the visual effects of such technology. Around the same time, Peter Sedgley (1930–) began to project programmed sequences of coloured light onto painted surfaces, creating pulsing colour transformations and the illusion of movement. Whereas Sedgley's intention was to counter the sensory barrage of light and colour in the urban environment, David Batchelor (1955–) confronts the artificiality of such phenomena directly, using coloured lights in his work to evoke the character of London's streets after dark. Also interested in exploring everyday experiences is Bruce Nauman (1941–), who draws attention to how the position, type and quality of light changes how we perceive our surroundings. Olafur Eliasson's (1967–) interest in colour perception is integral to his installation *Yellow versus Purple* 2003 in which viewers become surfaces for coloured light to be projected on to. Catherine Yass (1963–) meanwhile overturns colour relationships by combining a colour negative with a positive image in a single transparency to create strange, psychologically-charged scenes.

Dan Flavin 1933–96

Dan Flavin's name has become synonymous with his arrangements of fluorescent lights which engage with their surrounding architectural space. The first of these was *the diagonal of May 25, 1963 (to Constantin Brancusi)* 1963, a gold-coloured tube mounted diagonally on the wall. Flavin's neutral geometric forms, use of serialisation and reliance on industrially produced materials have often been associated with the rational aesthetics of the minimalism movement. However, Flavin referred to his work as 'maximalist', given the balance between his works' economy of means yet visual exuberance. While influenced by his Catholic upbringing, he always rejected interpretations of his work as spiritual, assumed by viewers given the immateriality of the light. Rather, Flavin preferred for his art to be taken at face value. Many of Flavin's works refer to significant figures of twentieth-century art, including Russian artist Vladimir Tatlin (1885–1953), to whom he dedicated his single most sustained series of pseudo-monuments. Flavin had a special admiration for Tatlin's proposed design for the *Monument to the Third International* 1919–20, designed to celebrate the Bolshevik Revolution in Russia and act as headquarters for the Communist International (Comintern). Flavin considered Tatlin's unbuilt monument to be under-appreciated and admired its practical occupation as a building-come-sculpture, and its engineered form as a revolving spiral. At 400 metres high, the spiral would have been taller than the Eiffel Tower, with which it would have competed as the ultimate symbol of modernity. Like all Flavin's sculptures, this work was made using prefabricated fluorescent tubes. He described it as a 'monument' partly as a joke, aware of the disparity between its modest materials and immateriality and the traditional grandeur and solidity of monumental sculpture.

'monument' for V. Tatlin 1966–9
Fluorescent tubes and metal
305.4 × 58.4 × 8.9

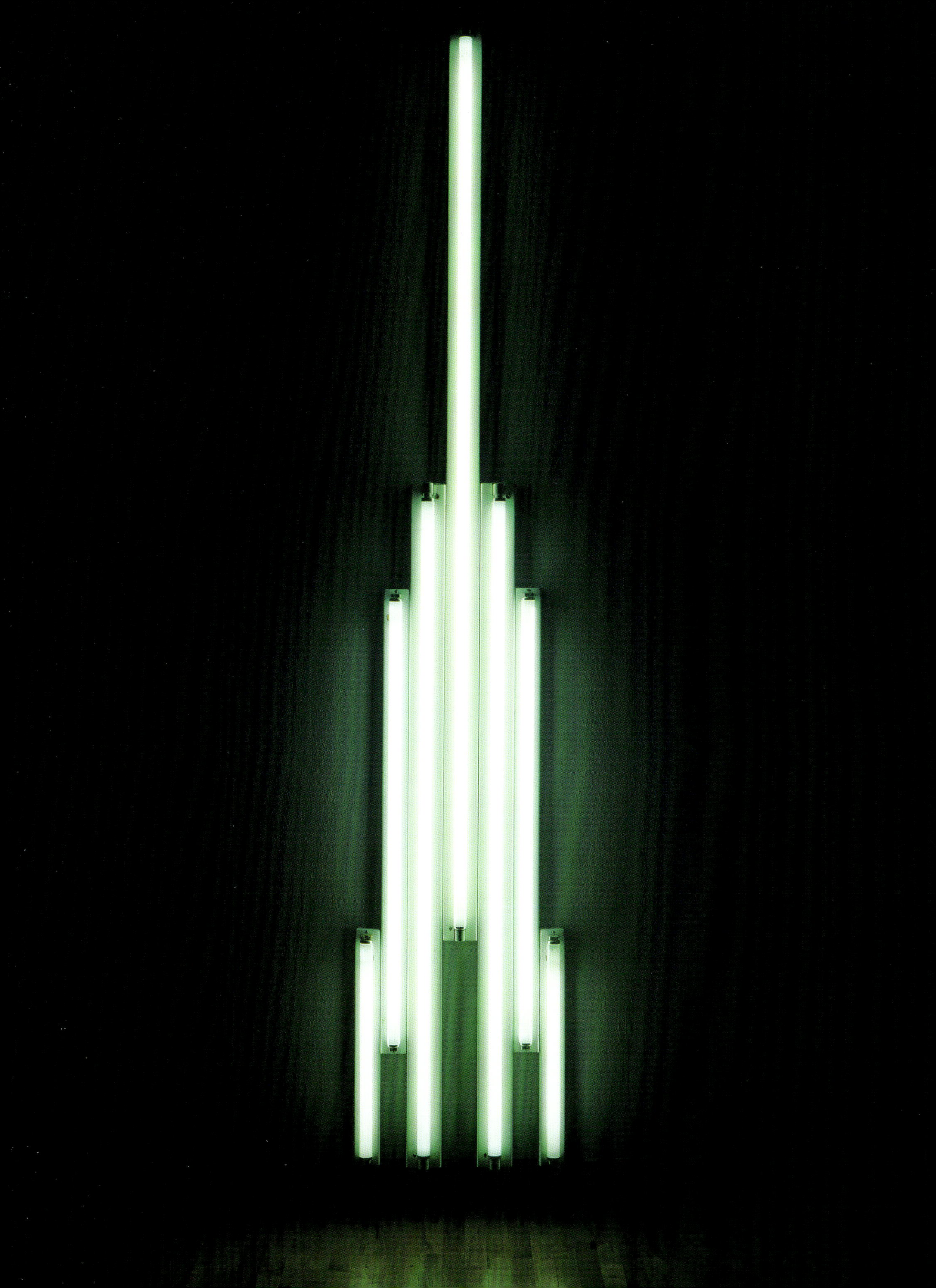

Bruce Nauman 1941–

Bruce Nauman first studied mathematics and physics at the University of Wisconsin–Madison (1960–4), before pursuing a career as an artist and dedicating himself to sculpture, performance and the moving image. Since then, the studio and the artist's body have been at the core of Nauman's practice. Early on he developed the notion that everything the artist did in the studio was art, thereby redefining art as an activity rather than a product. The realisation that he spent most of his time pacing in his studio led to his seminal film, video and photographic works of the late 1960s, featuring physical activities: walking, dancing, playing the violin, putting on make-up and making faces. From the late 1960s Nauman made a series of cages and corridors, often augmenting these works with texts, video or closed-circuit television, sound, mirrors and light. In his corridor pieces, Nauman's sculpture assumes the dimensions of architecture. The spaces are often claustrophobic, yet they seem to extend indefinitely, like a corridor seen in a dream. Here, the sense of infinite extension is created by a mirror set at an angle at the end of the corridor. The width of the corridor has been narrowed so that it is impossible to walk through it, heightening the sense of eerie isolation. Instead of being a 'performance area', it becomes a space which is inaccessible, and which appears to extend out of sight.

Corridor with Mirror and White Lights 1971
Wood, glass and fluorescent tubes
304.8 × 30.8 × 1219.2

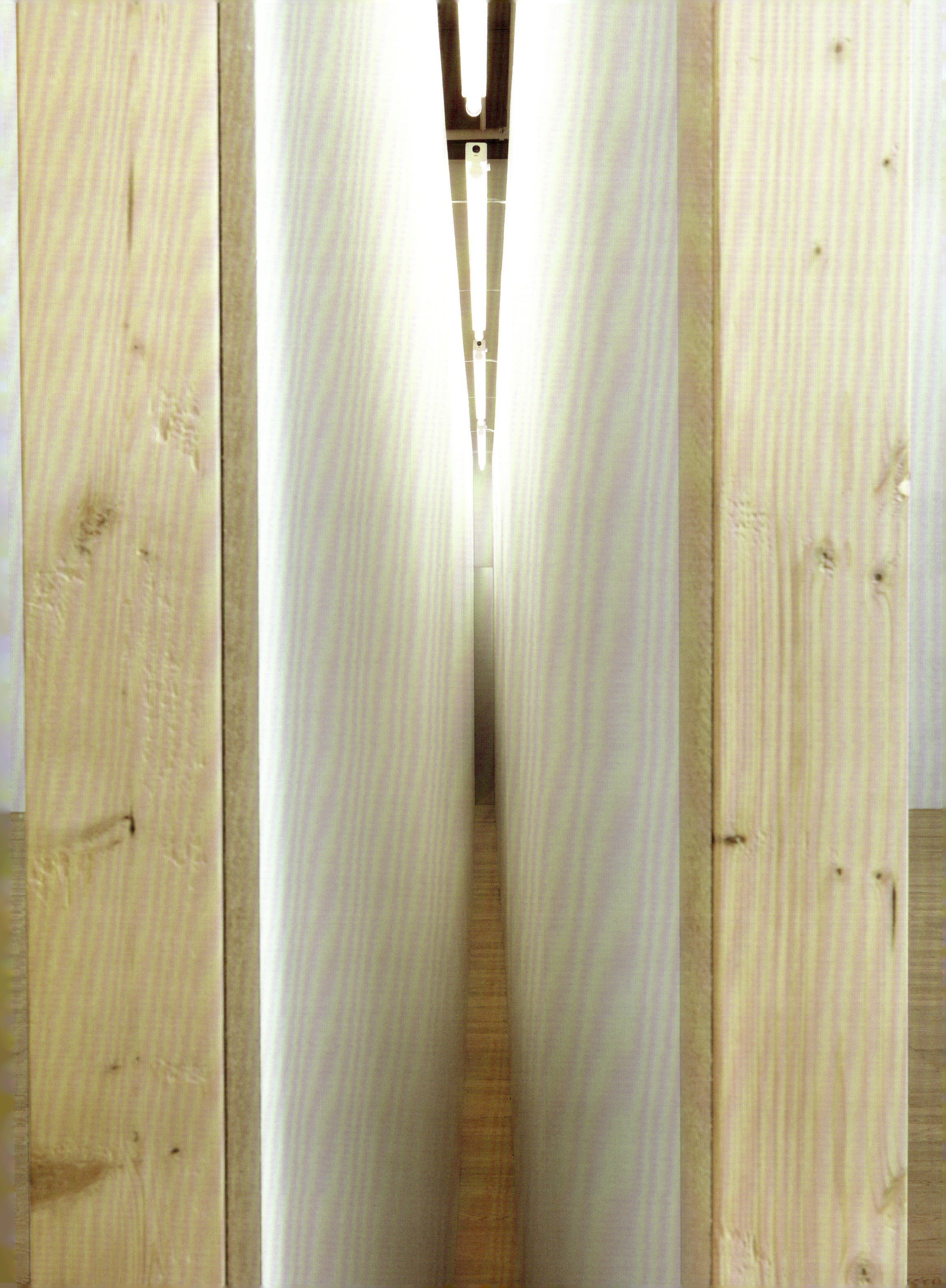

David Batchelor 1955–

Since the early 1990s, Scottish artist David Batchelor has been concerned with the way that colour and light are experienced in the urban environment. As his sculptures remind us, colour can only be perceived due to the presence of reflected light, the wavelength of which determines its hue. In 1997, Batchelor began exploring the artificiality of commercially produced colours by setting panels of glossy acrylic onto small wheeled dollies typically used in warehouses and factories. Batchelor dubbed his collections of coloured dollies 'monochromobiles' – monochromes on wheels – of which *I Love King's Cross and King's Cross Loves Me 08* (pp.174–5) is a typical example. Comprising six industrial dollies found on the streets near his London studio, the sculpture features bright orange, red, yellow, violet, mauve and apricot panels, which appear shiny and lustrous under the gallery's artificial lighting. Illuminated colour is also explored in works such as *Spectrum of Brick Lane 2*, which is inspired by busy London streets after dark. The tall column of coloured lightboxes evokes the illuminated signs of the many takeaways and curry restaurants for which east London's Brick Lane is renowned. Bright with seductive light on one side, dull and nondescript on the other, *Spectrum of Brick Lane 2* uses the presence and absence of light to reflect the contradictory character of England's capital – at once glitzy and unsavoury – and, indeed, cities all over the world. In this way, Batchelor ensures that the lights and colours he uses are not perceived as a transcendental presence, but rather rooted in everyday experiences.

Spectrum of Brick Lane 2 2007
Lightboxes, steel shelving, acrylic sheet, fluorescent lights, cable and plug boards
520 × 90 × 31

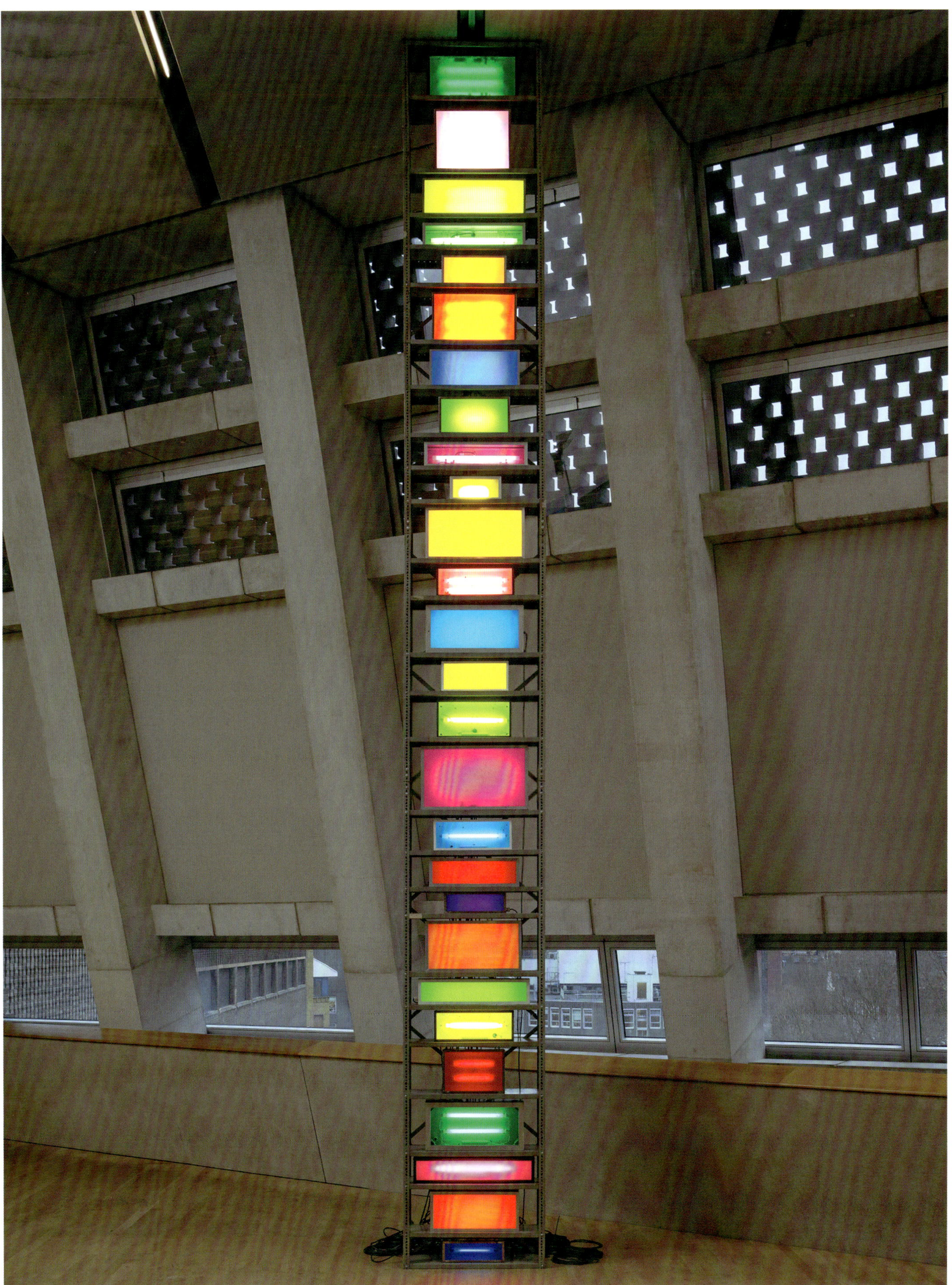

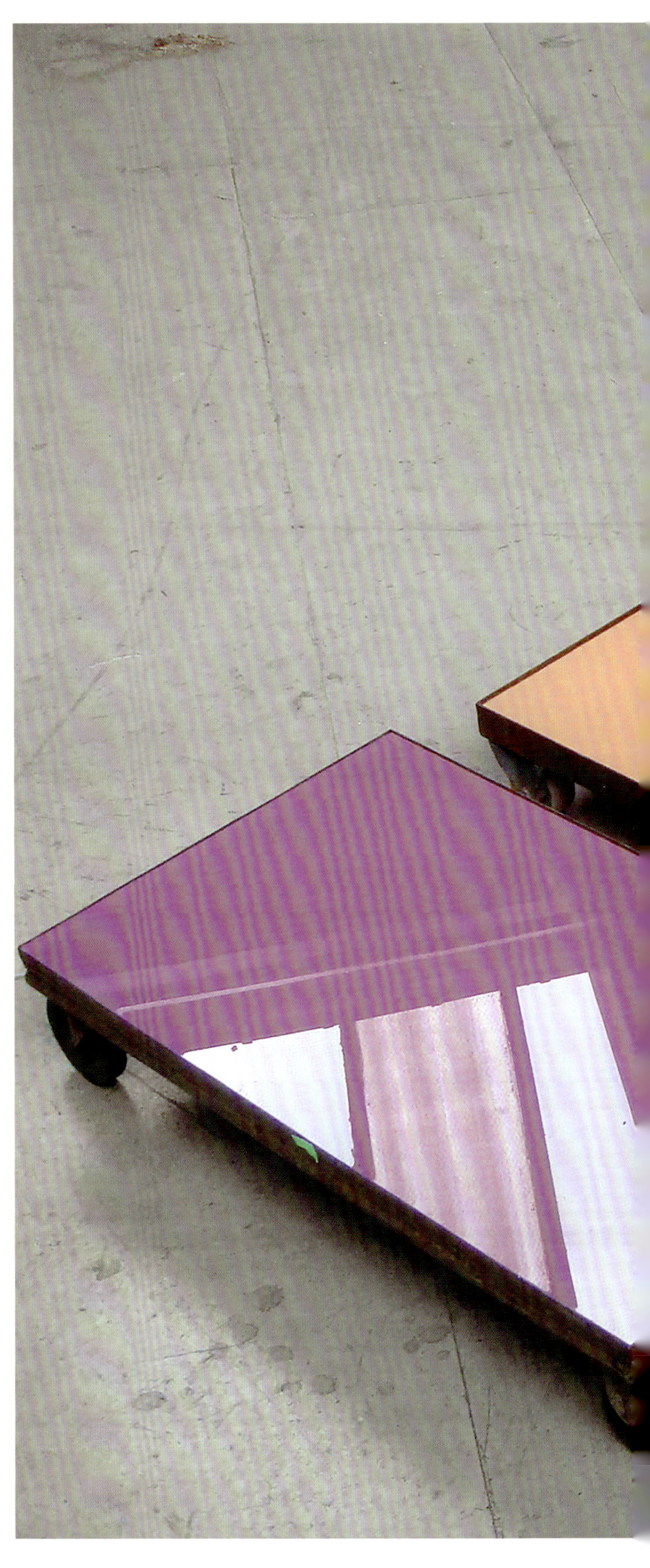

I Love King's Cross and King's Cross Loves Me 08 2002–7
6 steel, rubber and acrylic sheets
Each between: 12.5 × 65 × 55 and 16.5 x 76 x 46

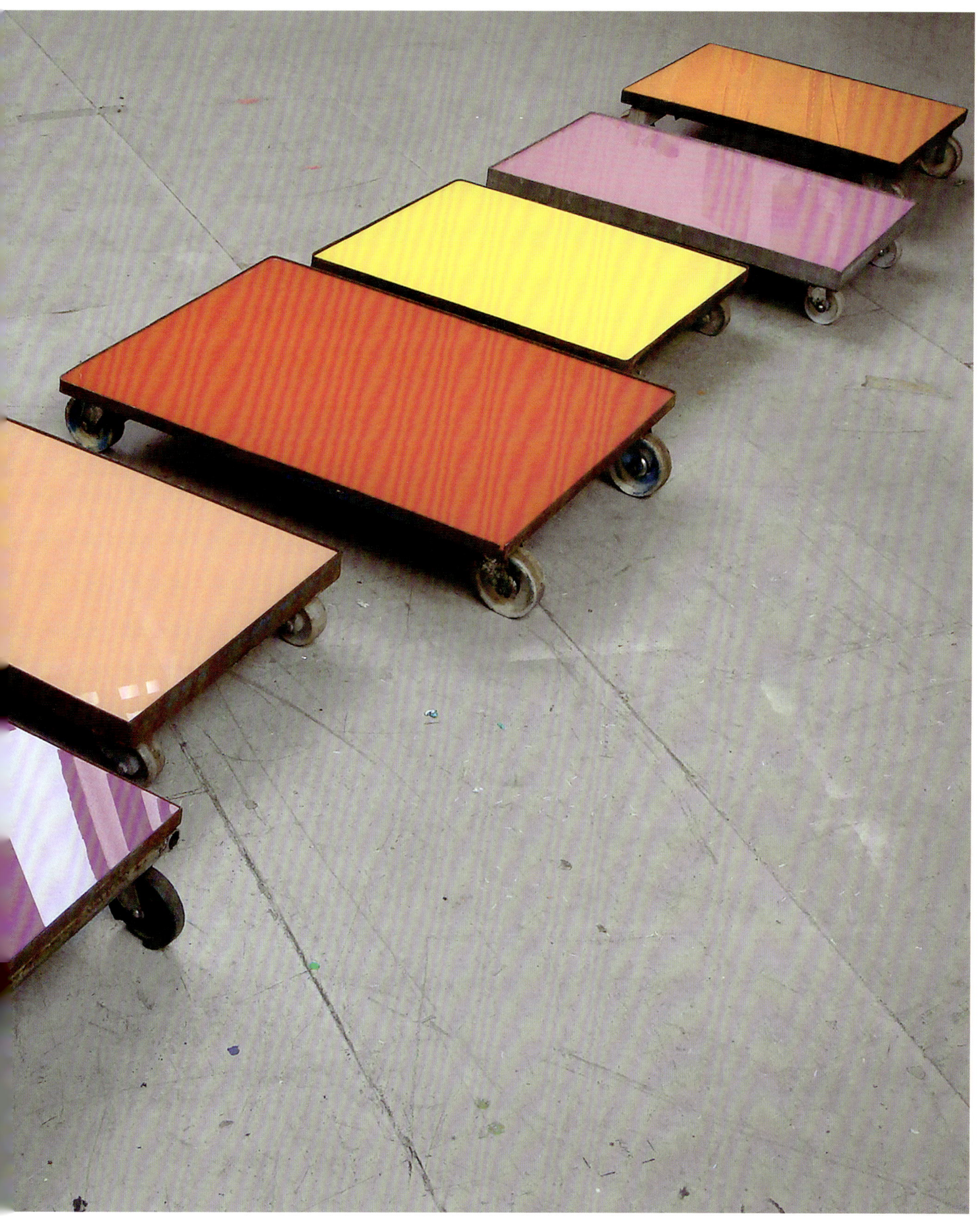

Peter Sedgley 1930–

Peter Sedgley is a self-taught artist who has devoted his career to explorations of colour and light. Having originally trained as an architect, Sedgley was to have been involved in the postwar rebuilding plans for Britain but resigned in protest, as he considered the plans too conservative in their attempts to recreate rather than innovate. He subsequently served in the Royal Air Force as a radar technician, and helped found a construction co-operative, before becoming an artist. Early in his artistic career, Sedgley began a series of what he later referred to as *Target Paintings*, in which he investigated colour theories espoused by Johann Wolfgang von Goethe (1749–1832) and Paul Klee (1879–1940). *Colour Cycle III* is part of this series, in which the canvas is painted with concentric circles of different colours.

Viewed in a darkened space, the work is lit by lights of changing colour in a programmed sequence. This creates a dialogue between colour illumination and the painted surface, the interaction between colour and light radically transforming what the naked eye perceives. Sedgley later stated that 'a cold light intensified some colours in my painting and modulated others and warm colours did the contrary, at the same time gave an apparent movement ... Something akin to tuning up a musical instrument.'[24] He conceived this work as an antidote to the assault on our senses by the commercial world, postulating that artists must utilise light to explore new landscapes, and in doing so, extend the practice of sculpture and painting.

Colour Cycle III 1970
Acrylic paint on canvas
184.1 × 182.9

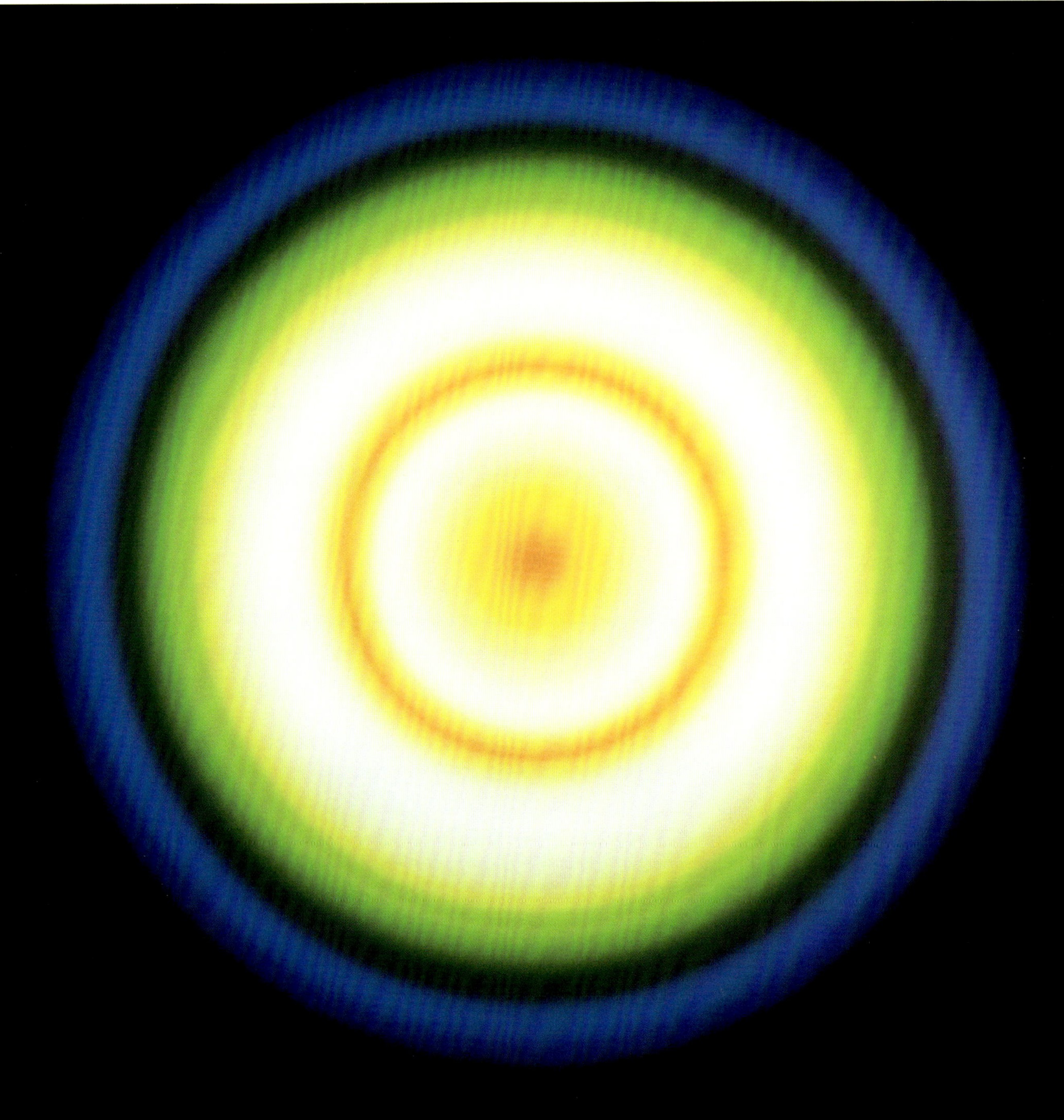

Olafur Eliasson 1967–

Olafur Eliasson has been investigating the artistic and scientific properties of light and colour since his student days at the Royal Danish Academy of Arts in Copenhagen (1989–1995), interests that remain central to his practice alongside social and environmental issues. In addition to physics and geometry, the Danish-Icelandic artist has drawn much inspiration from the light experiments of early twentieth-century European artists such as László Moholy-Nagy (1895–1946), as well as American pioneers including Robert Irwin (1928–), Douglas Wheeler (1939–) and James Turrell (1943–), who began investigating the material and immaterial properties of light in the 1960s and 1970s. In this work Eliasson seeks to explode the 'psychological and associative potential' of abstracted colour, and in doing so to highlight the 'extreme' differences in how individuals experience colours. He has explained that 'colour doesn't exist in itself, [it exists] only when looked at. The fact that "colour", uniquely, only materializes when light bounces off it into our retina indicates that analysing colours is in fact about analysing ourselves.'[25] Installed in a darkened room, *Yellow versus Purple* comprises a transparent yellow disc of colour-effect glass, suspended from a steel cable linked to a motor, and a floodlight. The light shining through the rotating disc makes a yellow shape on the wall while a special filter on the glass reflects the light and creates a purple shape that changes size as it orbits the room. Viewers can walk through the installation so that the shapes and colours cover their bodies. Visitors are not only viewers, but 'become projection surfaces themselves, which means they are simultaneously both subject and object'.[26] The choice of colours for *Yellow versus Purple*, and the title's playful suggestion of competition between them, reflects the fact that they occupy opposite positions on the colour wheel.

Yellow versus Purple 2003
Colour-effect filter glass, spotlight, tripod, motor, wire
Object diam. 75 cm; display dimensions variable

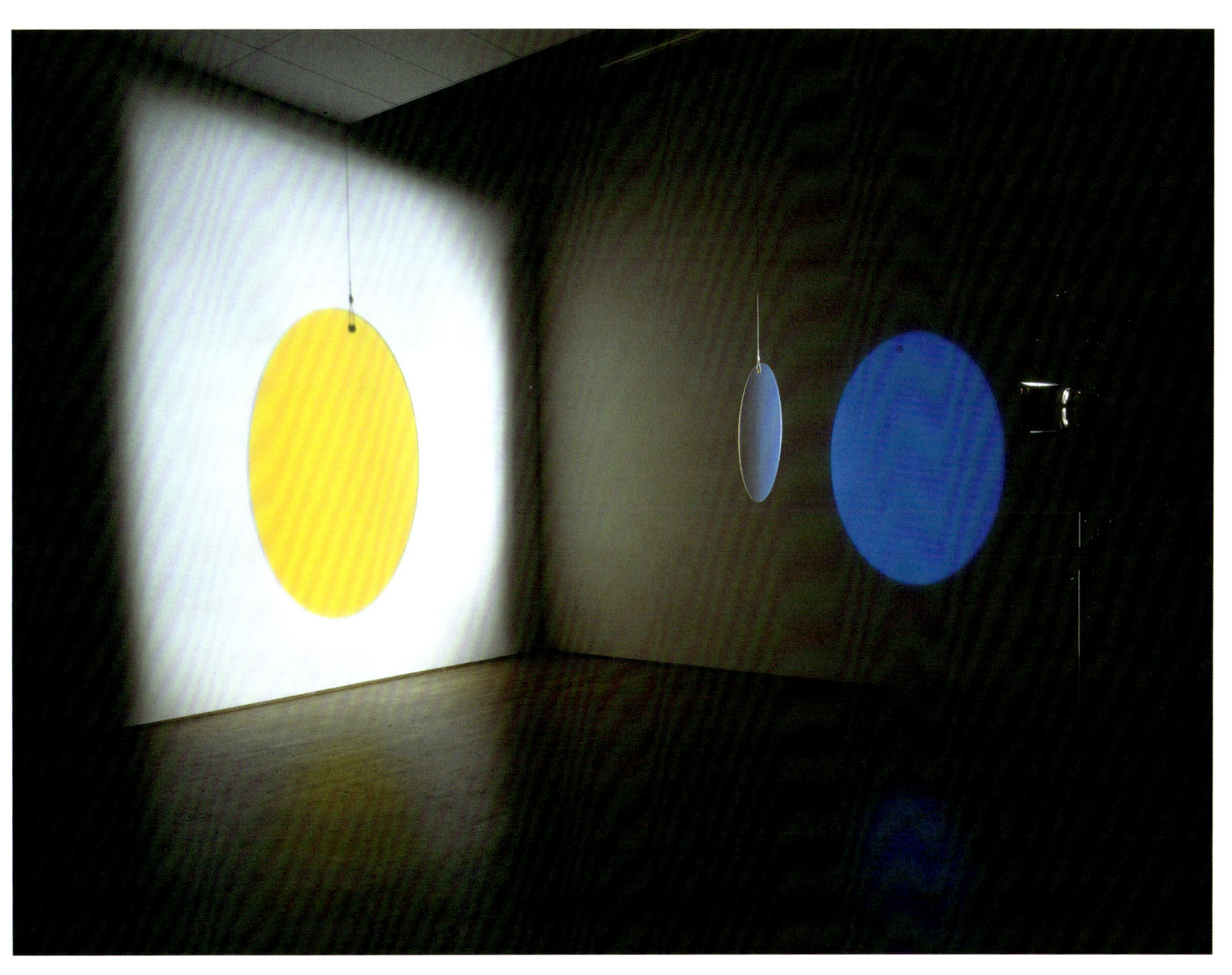

Catherine Yass 1963–

In 1994 Catherine Yass was commissioned to make a series of images for Springfield Hospital, a psychiatric hospital in London, with a history of using photography as a tool to classify mental illness according to its physical manifestations. To subvert this, Yass made six anonymous portraits of patients and hospital workers and mixed these together. The photographs used in *Corridors* were intended as backgrounds to these portraits. However, Yass became interested in the empty spaces as images in and of themselves, perceiving them as even more disorientating to the viewer without their intended subjects. She uses lightboxes to enhance this effect. The photographs are in sharp focus only in the foreground of the image, at the level of the corridor walls, and have been taken with a shallow depth of field. In most images the centre dissolves into an intense blue glow. Blue light, similar in shade to 'Chartres blue', a long-lasting blue stained-glass developed in the 1100s in France for church windows, has become a signature element of Yass's work. She creates these images by taking two photographs of her subject within seconds of each other and superimposing them. One is a 'positive' image, the normal form of a photographic image, and the other is a 'negative' image, where light and dark are inverted as on the negative of a photographic print. Yass has explained: 'I think of the space between positive and negative images as a gap.'[27] She has described this gap as 'an empty space left for the viewer to fall into'.[28]

Opposite and overleaf: *Corridors* 1994
Photographs, dye destruction prints on transparencies on lightboxes
89 × 72.5 × 14

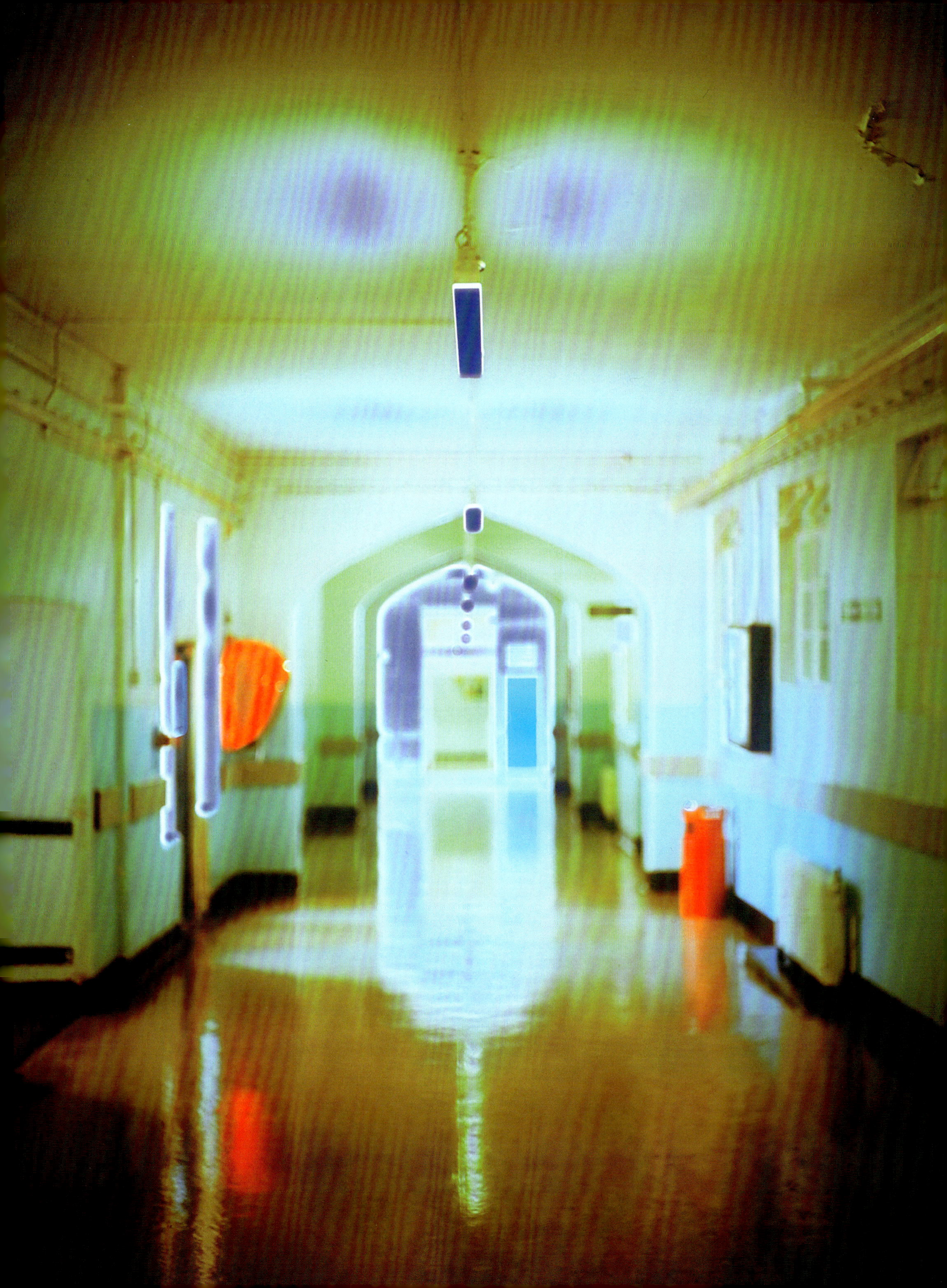

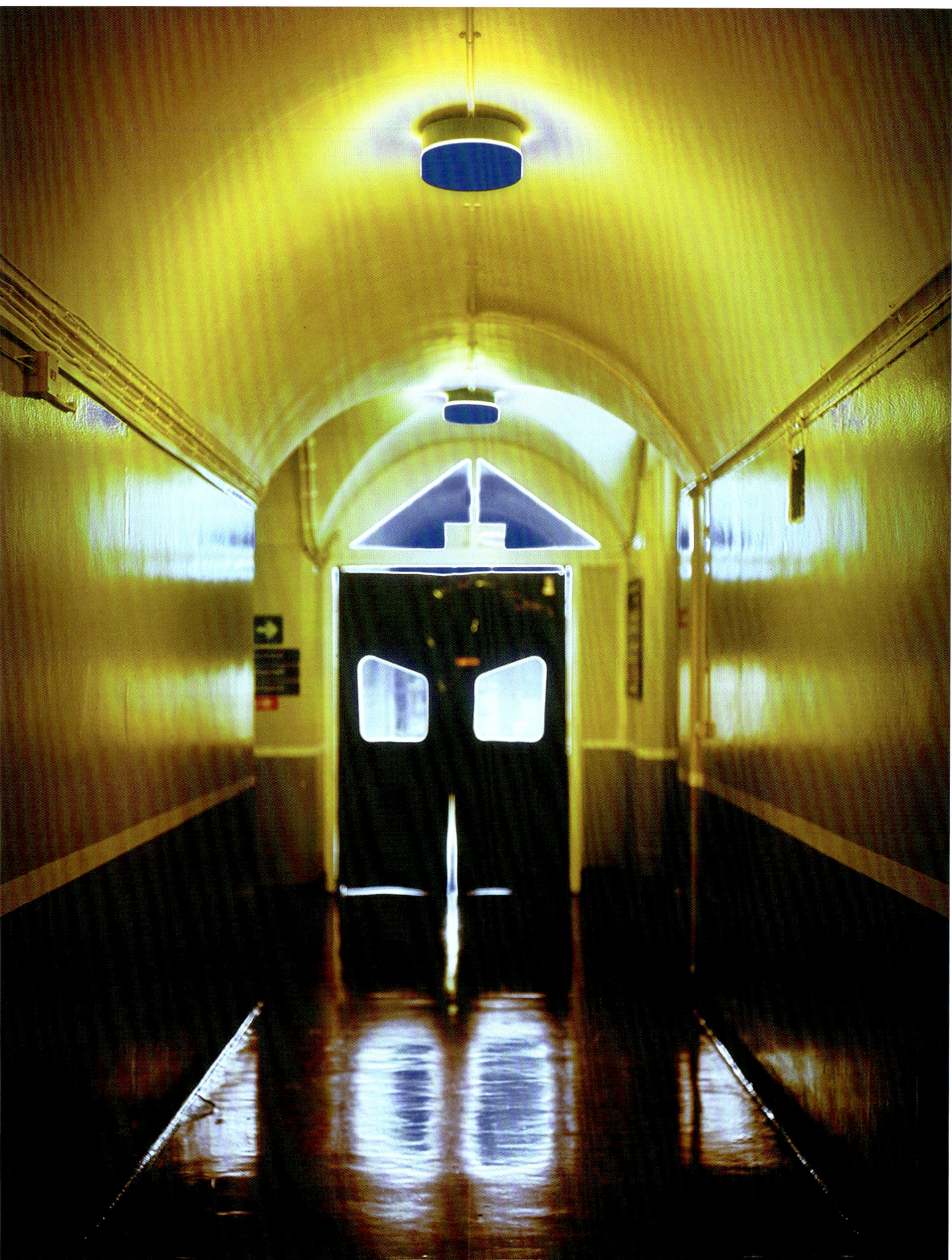

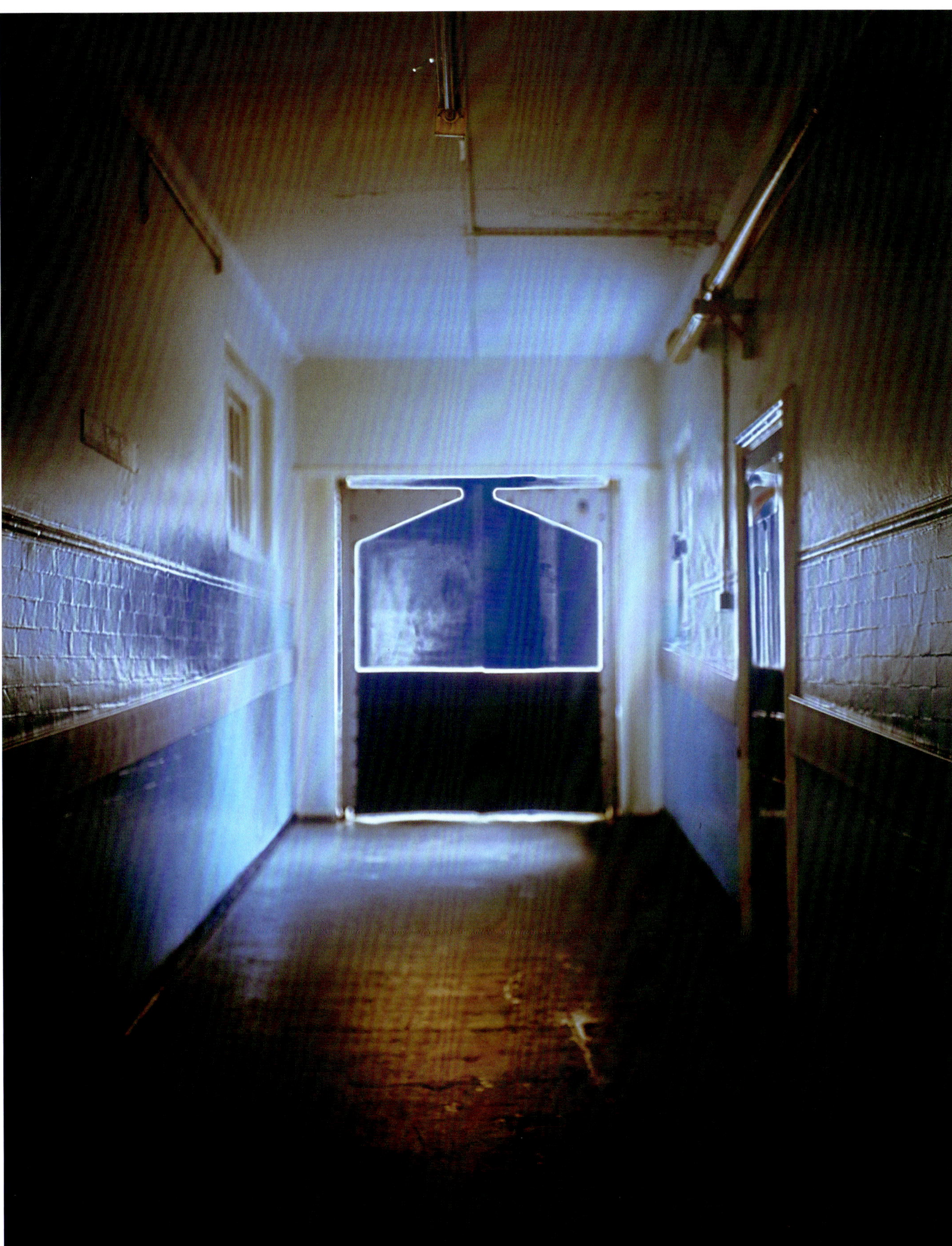

Expansive Light

Whether depicting a starry night sky, capturing a golden sunset on film, or immersing viewers in the warm glow of artificial illumination, contemporary artists have explored the role that light plays in revealing the expansiveness of our universe and the precariousness of our place within it. Lis Rhodes (1942–) and James Turrell (1943–) have made installations in which light envelops viewers, causing them to become a part of the work as they engage with it. Other artists employ reflective surfaces that emphasise the presence of light. Olafur Eliasson (1967–) has used such strategies in works that change the appearance of gallery architecture depending on the position of the viewer, reminding us that our actions, however small, have an impact on the world around us. The experience of light in the vast landscapes of the American West informed the photorealist drawings and prints for which Vija Celmins (1938–) is celebrated. Her painstakingly crafted images of cloud-filled skies, distant galaxies, parched deserts and choppy seas portray the immensity of the natural world, while also speaking to its indifference towards humanity. This theme is also present in the 16mm films made by Tacita Dean (1965–); her *Disappearance at Sea* 1996 contrasts the fading light of the sun setting over the ocean, with a coastal lighthouse beacon to comment on the fragility of life and the perils of the sea.

James Turrell 1943–

James Turrell, an avid pilot, works directly with light and space to create artworks that engage with atmospheric conditions. Having trained in perceptual psychology, Turrell began experimenting with light as a pure medium in the mid-1960s. The greatest expression of this is arguably Turrell's series of over eighty *Skyspaces*, conceived as an aperture installed in the gallery ceiling which allows viewers to witness the sky decontextualised of the horizon line; a pure expression of light and colour. Working with light as a medium, Turrell explains: 'My work has no object, no image and no focus. With no object, no image and no focus, what are you looking at? You are looking at you looking.'[29] *Raemar, Blue* is one of the earliest and most significant of Turrell's *Shallow Space Constructions*, works which combine architecture, sculpture, light and space to envelop the viewer in a coloured atmosphere that plays with the experience of perception and the effect of light in space. Blue light radiates from fluorescent tubes placed behind a partition, causing the partition to appear to float at the back of the gallery. Turrell found inspiration from his experience as a pilot: 'As you fly, you do see space that is determined not so much by physical confines, but by atmospheric and light phenomena within the space.'[30] His light installations are intended to produce a state of self-reflection and contemplation, encouraging viewers to become aware of the process of looking and the limits of perception.

Raemar, Blue 1969
Fluorescent light
Dimensions variable

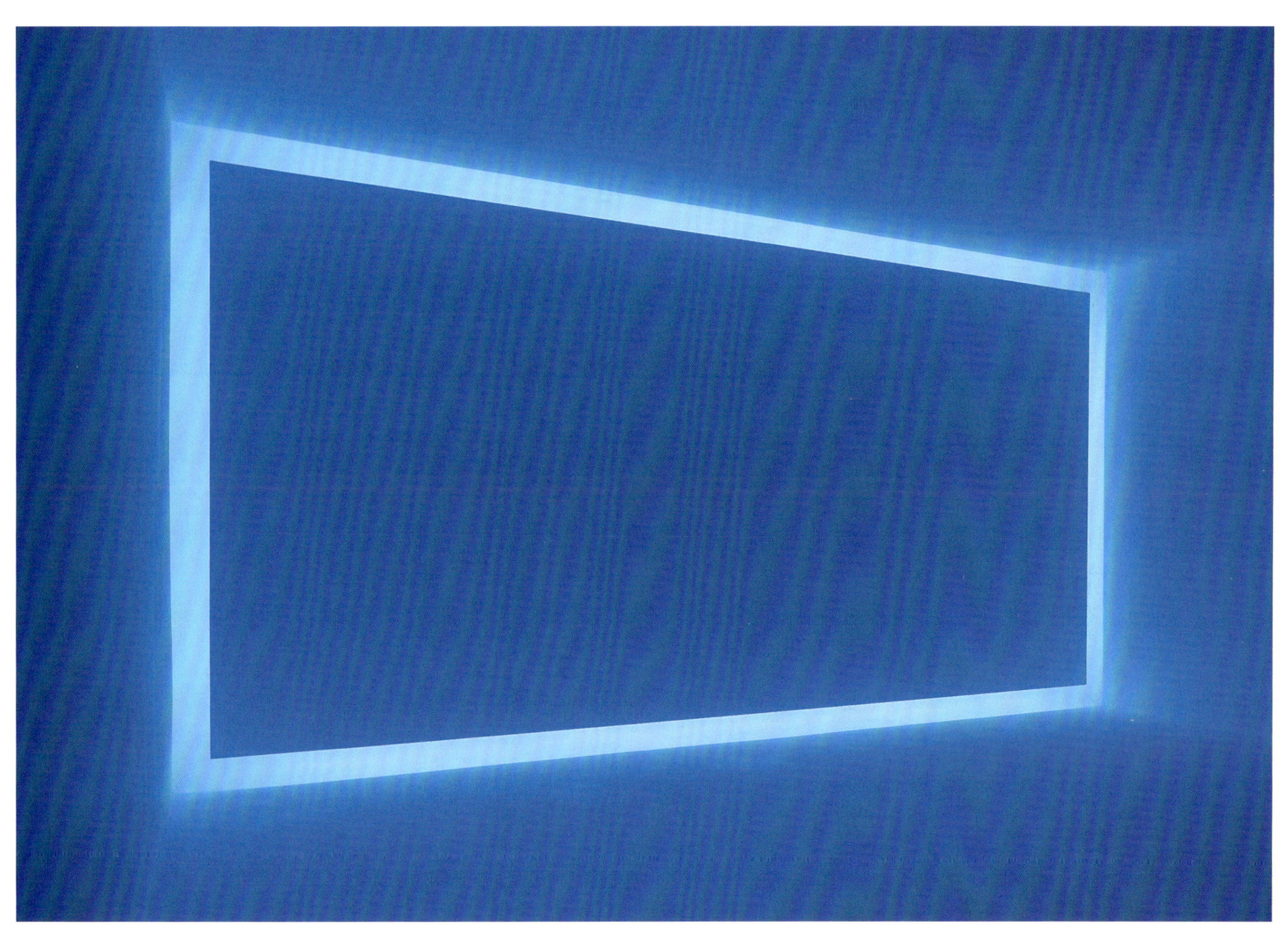

Lis Rhodes 1942–

Lis Rhodes began to incorporate performance, photography, text and spoken word into films in the late 1960s, while working as the cinema curator at the London Film-Makers' Co-op. There, alongside colleagues Peter Gidal (1946–) and Malcolm Le Grice (1940–), Rhodes helped to define the terms of film practice and discourse. Her works voice feminist ideas in relation to dominant cultural practices, and she has been instrumental in drawing attention to the lack of women's representation in the arts and filmmaking. *Light Music* is a seminal exploration of 16mm optical sound and expanded cinema. Rhodes adhered Letraset typefaces to the filmstrip, producing an onscreen abstraction of lines that is also read by the projector as audio. This creates a direct indexical relationship between what is seen and what is heard, as the stuttering sound corresponds to the space between the lines appearing on the screens. The room in which the work is shown is usually also filled with haze, giving the crossing projection beams a sculptural quality. Viewers are encouraged to move between the screens, engaging directly with the artwork. This is an early example of expanded cinema, where the viewer is both spectator and participant.

Light Music 1975
Film; 16mm, shown as video; 2 projections, black and white, and sound (dual mono)
25 min

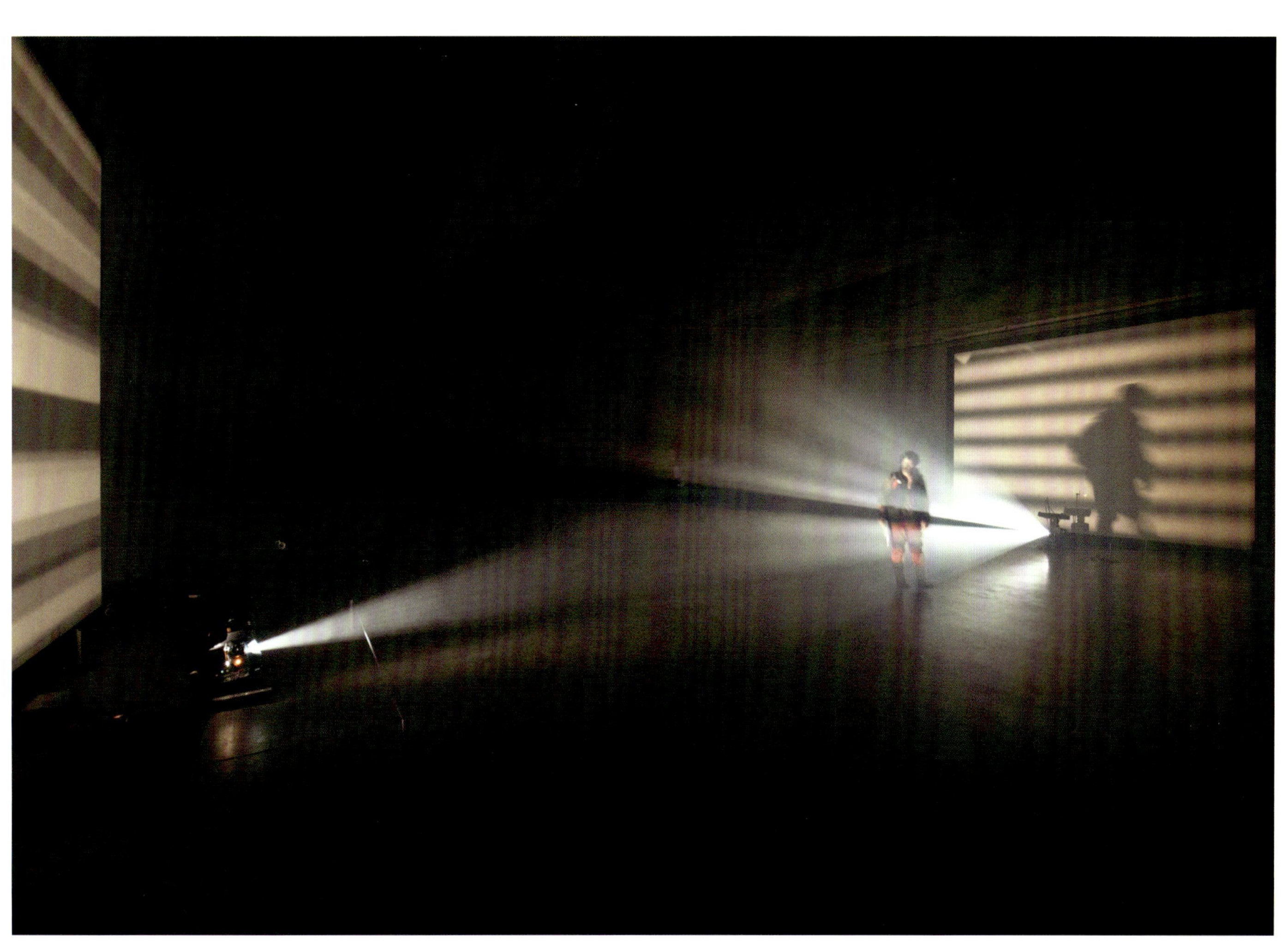

Olafur Eliasson 1967–

Light and colour have remained cornerstones of Eliasson's practice, as both media and subject matter. Initially it was the artistic and scientific properties of light and colour that were his primary interest; from 2003 onwards, however, he became more concerned with their psychological and physical effects – at their simplest, how light and colour can manipulate how one feels in a particular environment. His sculptures and large-scale light installations use light to alter the experience of space and architecture. For *Stardust particle*, Eliasson embedded a large, spherical polyhedron made of partially reflective glass into a larger, steel-frame polyhedron. The crystalline structure evokes the form of a greatly enlarged stardust particle – a remnant of an exploded star. Suspended from a motor, the translucent artwork rotates and glints like a mirrorball, throwing patterns of reflected light around the space in which it hangs. An adjacent spotlight pointed at the sculpture casts complex geometrical shadows, adding to the mesmerising effect. *Stardust particle* is similar in composition and operation to an earlier work, *Yellow versus Purple* 2003 (p.179), though it creates a different effect. *Stardust particle* was conceived for and first shown in the artist's solo exhibition *Contact* at Fondation Louis Vuitton, Paris, in 2014–15, in which Eliasson proposed contact as a form of social inclusion. He has said: 'Contact is not a picture, it is not a representation; it is about your ability to reach out, connect, and perhaps even put yourself in another person's place. For me, contact is where inclusion begins.'[31]

Stardust particle 2014
Stainless steel, translucent mirror-filter glass, wire, motor, spotlight
Diam. 176 cm

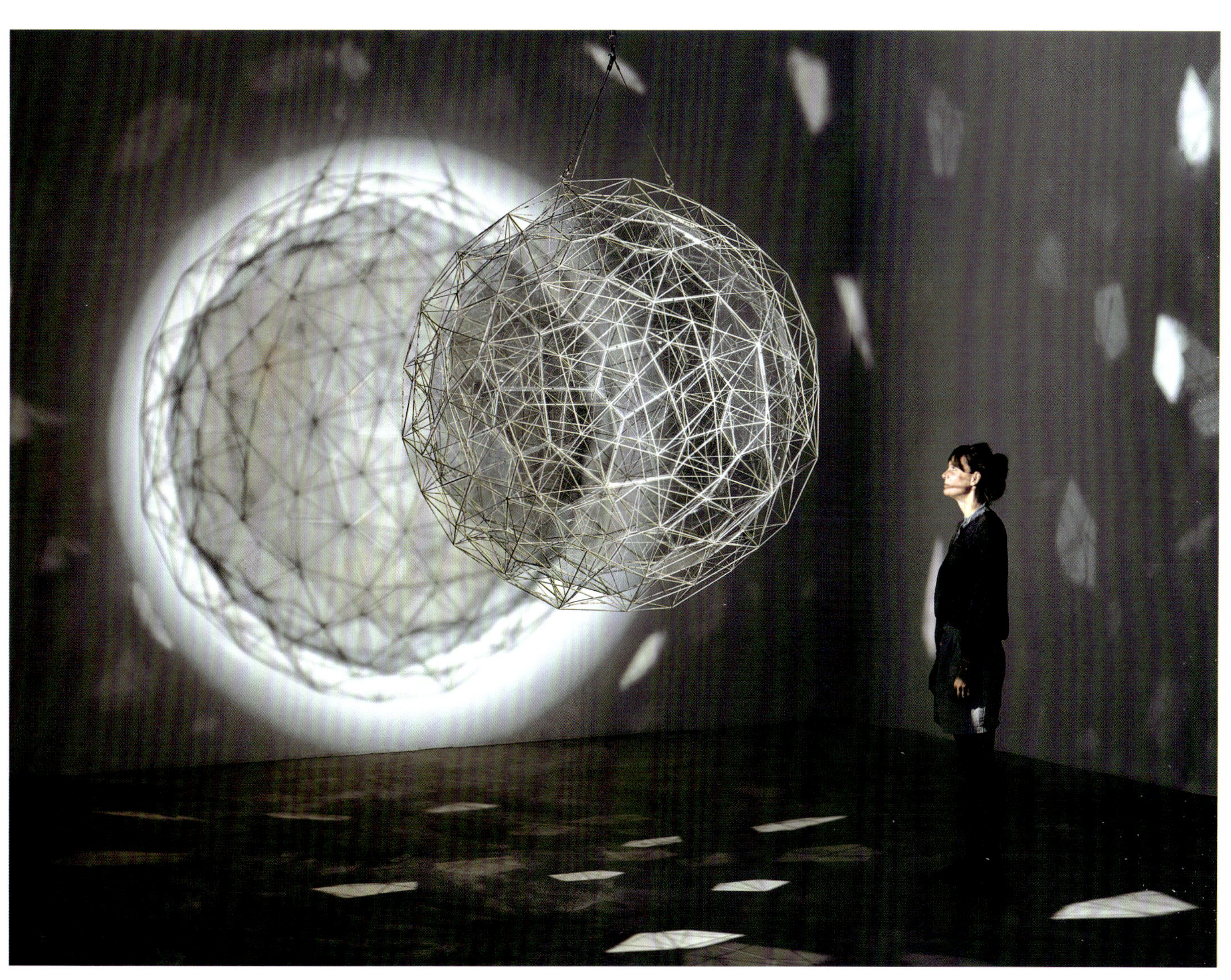

Vija Celmins 1938–

These four lithographs by Vija Celmins are derived from a series of meticulous, labour-intensive pencil drawings that the Latvian-American artist made in the 1970s. Rendered with exacting detail in a reduced palette of grey tones, each one shows an aspect of the natural environment under different lighting conditions. *Sky* depicts cumulus clouds drifting in a bright daytime sky, while *Galaxy* (the only image to depict light sources) shows a dark night sky illuminated by millions of burning stars, each one as powerful as our own sun yet millions of miles away from the earth. *Ocean* captures the light falling and glinting on the churning Pacific Ocean; the contrast between light and shadow gives definition to the mass of choppy waves. Similarly, in *Desert*, strong shadows enliven the stony ground of the arid Mojave Desert in south-eastern California. Light is central to these images, and although the vast spaces depicted are suggestive of freedom, they are simultaneously imbued with a sense of loneliness. This is emphasised by the photographic nature of the prints, where cropping lends them an abstract and impersonal quality. Celmins has always been interested in light, a theme that manifests itself in various ways in her drawings and paintings, combining pop art's interest in everyday life with the techniques of photorealism. However, it was her experiences of the vast landscapes of the American West while living in California in the 1970s that made her more sensitive to the effect of natural light on the landscape.

Opposite, top left: *Sky* 1975
Lithograph on paper
31.5 × 42

Opposite, top right: *Galaxy* 1975
Lithograph on paper
31.7 × 41.8

Opposite, below left: *Ocean* 1975
Lithograph on paper
31.7 × 42

Opposite, below right: *Desert* 1975
Lithograph on paper
31.5 × 41.6

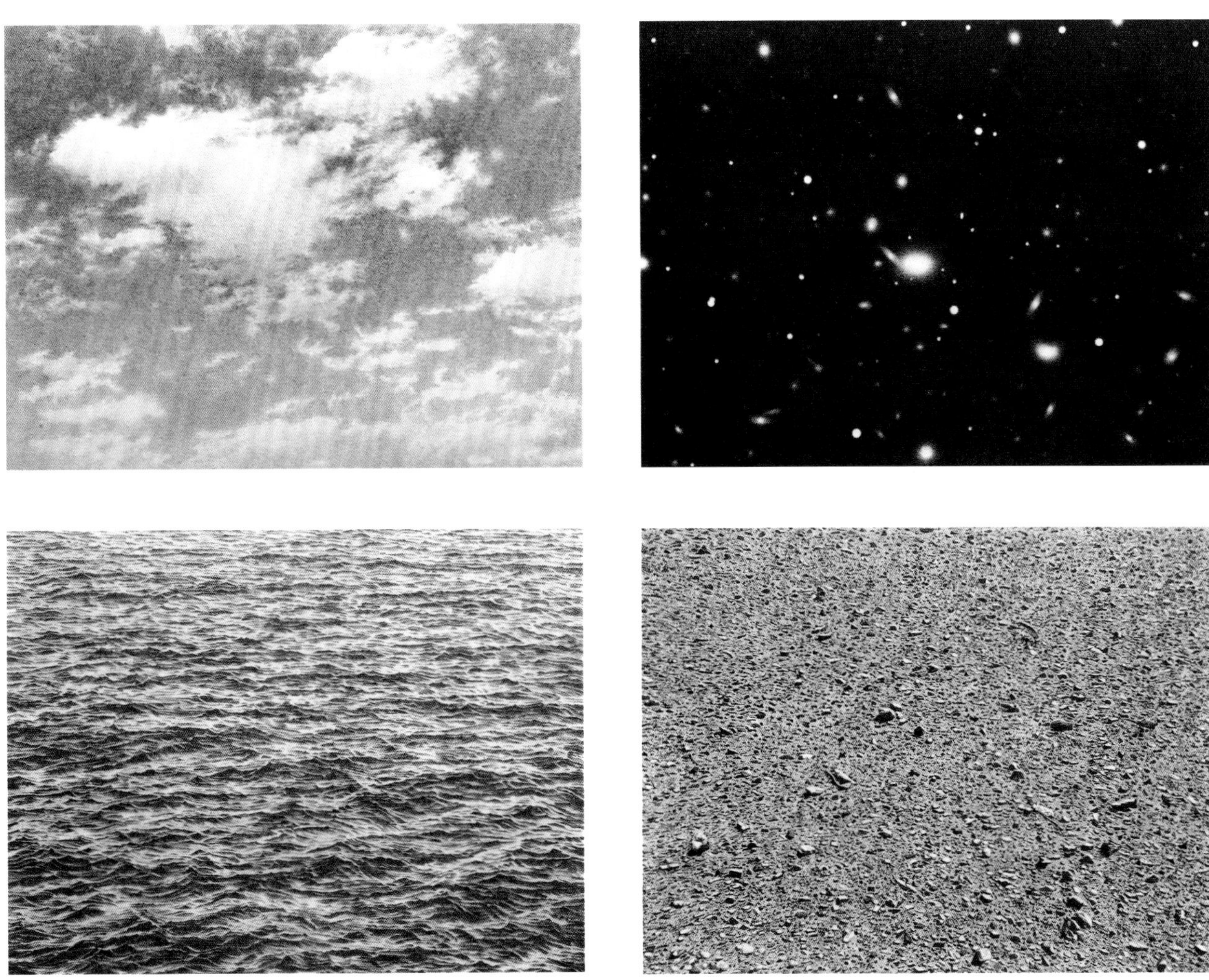

Tacita Dean 1965–

After training as a painter, Tacita Dean began making films in 1992, producing works characterised by long takes and an exploration of narrative, memory and history. Her continued interest in the relationship between filmic technology and notions of obsolescence can be seen in works such as *Kodak* 2006, which was shot at the Kodak factory in eastern France using the last 16mm film stock produced there. *Disappearance at Sea* is a 16mm colour film with sound shot at the lighthouse on St Abb's Head in Berwick-upon-Tweed in northern England. Shown on a loop, the fourteen-minute film consists of seven lengthy shots captured by a static camera that alternate between close-ups of the rotating lighthouse bulbs and footage looking out to sea. As the film progresses the scene changes from dusk to nightfall, with the colour of the sky shifting through a range of yellows, reds and purples. The film was inspired by the story of Donald Crowhurst (1932–1969), a British businessman and amateur sailor who died while attempting a voyage around the world during which he falsified his progress. In 1997 Dean explained how she interpreted Crowhurst's expedition: 'His story is about human failing; about pitching his sanity against the sea.'[32] The 'disappearance' referred to in the work's title is an allusion both to Crowhurst's death and to the sunset and eventual darkness the film depicts. Dean's fascination with the sea 'can be traced back to 1700s notions of the sublime, where elemental forces were viewed as emblems of turbulent and ungovernable human emotions'.[33]

Disappearance at Sea 1996
16mm colour anamorphic film, optical sound
14 min

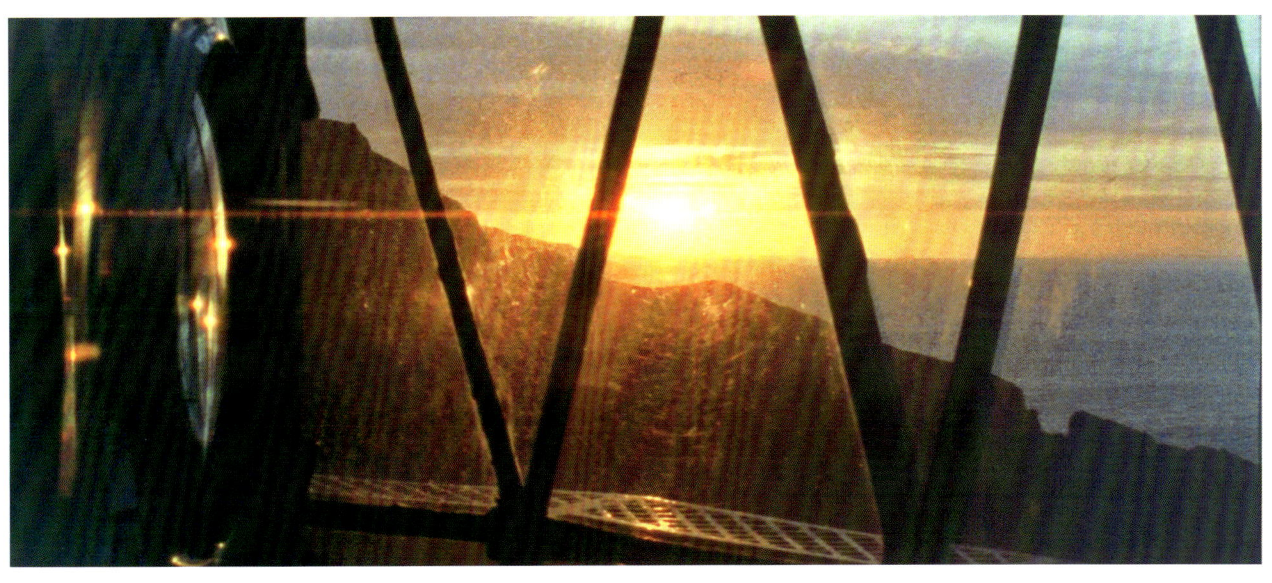

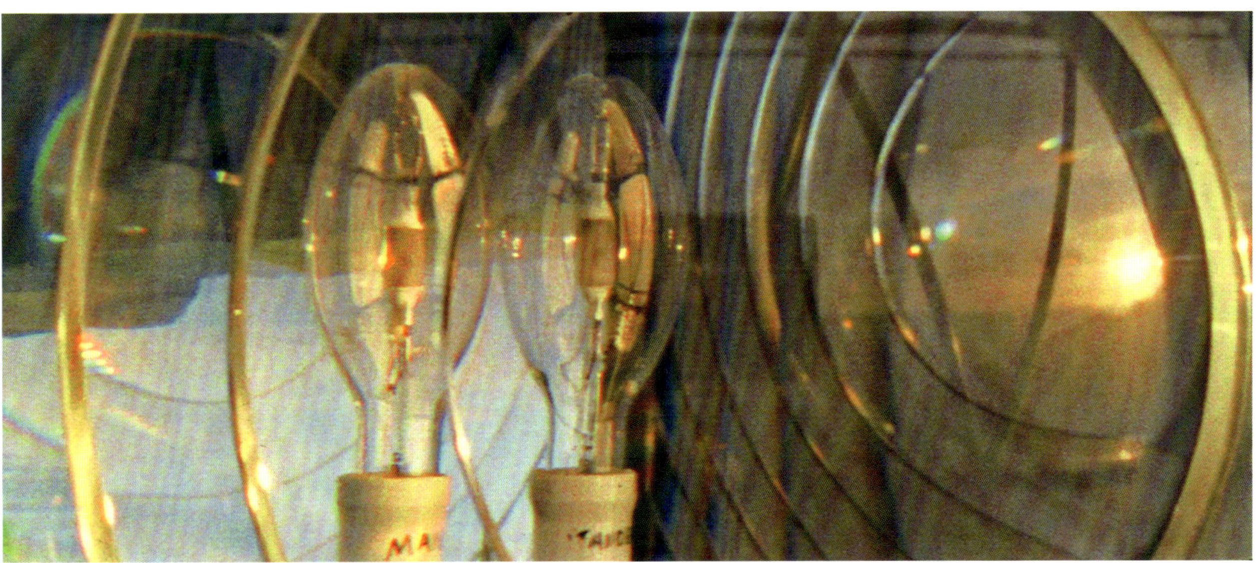

Notes

The Colours of Light, pp.8–31

1 René Descartes, *The World*, or *Treatise on Light*, translated by Michael S. Mahoney, https://www.princeton.edu/~hos/mike/texts/descartes/world/worldfr.htm, accessed 12 October 2020.

2 Christiaan Huygens, *Traité de la lumière ...*, Leiden 1690.

3 Isaac Newton, *Opticks*, London 1704.

4 Andreas Blühm and Louise Lippincott, *Light! The Industrial Age 1750–1900: Art & Science, Technology & Society*, New York 2001, p.46.

5 Ibid.

6 William Blake *Newton* 1795–c.1805. Colour print, ink and watercolour on paper 46 × 60. Tate. Presented by W. Graham Robertson 1939. N05058.

7 Blühm and Lippincott, p.60.

8 For example, 'You, Lord, are my lamp; the Lord turns my darkness into light' (Psalms 18:28). God 'reveals the deep things of darkness and brings utter darkness into the light' (Job 12:22). 'The commands of the Lord are radiant, giving light to the eyes' (Psalms 19:8).

9 Using steam power to run the machinery and replacing the printing flatbed with the rotary motion of cylinders altered the design of the printing press radically between 1802 and 1818.

10 The nineteenth century saw a serious campaign against the churches by the secularist movement. In the United Kingdom, the principal target was the state church, the Church of England, which was highly privileged and controlled key aspects of public life. For example, until 1828 no one could hold a public office without signing up to the beliefs of the Church.

11 Michaela Giebelhausen, *Painting the Bible: Representation and Belief in Mid-Victorian Britain*, Aldershot and Burlington, VT 2006, p.33.

12 Ibid., p.185.

13 John 8:12.

14 Matthew 5:16.

15 The original painting (1853) can be found in the side chapel at Keble College, Oxford. A second, smaller version (1851–6) is in the Manchester Art Gallery collection, while the final and largest version (c.1900–4) hangs in St Paul's Cathedral, London.

16 Claude Barbre, 'Constable's Skies', *Journal of Religion and Health*, vol.43, no.4, 2004, pp.390–2. http://www.jstor.org/stable/27512823, accessed 13 October 2020.

17 Catalogue entry for John Constable, *Cloud Study* 1822, https://www.tate.org.uk/art/artworks/constable-cloud-study-n06065, accessed 9 October 2020.

18 Joseph Jean Pichot, *Historical and Literary Tour of a Foreigner in England*, vol.1, London 1825, p.123.

19 Cian Duffy, 'Mount Vesuvius', *European Romanticisms in Association*, posted 3 April 2020, http://www.euromanticism.org/mount-vesuvius/, accessed 12 October 2020.

20 Catalogue entry for *Joseph Wright of Derby, Vesuvius in Eruption, with a View over the Islands in the Bay of Naples*, https://www.tate.org.uk/art/artworks/wright-vesuvius-in-eruption-with-a-view-over-the-islands-in-the-bay-of-naples-t05846, accessed 12 October 2020.

21 *Art Journal*, 1890, p.218, quoted in catalogue entry for John Everett Millais, '*The Moon is Up, and Yet it is not Night*' 1890, https://www.tate.org.uk/art/artworks/millais-the-moon-is-up-and-yet-it-is-not-night-n05632, accessed 19 October 2020.

22 Sue Roe, *The Private Lives of the Impressionists*, London 2007, p.129.

23 In a letter to Alice Monet dated 29 March 1893, Monet wrote of having worked on fourteen paintings in one day at Rouen and in 1918 talked of light effects which lasted 'sometimes three or four minutes at the most'. John House, *Monet: Nature into Art*, London 1986, pp.144 and 204.

24 https://en.wikipedia.org/wiki/Michel_Eugène_Chevreul, accessed 20 October 2020.

25 Ogden Rood, *Modern Chromatics, with Applications to Art and Industry*, published in 1879, with German and French translations appearing in 1880 and 1881, respectively.

26 *The Bridge at Courbevoie* 1886–7, https://www.beyondthelabel.info/artwork/the-bridge-at-courbevoie-1886-87/73/, accessed 19 October 2020.

27 Ibid.

28 https://courtauld.ac.uk/gallery/what-on/exhibitions-displays/archive/bridget-riley-learning-from-seurat, accessed 20 October 2020.

29 Catalogue entry for Bridget Riley *Late Morning* 1967–8, https://www.tate.org.uk/art/artworks/riley-late-morning-t01032, accessed 20 October 2020.

30 'Daguerreotype', https://www.britannica.com/technology/photography/Daguerreotype#ref416337, accessed 5 November 2020.

31 Elizabeth Palermo, 'Who Invented the Light Bulb', *Live Science*, 17 August 2017, https://www.livescience.com/43424-who-invented-the-light-bulb.html, accessed 23 October 2020.

32 Blühm and Lippincott, p.242.

33 Walter Gropius, 'Program of the Staatliche Bauhaus in Weimar', 1919, https://bauhausmanifesto.com, accessed 23 October 2020.

34 Josef Albers, *Interaction of Color*, revised and expanded edn, New Haven and London 2006, p.8.

35 Ibid. p.1.

36 Walter Gropius and Arthur S. Wensinger (eds), translated by Arthur S. Wensinger, *The Theater of the Bauhaus*, Middletown, CT 1961, p. 67, https://monoskop.org/images/a/a7/Gropius_Walter_ed_The_Theater_of_the_Bauhaus.pdf, accessed 29 October 2020.

37 Department of Photographs, The Metropolitan Museum of Art, 'Photography at the Bauhaus', *Heilbrunn Timeline of Art History*, October 2004, https://www.metmuseum.org/toah/hd/phbh/hd_phbh.htm, accessed 29 October 2020.

38 Nan R. Piene, 'Light Art', *Art in America*, May–June 1967, p.26.

39 László Moholy-Nagy, from John Szarkowski, *Looking at Photographs*, https://www.atgetphotography.com/The-Photographers/Laszlo-Moholy-Nagy.html, accessed 29 October 2020.

40 During the same period, Man Ray (1890–1976), working in Paris, also shone light on objects lying on photosensitive paper and called the printed result 'Rayographs'.

41 Piene, p.27.

42 '*Light Prop for an Electric Stage*: Past and Present', *Harvard Art Museums*, https://www.youtube.com/watch?v=gg5bahsq65A, accessed 3 November 2020.

43 https://en.wikipedia.org/wiki/Dan_Flavin#cite_note-17, accessed 4 November 2020.

44 Piene, p.30.

45 https://jamesturrell.com/about/introduction/, accessed 5 November 2020.

46 https://www.moma.org/audio/playlist/2/212, accessed 5 November 2020.

Artwork entries, pp.36–195

1 Geoffrey Keynes, *The Complete Writings of Blake*, London 1957, pp.224–5.

2 Martin Butlin, *William Blake 1757–1827*, Tate Gallery Collections, Vol.5, London 1990.

3 Johann Caspar Lavater, *Essays on Physiognomy*, 20th edn. Originally published by Thomas Tegg, London 1844, p.116.

4 David Irwin, 'Jacob More, Neo-Classical Landscape Painter', *The Burlington Magazine* 114, no.836 (1972), pp.775–9. www.jstor.org/stable/877183. Accessed 3 June 2020.

5 Turner's choice of subject may have been partly suggested by the leading English art critic of the Victorian era, John Ruskin's (1819–1900) reference to him as 'the great angel of the Apocalypse'.

6 Joseph Wright of Derby, *Vesuvius in Eruption, with a View over the Islands in the Bay of Naples* c.1776–80, in Nigel Llewellyn and Christine Riding (eds), *The Art of the Sublime*, Tate Research Publication, January 2013, https://www.tate.org.uk/art/research-publications/the-sublime/joseph-wright-of-derby-vesuvius-in-eruption-with-a-view-over-the-islands-in-the-bay-of-r1105581, accessed 2 August 2020.

7 Christopher Wood, *Victorian Painting*, Boston 1999, p.19.

8 Johann Wolfgang von Goethe, *Theory of Colours*, trans. Charles Lock Eastlake, Oxford 1840, p.777 (original), p.310 (translation).

9 Martin Butlin and Evelyn Joll, *The Paintings of J.M.W. Turner*, revised edn, New Haven and London 1984, pp.229–30.

10 Sisley, cited in R. Goldwater et al. (eds), *Artists on Art: From the Fourteenth to the Twentieth Centuries*, London 1976, pp.300–10.

11 Elizabeth Prettejohn, *The Art of the Pre-Raphaelites*, London 2000, pp.192–3.

12 Cornwall Artists Index, http://cornwallartists.org/cornwall-artists/frank-bramley, accessed 4 September 2020.

13 Mary Chamot, Dennis Farr and Martin Butlin, *The Modern British Paintings, Drawings and Sculpture*, Vol.2, London 1964.

14 J.M.W. Turner, 'Royal Academy Lectures', c.1807–38, Department of Western Manuscripts, British Library, London, ADD MS 46151 O ff.8 verso–11 verso. For an earlier version of this material, see BL MS H ff.10–14.

15 Ronald Alley, *Catalogue of the Tate Gallery's Collection of Modern Art other than Works by British Artists*, Tate Gallery and Sotheby Parke-Bernet, London 1981, pp.441–6, reproduced p.441.

16 László Moholy-Nagy, 'Photography is Manipulation of Light', *Photographische Korrespondenz*, vol.64, no.5, 1 May 1928. Translated in Andreas Haus, *Moholy-Nagy: Fotos und Fotogramme*, Munich 1978, p.48.

17 Yayoi Kusama, *Infinity Net: The Autobiography of Yayoi Kusama*, London 2011, p.69.

18 Chris Stephens and Katherine Stout (eds), *Art & the 60s: This Was Tomorrow*, London 2004, p.40.

19 Pae White website, https://www.1301pe.com/pae-white, accessed 4 September 2020.

20 Quoted in Alex Farquharson, 'About the Exhibition', https://hammer.ucla.edu/exhibitions/2004/hammer-projects-pae-white, accessed 21 September 2020.

21 Email to Tate curator Evi Baniotopoulou, 29 October 2004, Tate Gallery Records.

22 Ibid.

23 Ibid.

24 The Redfern Gallery, https://www.redfern-gallery.com/artists/66-peter-sedgley/#/overview/, accessed 4 September 2020.

25 Olafur Eliasson, '447 Words on Colour, 2001', in Madeleine Grynsztejn, Daniel Birnbaum and Michael Speaks, *Olafur Eliasson*, London 2002, p.130.

26 Holger Broeker, 'Light – Space – Color: Olafur Eliasson's Experiment Set-ups with Light', in exh. cat., Kunstmuseum Wolfsburg 2004, p.50.

27 Parveen Adams and Greg Hilty, *Catherine Yass: Works 1994–2000*, London 2000, pp.8, 84, reproduced (colour) p.81.

28 Ibid., reproduced (colour) p.84.

29 James Turrell website, http://jamesturrell.com/about/introduction/, accessed 4 September 2020.

30 Quoted in Richard Whittaker, 'Greeting the Light: An Interview with James Turrell', 1999, http://www.conversations.org/story.php?sid=32, accessed 4 September 2020.

31 Artist's statement, *Contact*, Fondation Louis Vuitton, Paris, 2014, http://www.fondationlouisvuitton.fr/en/expositions/exposition-olafur-eliasson-contact.html, accessed 4 September 2020.

32 Quoted in *Tacita Dean: Missing Narratives*, exh. cat., Frith Street Gallery, London 1997, p.17.

33 *Tacita Dean: Recent Films and Other Works*, exh. cat., Tate Britain, London 2001, p.9.

Further Reading

Parveen Adams and Greg Hilty, *Catherine Yass: Works 1994–2000*, London 2000.

Craig Adcock, *James Turrell: The Art of Light and Space*, Berkeley 1990.

Josef Albers, *Interaction of Color* [1963], revised and expanded edn, New Haven and London 2006.

Ronald Alley, *Catalogue of the Tate Gallery's Collection of Modern Art other than Works by British Artists*, Tate Gallery and Sotheby Parke-Bernet, London 1981.

Nicholas Baume (ed.), *Anish Kapoor: Past, Present, Future*, exh. cat., Institute of Contemporary Art, Boston 2008.

The British Art Show 4, exh. cat., Hayward Gallery, London 1995.

Martin Butlin and Evelyn Joll, *The Paintings of J.M.W. Turner*, revised edn, New Haven and London 1984.

Martin Butlin, *William Blake 1757–1827*, Tate Gallery Collections, Vol.5, London 1990.

J. Butterfield, *The Art of Light and Space*, Abbeville, New York 1993.

Germano Celant (ed.), *The Italian Metamorphosis 1943–1968*, exh. cat., Guggenheim Museum, New York 1994.

Mary Chamot, Dennis Farr and Martin Butlin, *The Modern British Paintings, Drawings and Sculpture*, Vol.2, London and New York 1964.

Martin Creed, *Martin Creed: Works*, London 2010.

Kathleen Crouan, *John Linnell: A Centennial Exhibition*, exh. cat., Fitzwilliam Museum, Cambridge 1982.

Directions: Virgil Marti and Pae White, exh. cat., Hirshhorn Museum and Sculpture Garden, Washington, D.C. 2007.

Judy Egerton, *Wright of Derby*, exh. cat., Tate Gallery, London 1991.

Olafur Eliasson and Philip Ursprung (eds), *Studio Olafur Eliasson: An Encyclopedia*, London 2016.

Olafur Eliasson, Gijs van Tuyl and Holger Broeker, *Your Lighthouse: Works with Light 1991–2004*, London 2004.

Alexander Farquharson, *Pae White*, exh. cat., Armand Hammer Museum of Art and Cultural Center, Los Angeles 2004.

William Feaver, *The Art of John Martin*, Oxford and New York 1975, pp.55–9.

Briony Fer, Robert Gober and Lane Relyea, *Vija Celmins*, London 2004.

John Gage, *Colour in Turner: Poetry and Truth*, London 1969.

J.W. von Goethe, *Theory of Colours* (C.L. Eastlake and J. Murray, trans. from German with notes), London 1840.

J.W. von Goethe, *Poetry and Truth*, Vol.1, London 1848.

Madeleine Grynsztejn (ed.), *Take Your Time: Olafur Eliasson*, exh. cat., San Francisco Museum of Modern Art, 2007.

Tone Hansen and Milena Hoegsberg (eds), *Josef Albers: No Tricks, No Twinkling of the Eyes*, exh. cat., Henie Onstad Kunstsenter, Oslo 2014.

Andreas Haus, *Moholy-Nagy: Photographs and Photograms*, trans. Frederic Samson, New York 1980.

Raoul Hausmann, Hans Arp, Ivan Puni, László Moholy-Nagy, 'Manifesto of Elemental art' (originally published as 'aufruf zur elementaren Kunst', *DE STIJL* No.10 [1921]), reprinted in Krisztina Passuth, *Moholy-Nagy*, London 1985.

Renate Heyne and Floris M. Neusüss (eds), *Moholy-Nagy: The Photograms, Catalogue Raisonné*, Ostfildern 2009.

Hospital Projects: Zarina Bhimji, Tania Kovats, Catherine Yass, Public Art Development Trust, London 1995.

Italian Photography 1930–1970s, exh. cat., Manezh Central Exhibition Centre, Moscow 2007.

James Turrell: Light & Space, exh. cat., Whitney Museum of American Art, New York 1980.

Japanese Photography in the 1930s, exh. cat., Museum of Modern Art, Kamakura 1988, pp.238–40.

Josef Albers: Paintings, exh. cat., Waddington Galleries, London 2009.

David Linnell, *Blake, Palmer, Linnell and Co.: The Life of John Linnell*, Lewes 1994.

Michaëlis, Sophus and Alfred Bramsen, *Vilhelm Hammershøi*, Copenhagen–Christiana 1918.

Martin Myrone (ed.), *John Martin: Apocalypse*, exh. cat., Tate Britain, London 2012.

Olafur Eliasson: Your Rainbow Panorama: 360°, exh. cat., ARoS Aarhus Kunstmuseum, Aarhus 2011.

Erwin Panofsky, *Perspective as Symbolic Form*, trans. Christopher S. Wood, New York 1991.

Leslie Parris, *The Tate Gallery Constable Collection*, London 1981.

Philippe Parreno, exh. cat., Centre Georges Pompidou, Paris 2009.

Paul Signac, 'The Neo Impressionist Movement', in *Seurat and his Contemporaries*, exh. cat. Wildenstein Gallery, London 1937.

Robert Speaight, *William Rothenstein: The Portrait of an Artist in his Time*, London 1962.

Tacita Dean: Recent Films and Other Works, exh. cat., Tate Britain, London 2001.

M. Tuchman (ed.), *The Spiritual in Abstract Art. Abstract Painting 1890–1985*, New York 1999.

Viewpoints: Italy in Black and White, exh. cat., The Estorick Collection of Modern Italian Art, London 2005.

Vija Celmins, exh. cat., Institute of Contemporary Arts, London 1996.

Judith Wechsler, *György Kepes, The MIT Years: 1945–1977*, Cambridge, MA 1978.

Yayoi Kusama, exh. cat., Tate Modern, London 2012.

Illustrated Works

The works are listed alphabetically by artist, and then chronologically. Measurements are given in centimetres, height before width. Page references are given at the end of the entries. The list does not include illustrations on pp.8–31. All information was correct at the time of going to print.

Josef Albers 1888–1976

Study for Homage to the Square: Beaming 1963
Oil paint on fibreboard 76.2 × 76.2. Tate. Presented by Mrs Anni Albers, the artist's widow and the Josef Albers Foundation 1978, T02310. p.153

Study for Homage to the Square 1964
Oil paint on fibreboard 76.2 × 76.2. Tate. Presented by Mrs Anni Albers, the artist's widow and the Josef Albers Foundation 1978, T02312. p.155

Study for Homage to the Square: Departing in Yellow 1964
Oil paint on fibreboard 76.2 × 76.2. Tate. Purchased 1965, T00783. p.154

David Batchelor 1955–

I Love King's Cross and King's Cross Loves Me 08 2002–7
6 steel, rubber and acrylic sheets. Each between: 12.5 × 65 × 55 and 16.5 x 76 x 46. Tate. Presented by Tate Patrons 2009, T12801. pp.174–5

Spectrum of Brick Lane 2 2007
Lightboxes, steel shelving, acrylic sheet, fluorescent lights, cable and plug boards 520 × 90 × 31. Tate. Presented by Tate Patrons 2009, T12800. p.173

William Blake 1757–1827

God Judging Adam 1795
Relief etching, ink and watercolour on paper 43.2 × 53.5. Tate. Presented by W. Graham Robertson 1939, N05063. p.39

The Good and Evil Angels 1795–c.1805
Colour print, ink and watercolour on paper 44.5 × 59.4. Tate. Presented by W. Graham Robertson 1939, N05057. p.39

Frank Bramley 1857–1915

A Hopeless Dawn 1888
Oil paint on canvas 122.6 × 167.6. Tate. Presented by the Trustees of the Chantrey Bequest 1888, N01627. p.111

John Brett 1831–1902

The British Channel Seen from the Dorsetshire Cliffs 1871
Oil paint on canvas 106 × 212.7. Tate. Presented by Mrs Brett 1902, N01902. p.79 (and cover)

Vija Celmins 1938–

Desert 1975
Lithograph on paper 31.5 × 41.6. Tate. Purchased 1999, P78337. p.193

Galaxy 1975
Lithograph on paper 31.7 × 41.8. Tate. Purchased 1999, P78335. p.193

Ocean 1975
Lithograph on paper 31.7 × 42. Tate. Purchased with assistance from the American Fund for the Tate Gallery, courtesy of the Judith Rothschild Foundation 1999, P78336. p.193

Sky 1975
Lithograph on paper 31.5 × 42. Tate. Purchased 1999, P78334. p.193

Edmund Collein 1906–92

Untitled (Material Study by Otti Berger, Josef Albers' Preliminary Course, Bauhaus Dessau) c.1927
Photograph; gelatin silver print on paper 8.6 × 6.5. Tate. Purchased with funds provided by the Photography Acquisitions Committee 2012, P80042. p.131

John Constable 1776–1837

Harwich Lighthouse ?exh.1820
Oil paint on canvas 32.7 × 50.2. Tate. Presented by Miss Isabel Constable as the gift of Maria Louisa, Isabel and Lionel Bicknell Constable 1888, N01276. pp.59–61

Branch Hill Pond, Hampstead Heath, with a Boy Sitting on a Bank c.1825
Oil paint on canvas 33.3 × 50.2. Tate. Bequeathed by Henry Vaughan 1900, N01813. p.59

Salisbury Cathedral from the Meadows exh.1831
Oil paint on canvas 153.7 × 192. Tate. Purchased by Tate with assistance from the National Lottery through the Heritage Lottery Fund, The Manton Foundation, Art Fund (with a contribution from the Wolfson Foundation) and Tate Members in partnership with Amgueddfa Cymru-National Museum Wales, Colchester and Ipswich Museums Service, National Galleries of Scotland, and The Salisbury Museum 2013, T13896. pp.63–5

John Constable 1776–1837 and David Lucas 1802–81

Spring published 1830
Part of *Various Subjects of Landscape, Characteristic of English Scenery ('English Landscape')*
Mezzotint on paper 12.7 × 24.5. Tate. Purchased 1985, T03986. p.69

A Heath published 1831
Part of *Various Subjects of Landscape, Characteristic of English Scenery ('English Landscape')*
Mezzotint on paper 14.1 × 19. Tate. Purchased 1985, T04013. p.68

River Stour, Suffolk published 1831
Part of *Various Subjects of Landscape, Characteristic of English Scenery ('English Landscape')*
Mezzotint on paper 14.5 × 22.2. Tate. Purchased 1985, T03996. p.68

Summer, Afternoon – After a Shower published 1831
Part of *Various Subjects of Landscape, Characteristic of English Scenery ('English Landscape')*
Mezzotint on paper 14.3 × 19. Tate. Purchased 1985, T04052. p.67

Tacita Dean 1965–

Disappearance at Sea 1996
Film; 16mm colour anamorphic film, optical sound. 14 min. Tate. Purchased 1998, T07455. p.195

Olafur Eliasson 1967–

Yellow versus Purple 2003
Colour-effect filter glass, spotlight, tripod, motor, wire. Object diam. 75 cm; display dimensions variable. Tate. Purchased using funds provided by the 2003 Outset/Frieze Art Fair Fund to benefit the Tate Collection 2003, T11806. p.179

Stardust particle 2014
Stainless steel, translucent mirror-filter glass, wire, motor, spotlight. Diam. 176 cm. Tate. Presented by the artist in honour of Sir Nicholas Serota 2018, T15131. pp.6, 191

Dan Flavin 1933–96

'monument' for V. Tatlin 1966–9
Fluorescent tubes and metal 305.4 × 58.4 × 8.9. Tate. Purchased 1971, T01323. p.169

Armand Guillaumin 1841–1927

Moret-sur-Loing 1902
Oil paint on canvas 60 × 73. Tate. Purchased 1936, N04824. p.99

Vilhelm Hammershøi 1864–1916

Interior, Sunlight on the Floor 1906
Oil paint on canvas 51.8 × 44. Tate. Purchased 1930, N04509. p.115

William Holman Hunt 1827–1910

The Awakening Conscience 1853
Oil paint on canvas 76.2 × 55.9. Tate. Presented by Sir Colin and Lady Anderson through the Friends of the Tate Gallery 1976, T02075. p.105

Hanaya Kanbee 1903–91

Light B 1930, printed 1970s
Photograph; gelatin silver print on paper 25.7 × 20.3. Tate. Presented anonymously 2015, T14390. p.139

Wassily Kandinsky 1866–1944

Swinging 1925
Oil paint on board 70.5 × 50.2. Tate. Purchased 1979, T02344. p.159

Anish Kapoor 1954–

Ishi's Light 2003
Fibreglass, resin and lacquer 315 × 250 × 224. Tate. Presented by Tate International Council 2005, T12004. p.43

György Kepes 1906–2001

Blobs 3 c.1939–40
Photograph; gelatin silver print on paper 35.5 × 28.4. Tate. Purchased with funds provided by the Russia and Eastern European Acquisitions Committee and the Photography Acquisitions Committee 2013, P80545. p.137

Branches c.1939–40
Photograph; gelatin silver print on paper 35.5 × 28.3. Tate. Purchased with funds provided by the Russia and Eastern European Acquisitions Committee and the Photography Acquisitions Committee 2013, P80557. p.135

Circles and Dots c.1939–40
Photograph; gelatin silver print on paper 35.3 × 28.3. Tate. Purchased with funds provided by the Russia and Eastern European Acquisitions Committee and the Photography Acquisitions Committee 2013, P80556. pp.2, 137

Structure Photogram c.1939–40
Photograph; gelatin silver print on paper 25.4 × 20.3. Tate. Purchased with funds provided by the Russia and Eastern European Acquisitions Committee and the Photography Acquisitions Committee 2013, P80554. p.137

Light Reflection 1941
Photograph; gelatin silver print on paper 35.5 × 28.4. Tate. Purchased with funds provided by the Russia and Eastern European Acquisitions Committee and the Photography Acquisitions Committee 2013, P80567. p.137

Yayoi Kusama 1929–

The Passing Winter 2005
Mirror and glass 180 × 80.5 × 80.5. Tate. Purchased with funds provided by the Asia Pacific Acquisitions Committee 2008, T12821. pp.145–7

Liliane Lijn 1939–

Liquid Reflections 1968
Perspex, metal, water, liquid paraffin, motor, electrical components and lamp. Diam. 106.2 cm. Tate. Purchased 1973, T01828. p.125

John Linnell 1792–1882

Kensington Gravel Pits 1811–12
Oil paint on canvas 71.1 × 106.7. Tate. Purchased 1947, N05776. p.71

Landscape (The Windmill) 1844–5
Oil paint on canvas 38.1 × 45.7. Tate. Presented by Robert Vernon 1847, N00439. pp.72–3

John Martin 1789–1854

The Destruction of Pompeii and Herculaneum 1822
Oil paint on canvas 161.6 × 253. Tate. Purchased 1869, N00793. pp.53–5

John Everett Millais, 1829–96

Mariana 1851
Oil paint on mahogany 59.7 × 49.5. Tate. Accepted by HM Government in lieu of tax and allocated to the Tate Gallery 1999, T07553. p.103

Ophelia 1851–2
Oil paint on canvas 76.2 × 111.8. Tate. Presented by Sir Henry Tate 1894, N01506. pp.81–3

László Moholy-Nagy 1895–1946

K VII 1922
Oil paint and graphite on canvas 115.3 × 135.9. Tate. Purchased 1961, T00432. p.151

Claude Monet 1840–1926

Poplars on the Epte 1891
Oil paint on canvas 92.4 × 73.7. Tate. Presented by the Art Fund 1926, N04183. p.87

The Seine at Port-Villez 1894
Oil paint on canvas 65.4 × 100.3. Tate. Purchased 1953, N06182. p.85

Jacob More 1740–93

The Deluge 1787
Oil paint on canvas. 150.4 × 204.6. Tate. Purchased with assistance from Tate Patrons and Tate Members 2008, T12758. p.41

Bruce Nauman 1941–

Corridor with Mirror and White Lights 1971
Wood, glass and fluorescent tubes 304.8 × 30.8 × 1219.2. Tate. Purchased 1973, T01753. p.171

Philippe Parreno 1964–

6.00 PM 2000–6
Carpet. Dimensions variable. Tate. Purchased using funds provided by the 2006 Outset/Frieze Art Fair Fund to benefit the Tate Collection 2007, T12411. p.113

Camille Pissarro 1830–1903

The Pilots' Jetty, Le Havre, Morning, Cloudy and Misty Weather 1903
Oil paint on canvas 65.1 × 81.3. Tate. Presented by Lucien Pissarro, the artist's son 1948, N05833. p.95

Lis Rhodes 1942–

Light Music 1975
Film; 16mm, shown as video; 2 projections, black and white, and sound (dual mono). 25 min. Tate. Presented by Tate Members 2012, T13857. p.189

George Richmond 1809–96

The Creation of Light 1826
Tempera, gold and silver on mahogany 48 × 41.7. Tate. Purchased 1986, T04164. p.37

Bridget Riley 1931–

Nataraja 1993
Oil paint on canvas 165.1 × 227.7. Tate. Purchased 1994, T06859. p.165

William Rothenstein 1872–1945

Mother and Child 1903
Oil paint on canvas 96.9 × 76.5. Tate. Purchased 1988, T05075. p.117

Peter Sedgley 1930–

Colour Cycle III 1970
Acrylic paint on canvas 184.1 × 182.9. Tate. Purchased 1970, T01237. p.177

Alfred Sisley 1839–99

The Path to the Old Ferry at By 1880
Oil paint on canvas 49.8 × 65.1. Tate. Bequeathed by Montague Shearman through the Contemporary Art Society 1940, N05144. pp.92–3

The Small Meadows in Spring 1880
Oil paint on canvas 54.3 × 73. Tate. Presented by a body of subscribers in memory of Roger Fry 1936, N04843. pp.89–91

Philip Wilson Steer 1860–1942

A Procession of Yachts 1892–3
Oil paint on canvas 62.9 × 76.2. Tate. Purchased 1922, N03668. p.97

Stefan Themerson 1910–88

Untitled 1930, printed later
Photograph; gelatin silver print on paper 19.2 × 24.5. Tate. Purchased with funds provided by the Russia and Eastern Europe Acquisitions Committee 2016, P81616. p.133

Joseph Mallord William Turner 1775–1851

The Deluge ?exh.1805
Oil paint on canvas 142.9 × 235.6. Tate. Accepted by the nation as part of the Turner Bequest 1856, N00493. pp.44–5

Lecture Diagram 61: A Cube with Shadow c.1810–11
Part of *I. Numbered Perspective Diagrams*
Graphite and watercolour on paper 67.5 × 101. Tate. Accepted by the nation as part of the Turner Bequest 1856, D17086. p.121

Lecture Diagram 62: Various Forms with Shadows c.1810
Part of *I. Numbered Perspective Diagrams*
Graphite and watercolour on paper 67 × 99.9. Tate. Accepted by the nation as part of the Turner Bequest 1856, D17087. p.121

Lecture Diagram 63: Various Forms with Shadows c.1810
Part of *I. Numbered Perspective Diagrams*
Graphite and watercolour on paper 67 × 100. Tate. Accepted by the nation as part of the Turner Bequest 1856, D17088. p.121

Lecture Diagram 64: Various Forms with Shadows c.1810
Part of *I. Numbered Perspective Diagrams*
Graphite and watercolour on paper 67.1 × 100.5. Tate. Accepted by the nation as part of the Turner Bequest 1856, D17089. p.121

Lecture Diagram 65: Interior of a Prison c.1810
Part of *I. Numbered Perspective Diagrams*
Gouache, graphite and watercolour on paper 48.7 × 68.7. Tate. Accepted by the nation as part of the Turner Bequest 1856, D17090. p.123

Lecture Diagram 66: Interior of a Prison (after Giovanni Battista Piranesi) c.1810
Part of *I. Numbered Perspective Diagrams*
Graphite and pen and ink on paper 44.3 × 59.5. Tate. Accepted by the nation as part of the Turner Bequest 1856, D17091. p.123

Lecture Diagram: Reflections in a Single Polished Metal Globe and in a Pair of Polished Metal Globes c.1810
Part of *II. Various Perspective Diagrams*
Oil paint and graphite on paper 64 × 96.8. Tate. Accepted by the nation as part of the Turner Bequest 1856, D17147. p.122

Sun Setting over a Lake c.1840
Oil paint on canvas 91.1 × 122.6. Tate. Accepted by the nation as part of the Turner Bequest 1856, N04665. pp.32–3, 76

Shade and Darkness – the Evening of the Deluge exh.1843
Oil paint on canvas 78.7 × 78.1. Tate. Accepted by the nation as part of the Turner Bequest 1856, N00531. p.76

Light and Colour (Goethe's Theory) – the Morning after the Deluge – Moses Writing the Book of Genesis exh.1843
Oil paint on canvas 78.7 × 78.7. Tate. Accepted by the nation as part of the Turner Bequest 1856, N00532. p.77

The Angel Standing in the Sun exh.1846
Oil paint on canvas 78.7 × 78.7. Tate. Accepted by the nation as part of the Turner Bequest 1856, N00550. p.47

James Turrell 1943–

Raemar, Blue 1969
Fluorescent light. Dimensions variable. Tate. Presented by the Tate Americas Foundation, partial purchase and partial gift of Doris J. Lockhart 2013, T14268. p.187

Luigi Veronesi 1908–98

Construction 1938
Photograph; gelatin silver print on paper 28.6 × 38.8. Tate. Accepted under the Cultural Gifts Scheme by HM Government from Massimo Prelz Oltramonti and allocated to Tate 2015, P13674. p.142

Untitled (Spiral) 1938
Photograph; gelatin silver print on paper 29.8 × 23.5. Tate. Accepted under the Cultural Gifts Scheme by HM Government from Massimo Prelz Oltramonti and allocated to Tate 2015. p.143

Photo n.145 1940, printed 1970s
Photograph; gelatin silver print on paper 31.8 × 28.7. Tate. Accepted under the Cultural Gifts Scheme by HM Government from Massimo Prelz Oltramonti and allocated to Tate 2015, P13675. p.141

Henry Wallis 1830–1916

Chatterton 1856
Oil paint on canvas 62.2 × 93.3. Tate. Bequeathed by Charles Gent Clement 1899, N01685. pp.107–9

Pae White 1963–

Morceau Accrochant 2004
Paper and thread. Display dimensions variable. Tate. Purchased using funds provided by the 2004 Outset/Frieze Art Fair Fund to benefit the Tate Collection 2005, T11918. pp.161–3

Stephen Willats 1943–

Visual Field Automatic No.1 1964
Plywood, wood, plastic, metal, light bulbs and circuit board 191 × 122 × 22. Tate. Purchased from funds provided by the Knapping Fund 2004, T11786. p.157

Joseph Wright of Derby 1734–97

Vesuvius in Eruption, with a View over the Islands in the Bay of Naples c.1776–80
Oil paint on canvas 122 × 176.4. Tate. Purchased with assistance from the National Heritage Memorial Fund, the Art Fund, Friends of the Tate Gallery, and Mr John Ritblat 1990, T05040. p.49

A Moonlight with a Lighthouse, Coast of Tuscany exh.1789
Oil paint on canvas 101.6 × 127.6. Tate. Purchased 1949, N05882. pp.50–1

Iwao Yamawaki 1898–1987

Set of Bowls 1930–2
Photograph; gelatin silver print on paper 12.7 × 10. Tate. Presented by Jacqui Brantjes and Daniel Pittack 2012, P13184. p.129

Untitled (Composition with Eggs and String, Bauhaus) 1930–2
Photograph; gelatin silver print on paper 11.3 × 8. Tate. Purchased with funds provided by the Asia Pacific Acquisitions Committee 2010, P79897. p.129

Untitled (Interior, Bauhaus, Dessau) 1930–2
Photograph; gelatin silver print on paper 23.3 × 15.2. Tate. Purchased with funds provided by the Asia Pacific Acquisitions Committee 2010, P79895. p.127

Catherine Yass 1963–

Corridors 1994
Photograph; dye destruction print on transparency on lightbox 89 × 72.5 × 14. Tate. Presented by the Patrons of New Art (Special Purchase Fund) through the Tate Gallery Foundation 1996, T07068. p.181

Corridors 1994
Photograph; dye destruction print on transparency on lightbox 89 × 72.5 × 14. Tate. Presented by the Patrons of New Art (Special Purchase Fund) through the Tate Gallery Foundation 1996, T07072. p.182

Corridors 1994
Photograph; dye destruction print on transparency on lightbox 89 × 72.5 × 14. Tate. Presented by the Patrons of New Art (Special Purchase Fund) through the Tate Gallery Foundation 1996, T07070. p.183

Credits

Artists' credits

© The Josef and Anni Albers Foundation / DACS 2022 pp.153–5

© David Batchelor. All Rights Reserved, DACS 2022 pp.173, 174–5

© Vija Celmins, Courtesy Matthew Marks Gallery p.193

© Tacita Dean Courtesy the artist; Frith Street Gallery, London and Marian Goodman Gallery, New York/Paris p.195

© 2014 Olafur Eliasson pp.6, 9, 179, 191

© Stephen Flavin / Artists Rights Society (ARS), New York 2022 p.169

© Yamawaki Iwao & Michiko Archives pp.127, 129

© Anish Kapoor. All Rights Reserved, DACS 2022 p.43

© Hanaya Kanbee p.139

© Estate of György Kepes (Imre Kepes and Juliet Kepes Stone) pp.2, 135, 137

© Ursula Kirsten-Collein p.139

© YAYOI KUSAMA pp.145–7

© Liliane Lijn. All Rights Reserved, DACS 2022 p.125

© COMITATO LUIGI VERONESI, MILANO pp.141–3

© Bruce Nauman / Artists Rights Society (ARS), New York and DACS, London 2022 p.171

© Philippe Parreno, courtesy Esther Schipper, Berlin p.113

© Lis Rhodes p.189

© Bridget Riley 2022. All rights reserved. pp.24–5, 165

© Peter Sedgley p.177

© Themerson Estate p.133

© 2022 James Turrell p.187

© Stephen Willats. Courtesy the artist and Victoria Miro p.157

© Pae White pp.161–3

© Catherine Yass. All Rights Reserved, DACS 2022 pp.181–3

Photo credits

All images © Tate Images unless otherwise stated

ACTIVE MUSEUM / Alamy Stock Photo p.12

Artimage 2022 pp.174–5

© Bridgeman Images pp.23, 26

Harvard Art Museums/Busch-Reisinger Museum, Gift of Sibyl Moholy-Nagy © President and Fellows of Harvard College p.29

© Manchester Art Gallery p.14

Photo Ann Ronan/Heritage Images/Scala, Florence p.10

© Scala, Florence p.21

Photo Scala, Florence/bpk, Bildagentur fuer Kunst, Kultur und Geschichte, Berlin p.11

Photo: Elke Walford. © 2022. Photo Scala, Florence/bpk, Bildagentur für Kunst, Kultur und Geschichte, Berlin p.16

Photo: Jens Ziehe, 2017 pp.6, 191

Index

Page references in *italics* indicate pages on which artworks appear.